"Karnazes is revolutionizing [ultrarunning], inspiring many weekend warriors to take it up a notch . . . Money and fame aside, Karnazes [is] motivated by primal need more than anything else." —*Outside*

"Run, Karnazes, run!" —*FHM*

"Ultra-inspirational." —*Odyssey* **(Greece)**

"[Dean is] like a comic-book superhero who remains undercover by day, every bit the unremarkable family man." —*London Daily Telegraph*

"A real-life Forrest Gump . . . [Karnazes] has pushed his body to limits that are beyond masochistic. They're inhuman." —*Newsday*

"Superhuman." —*Boston Globe*

"Superstar." —*Oregonian*

"Superman." —*Gazzetta dello Sport Week* **(Italy)**

"Ultrarunning legend." —*Men's Journal*

"One of the sexiest men in sports."

—*Sports Illustrated Women*

"The undisputed king of the ultras, who has not only pushed the envelope but blasted it to bits."

—*Philadelphia Inquirer*

Secrets I Learned
Running 50 Marathons in 50 Days—
and How You Too
Can Achieve Super Endurance!

DEAN KARNAZES
With Matt Fitzgerald

GRAND CENTRAL
Life & Style

NEW YORK · BOSTON

Dean's blood work summary, in Appendix E, is included courtesy of Bryan Bergman, PhD, University of Colorado Assistant Professor of Medicine.

Grand Central Life & Style
Hachette Book Group
237 Park Avenue
New York, NY 10017

www.HachetteBookGroup.com

Grand Central Life & Style is an imprint of Grand Central Publishing.
The Grand Central Life & Style name and logo are trademarks of Hachette Book Group, Inc.

The publisher is not responsible for websites (or their content) that are not owned by the publisher.

Printed in the United States of America

Originally published in hardcover by Hachette Book Group.

First Trade Edition: August 2009
10 9 8 7 6 5

The Library of Congress has cataloged the hardcover edition as follows:
Karnazes, Dean, 1962-
    50/50 : secrets I learned running 50 marathons in 50 days—and how you too can achieve super endurance! / Dean Karnazes with Matt Fitzgerald.—1st ed.
        p. cm.
    ISBN 978-0-446-58183-7
1. Marathon running. 2. Physical fitness. 1. Fitzgerald, Matt. II. Title. III. Title: Fifty/ fifty. IV. Title: Fifty in fifty. V. Title: secrets I learned running 50 marathons in 50 days, and how you too can achieve super endurance.
    GV1065.K37 2008
    796.42'52—dc22
                            2008001291

ISBN 978-0-446-58184-4 (pbk.)

This book is dedicated to my mom and dad,

who always gave me the liberty to wander freely.

May our adventures never end . . .

Acknowledgments

I'll preface these acknowledgments by saying that I'm one of the luckiest men on earth. Why? Because I'm surrounded by some of the greatest people on earth. To them, I owe everything. The list is long, and at the top would be my wife, Julie, and my daughter and son, Alexandria and Nicholas. Your ongoing support, encouragement, and positive spirit have provided me with immeasurable inspiration and motivation. I can never thank you enough.

To the entire team at The North Face, and especially Topher Gaylord and Steve Rendle, I am forever grateful. It has been fun, and we're not done yet!

Many thanks to Matt Fitzgerald for helping me with this book, and my gratitude goes out to Chris Carmichael and Jason Koop for helping me get through fifty consecutive marathons without a single leg cramp!

To the dynamic duo over at Grand Central Publishing, Natalie Kaire and Jimmy Franco; your tireless marathon efforts in bringing this book to life have been extraordinary. Thank you for all that you've done, and continue to do, every day. And I owe a world of gratitude to my faithful agent, Carole Bidnick, whose dedication and commitment has been unwavering throughout this very long run together.

Lastly, I want to thank the thousands of athletes who joined me along the road. Together, we made a difference.

Contents

Preface

Men's Fitness has stated that I might just be the fittest man on the planet. *Time* once claimed that I'm no mere mortal. *Wired* hailed me as the perfect human. Let me share a little secret with you: I'm really just average. Perhaps even a little below average. I know this better than anyone. I'm not bestowed with any superhuman powers. I don't have any special gifts. There is no magic in my genetic makeup. I'm just an average guy.

So how am I able to run hundreds of miles at a clip? How was I able to complete fifty marathons, in fifty states, in fifty consecutive days? Just how do I do these things? I wrote this book to answer that question. There are lessons I've learned along the way that can help you achieve your own amazing feats of endurance, however you define them. Some of these lessons are nothing more than practical tips that I've picked up along the road, as all runners do; others come out of challenging experiences and help illustrate an approach or attitude that has proven effective for me. In either case, the aim of this book is to share with you the things that have helped me accomplish my goals, in the hope that you will be able to accomplish yours, no matter the scale.

Just remember, as extreme as some of my accomplishments have been, you are reading about an average guy. An extremely average guy.

50/50

Road Trip

O n a bright Saturday morning in February 2002, we set out on another road trip—Karnazes family–style. No bags were packed the night before our departure. No alarms were set to help us get an early start. Everyone rolled out of bed on his or her own schedule. And then chaos erupted. There was a mad scramble to fill bags and load them onto the Mother Ship, our beloved twenty-seven-foot RV. In the kitchen of our house, food appeared on burners, countertops, and tables and promptly disappeared into mouths. Children's laughter rang out frequently, and the occasional ball or other projectile toy sailed across a room.

Every few minutes, my dad asked one of us if we'd seen some item he desperately needed and couldn't find. The last of these items was the keys to the Mother Ship. He had just left the kitchen in search of them when my wife, Julie, entered.

"Is Popou ready?" she asked, her use of the Greek word for "dad" a sure indication that she was getting in the spirit of the weekend. The unstructured Grecian chaos of my family's operations sometimes unnerved her, but at other times, like now, she happily joined right in and became one of us.

"Popou's looking for the keys," said Alexandria, our seven-year-old.

"Who's got Nicholas?" Julie asked frantically, suddenly realizing she hadn't seen our four-year-old son for quite some time.

"Popou said he's already in the RV with Yiayia," Alexandria replied, referring to her grandmother, my mother, in Greek as well.

Young as he was, Nicholas was already showing signs of having inherited his father's insatiable wanderlust: He would walk right out the front door if left unattended for more than a few seconds.

"Wait a minute," Alexandria continued. "If Nicholas and Yiayia are already inside the Mother Ship, they must have the keys. How else could they unlock the door?"

She was, of course, correct. Being outwitted by a child was hardly a blow to Popou's pride, however. He didn't really care; he just wanted to get on with the adventure and was glad that someone had finally located those stinking keys he'd been searching all over for, for the past ten minutes.

At last we buckled ourselves into the Mother Ship and Popou began to guide the vehicle northward with sure hands. We sang and joked and quoted movies as he expertly piloted the craft along the highway.

Over the years, what I've come to realize is that the difference between a runner and a jogger is that a jogger still has control of his life. A scant hour after we had left our home in San Francisco, I was already stirring, my initial contentment replaced by a familiar restlessness. "Pull over," I said.

Having anticipated the inevitable, I was already dressed in my running gear. At the first available turnout, Dad guided the Mother Ship off the road. We had perfected our routine on many past family road trips. Sometimes I would leave home on foot before the family, and they'd pick me up along the roadside a few hours later. Other days I would wait until we reached our destination and then take flight. Once in a while, I would run all night and meet them in the morning. Today the formula was pretty simple: I'd run up the highway while they went shopping for supplies, secured our campsite, and prepared a gourmet lunch.

I gave Alexandria and Nicholas each a quick peck on the cheek while dashing toward the exit. I squeezed my mom's hand, embraced Julie, and saluted my dad.

"See you guys in a bit," I said, and I was out the door.

Today I would cover twenty-six or twenty-seven miles—roughly a marathon. The ultimate challenge for many runners, this distance represented a typical weekend long run for me. Sometimes I would run a marathon on Saturday and another on Sunday. I had run two hundred miles nonstop more than once and I was completing several one-hundred-mile races in extreme environments each year, so a leisurely run of just a fraction of that length wouldn't take much out of me. I could just enjoy the hypnotic cycle of my breathing, the rhythmic contractions of my muscles, and the splendor of the day. It was a typically perfect Napa Valley winter morning, not a cloud in the sky, the air dry and neither cool nor warm, a gentle breeze refreshing my exposed skin.

There were two pieces of mandatory equipment I always carried with me on these runs: a cell phone and a credit card. Three hours into my workout, the phone rang.

"Hey, hon, we forgot to get Parm—" A convoy of semis roared by, drowning out the rest of her sentence.

I stuck a finger in one ear and pressed the phone against the other. *"Say again?"*

"We forgot to get Parmesan. You know, cheese."

"Ohhh!"

"Could you stop and grab some on the way?"

"Sure thing."

Then another fortunate accident happened: I wrote a book that, almost overnight, made me one of the better-known runners in America—one of the few whom nonrunners actually knew about. The book chronicled my wild adventures as an all-night runner and became a surprise best seller. Suddenly the crazy long runs that I'd been doing for the past decade became "news." I was interviewed on the *Late Show with David Letterman*, on *60 Minutes*, and by Howard Stern. Race directors and running club presidents around the world began inviting me to give motivational talks for their participants and members, which often attracted standing-room-only audiences. *Runner's World* and *Outside* put me on their covers, and *Time* ran a feature story about me. *Time* magazine! My private adventures were now a public curiosity.

My visibility within The North Face also got a strong boost. Then, in 2005, three years after I had first conceived my big idea, a man named Joe Flannery became the company's new vice president of marketing. He took one look at my moth-eaten proposal and had a vision of his own.

I was a bundle of nerves when I sat down in Joe's roomy center office to talk about it.

"I want to make this bigger," Joe said.

"What, you want me to run more than fifty?" I joked.

Joe laughed briefly. "Not longer, bigger," he said.

Joe's vision was to transform my eccentric family vacation into a massive transcontinental fitness lollapalooza and media extravaganza called The North Face Endurance 50. Instead of running fifty arbitrary solo marathons measured by the Mother Ship's odometer wherever I felt like stretching my legs in a given state, I would run fifty official, certified marathon events that would be open to other participants. There would be pre- and post-marathon activities and additional events, just like at other marathons. Local and state government agencies at each marathon location would be brought on board. Joe and his staff would design an aggressive media campaign whose objective was to ensure that every man, woman, and child in the United States heard about the Endurance 50 at least once. The brand exposure for The North Face would be tremendous!

Great, I thought. *My family vacation has just run amok.* Joe must have seen my face fall. That's when he played his full hand.

"Dean, you've become an inspirational figure for a lot of people," he said earnestly. "This is an opportunity to inspire more folks than you ever dreamed you could reach. Not to mention, a big fund-raiser for Karno's Kids," he added, referring to the charity I had created to motivate and empower young boys and girls to become physically active.

That settled it. I was back on board, with a vengeance. If I die having contributed nothing more to the world than inspiring a handful or more of nonrunners to become runners, I will die knowing I did what I could to make the world a better place. It's not that I lack the imagination to find a bigger cause. It's that I believe there is no bigger cause. Running is much more than a good way to lose weight. It's a cure for depression and a potential path to personal growth and self-fulfillment. It's my recipe for making this world a more harmonious home to the human species.

"I'm in," I said.

Joe's first move was to call Merrill Squires, founder of the Squires Sports Group. I guess you would classify SSG as an event production company. They're logistics experts with extensive experience in creating roaming festivals, like the 2002 Olympic torch relay run across America.

"Sure, we can do this," Merrill told Joe confidently. But SSG had never undertaken anything quite like the Endurance 50 before. They had never even *heard* of anything like it being attempted. I later learned that, behind his back, Merrill's friends were giving him one-in-twenty odds of pulling it off.

The challenges were enormous. First, we had to find fifty marathon directors willing to re-create their events on a smaller scale on a date we suggested, or allow us to run our event concurrently with their normally scheduled marathon. Then we had to sequence these events so that it was feasible to caravan from one to the next in time to set up and run each marathon during the small window of opportunity that police support, local permits, and road closures afforded. Infinite details of transportation, supply sourcing, insurance, and personnel had to be worked out. And not least, we had to recruit enough sponsors to cover the whopping $1.2 million price tag for our unprecedented "expedition," as it came to be designated.

Fortunately, I was not personally responsible for making all these things happen. The role I was destined to play in The North Face Endurance 50 was decidedly different from the one I had envisioned for my family vacation. If the Endurance 50 was a movie, then others would take on the responsibilities of producer, director, location scout, set crew, and camera operator. I would be the so-called talent. The small star of a very big show.

The fifteen months of intensive preparation—which included some six thousand miles' worth of training runs and ultra-endurance tune-up races—that I endured between the time Joe Flannery layered his vision on top of mine and the start of marathon number one are a blur in my memory. The fast-forward button finally was released in September 2006, when I flew to St. Louis, Missouri, and from there drove to the bucolic town of St. Charles to begin what would turn out to be the most intense fifty days of my life, hands-down.

St. Charles was the site of the Lewis & Clark Marathon, which would be one of eight "live events" on our tour. A popular twelve-year-old event, it attracted roughly five thousand participants. St. Charles was also the starting site of the historic Lewis and Clark expedition. This year marked the two hundredth anniversary of that remarkable journey, so starting the Endurance 50 there seemed fitting.

The morning after arriving, I met up with Joe Flannery in a large parking lot. "There it is," he said, "your new home for fifty days." He was pointing at a huge tour bus fully cocooned in vinyl wrapping that displayed colorful graphics and attention-grabbing sponsor logos. "And here are your new friends," he added.

Before me stood a motley crew of scruffy-looking guys, mostly in their twenties, some of whom I had met once or twice before, others of whom were complete strangers to me. I would spend the majority of the next fifty days and nights within breath-smelling distance of these fellows in a cramped, mobile locker room, complete with barracks-style bunk beds stacked three-high. I hoped we wouldn't kill one another.

Among the crew members I knew slightly already were Jason Koop and Jimmy Hopper. With his lanky build, square jaw, and matted hair, "Koop" looked like he'd just walked off the set of *Chariots of Fire*. An accomplished former collegiate runner now working with Chris Carmichael, Lance Armstrong's personal coach and trainer, Koop was here principally to monitor my nutrition and physiological adaptations. "Hopps" had the look of a Southern California surfer dude, with a nest of blond hair that he would inexplicably shave off before I saw him again the next morning.

New to me were English, our English bus driver (it took me all too long to discern that the man was from England *and* his name was English), and Dave, veteran manager of many a rock band tour who had been hired to manage our expedition because, well, a rock band tour was the closest model for our expedition we could think of. English had feathery silver hair, a matching goatee, and a meaty handshake. Dave had darting eyes, slicked-back hair, and a way of seeming to hover in the background even as he stood and spoke with everyone else. They were the two elders in the group.

Unbeknownst to me, the younger members of the crew had already devised their own unique version of the Endurance 50: fifty states, fifty days, fifty phone numbers! They were hoping to entice some unsuspecting volunteer into giving them her phone number in each of the states across this great nation of ours. An ambitious goal, no doubt, but as I came to learn, they were every bit as determined as I was—darn resourceful too.

Dave explained that they were going to set up the "Finish Festival" in this parking lot as a sort of dress rehearsal for the performance that would be repeated tomorrow and again daily for seven weeks afterward. I then left for last-minute logistical meetings. When I returned two hours later, I couldn't believe my eyes. The gang had erected a small city of tents, carpets, banners, and stages. The scene looked more like a corporate-sponsored Moroccan street bazaar than a hotel parking lot. People scurried around with hammers, drills, and other tools, lugged coolers filled with food and drink, and squinted at assembly instruction papers. Music blared from zillion-watt loudspeakers. Everybody was drenched in perspiration from hauling all this stuff around. A towering inflatable finish arch that served as a makeshift entrance to the dream city teetered back and forth like a blimp getting ready for flight as two local volunteers brought on board just for the weekend (a tactic we would repeat at each venue) struggled to stake it down.

I stood in silence, taking in the chaotic tableau, my stomach alive with a gnawing sense of foreboding.

That evening was to be my last chance to get a full night's rest for nearly two months. My mind raced as I lay awake in our hotel room next to Julie. It hit me suddenly: *I have to run fifty marathons in fifty states in the next fifty days!* I believed then that I could do it, but I knew there were dozens of possible mishaps that might cause me to fail. Anything from a twisted ankle to out-of-control blistering to being hit by a car could bring the whole extravaganza crashing to a premature halt. And I was aware that the running would be the "easy" part of this quest. Running fifty marathons in fifty days from my front door would be one thing; running them between frenzied Finish Festivals and multi-hour bus drives would be quite another.

I had failed before, but never with so many people counting on me to succeed. I thought of the thousands of runners who had signed up to run with me at the forty-two specially created events, the teachers all around the country who'd designed activities for their students centered on the Endurance 50, the scores of magazines, newspapers, and radio and TV stations that had budgeted space and time to cover my exploits, and the sponsors that had shelled out great sums of cash to make the whole thing possible.

When you spend as much time anticipating a major undertaking as I spent anticipating the Endurance 50, your mind imagines so many possible scenarios that, by the time you actually begin, you're half convinced that the event can offer no surprises. But it always does. The Endurance 50 surprised me in many ways, but above all by the way it challenged me to apply virtually every lesson about running, and about life, that I had ever learned, and taught me countless new lessons to apply in the future. Lessons worth sharing. So, here goes . . .

CHAPTER 1

The Right Foot

Day 1
September 17, 2006
Lewis & Clark Marathon
St. Charles, Missouri
Elevation: 989'
Weather: 82 degrees; humid
Time: 3:50:52
Net calories burned: 3,187*
Number of runners: 4,800

I sat stiffly in a cold hotel conference room with a needle in my arm. It was five thirty in the morning on Day 1 of The North Face Endurance 50. The phlebotomist who had been hired to stick this needle in my arm—a stout, thin-lipped woman in her mid fifties—filled three vials with blood and then handed me a small plastic cup.

"Urinate into this," she said drily.

I would have to endure a version of this morning ritual roughly twice a week throughout my autumn tour of America.

Fifty days, fifty states, untold needle-sticks.

The idea was to monitor some of my body's important health indicators over the next seven weeks. A couple of recent medical studies had suggested that running long distances might be physiologically damaging. I wanted to prove them wrong— or die trying.

---

*This number represents the accumulated number of calories I burned to this point in the Endurance 50 marathons. My source for the calculations was www.coolrunning.com.

I felt light-headed and mildly queasy as I made my way toward the marathon expo and starting area. But I had other reasons for that. The scene was chaotic. Runners, their supporters, race officials, and volunteers darted in every direction with harried determination. The Endurance 50 festival area was packed. That familiar-looking Moroccan street bazaar was now in full swing. I'd had no idea it would be this hectic.

Making my way through the crowd, I nearly ran headlong into a lean man wearing a priest's robe. It was my dear friend, fellow ultrarunner, and licensed justice of the peace Topher Gaylord.

"Gaylord!" I exclaimed. "Er . . . I mean, Father! Man, am I glad to see you."

"Follow me, son," he said. Topher had flown from Italy to be here, clerical robe snugly packed in his suitcase.

We found a break in the crowd, and there stood my family: Julie, the kids, and my parents. Topher took hold of a microphone and began reading aloud from a prepared text as I put an arm around Julie's waist, Alexandria produced a bouquet of flowers, and Nicholas offered up a velvet-covered ring box. Julie's face took on a stunned expression as her eyes darted from Topher's robe to the flowers to the ring box and finally my face. Then they filled with tears. Surprise, Julie! We were renewing our wedding vows.

Attracted by the words of Topher's heartfelt sermon as they rang out from the PA system, a crowd of hundreds formed around us. Moments after the "I do's" had been exchanged, as though it'd been choreographed, the race announcer's voice called out, "Five minutes to race start!"

In marathon running, few things are more important than starting on the right foot. Physically and mentally, you have to be in the game. You can't really control what happens after eighteen or twenty miles. That's when the real suffering begins, and it's always worse than expected, even if you've run many marathons before. You just have to push through it with all the strength you have in your body and mind.

You can, however, control the first part of a marathon, and if you're wise you will control it in ways that make the last part—well, not easier, but better. You can resist the urge to start too fast, make sure you drink enough fluids, run the tangents, and so forth.

The surprise wedding reenactment I laid on Julie this morning was my way of starting this marathon of marathons on the right foot. The Endurance 50 was conceived as a dream family vacation, but it had become something different. Julie hadn't been able to take a leave from her practice as a dentist, so the rest of us would see her mostly on weekends. But her inability to come along for the full journey hadn't stopped Julie from playing a hero's role in planning the family side of the adventure. She had worked tirelessly for months on end. One night I stumbled home from a run at 1:30 AM to find her on the phone with Travelocity, arranging flights, car rentals, and hotel stays for my parents and the kids. Her generous heart deserved to be honored—publicly—and now it had been.

Upon hearing the announcer's five-minute notice, the crowd quickly began moving toward the starting line. My entire family exchanged one last hug. Topher whipped off his gown to expose the running gear he wore underneath. The two of us made our way to the starting chute, saying little. The gun went off, the crowd surged forward, and my five-year-old dream took one step into reality, and then another, and another.

Topher and I found a comfortable groove at a slightly sub-four-hour marathon pace. The first miles followed flat roads that passed through the historic section of St. Charles. The air was warm, wet, and still. Soon it would be hot, wet, and still.

A number of the runners in our vicinity spotted me and sidled up to offer and receive encouragement. Five miles into the race, a lanky boy of twelve or thirteen years found a slot on my shoulder.

"Are you Dean?" he asked.

"Yes, I'm Dean," I confirmed.

"I'm John," said the boy. He told me he was running the one-loop half-marathon that was being held on the same course as the marathon, which covered the same loop twice. John added that I was an inspiration to him, and he had come here with his mother in the hope of meeting me. I felt a rush of inspiration from the boy as his words sank in.

"You're doing great!" I said. Topher seconded that opinion. And he *was* doing great—for a while. John was all smiles as we passed by his mother at the ten-mile mark. She hollered and held up a sign that read GO TEAM DEAN! But the sun's rays were becoming mercilessly intense. John had never run so far before, and it appeared he was pushing harder than his natural pace to stay alongside us.

At eleven miles, his breathing was labored and his shoes clomped heavily on the road. At twelve miles, he was hunchbacked and grunting with effort.

"You can do it!" we yelled.

With a quarter mile left to the finish, John began weaving, and his stride fell apart completely. He was no longer running but lurching forward like a man on fire.

"Come on! You can do it!" we shouted.

With only one hundred yards to go, John stopped abruptly in the middle of the road and sent a cone-shaped torrent of vomit shooting to the ground with the force of a fire hose.

"Are you okay?" I asked. "Do you want to sit down for a minute?"

"Go ahead. I'll walk," John finally managed as several concerned spectators gathered around him to provide support. Topher and I resumed running, and I silently wondered whether we had just committed some form of child abuse. *Some inspiration I am*, I thought.

The carnage spread among the marathon runners on the second loop. By now the temperature was in excess of eighty

How to Avoid Sickness During a Race

- Eat your pre-race meal at least an hour beforehand.
- Avoid milk and lactose, as well as highly fibrous foods, for at least twenty-four hours prior.
- Consume easily digested foods such as instant oatmeal, bananas, and energy bars in your pre-race meal. If you eat your pre-race meal within an hour of the race, it should contain no more than five hundred calories.
- Don't drink too much fluid during the run. Let your thirst guide your drinking rate. Drink only water or a sports drink such as Accelerade.
- Train properly for the race so your body is accustomed to the level of exertion that will be called for. For example, complete at least one training run of twenty miles or more before running a full marathon.

degrees. Topher and I began passing struggling runners at the rate of two or three per mile. These poor folks had not started on the right foot. Many of them had come here with time goals that were no longer realistic in the conditions, but had refused to adjust their pace. Now they were paying the price.

"This is kind of brutal," Topher said.

"Yeah, man, it's toasty out here. I feel sorry for these people."

We crossed the finish line ten minutes faster than planned—perhaps a little too fast, given what still lay in front of me.

I spent the next two hours giving interviews, smiling for photos, signing books and posters, and chatting with fellow runners. At one point, I looked up from my seat to find John the twelve-year-old runner and his mother standing before me. He looked as good as new.

"Did you finish?" I asked hopefully.

"Piece of cake," he replied. He was beaming from ear to ear.

As I signed his well-worn copy of my book, John told me excitedly about his future race plans. It's a funny thing: If you're truly born to run, erupting within sight of the finish line can be as likely to hook you on the sport as winning the race.

> **QUICK TAKE:** *Raw ginger is a wonderful digestive aid for minor upset stomach and nausea. Try pickled ginger and ginger chews for a gentler response, or use freshly cut gingerroot if you're seeking stronger relief. Use it either before you run to prevent problems, or during a run at the first sign of trouble.*

Moments after John and his mother bid me farewell, I felt raindrops against my skin. At first, it was just a misty sprinkle, but within fifteen minutes it was pouring buckets.

The crowd scattered. The Endurance 50 crew sprang into action, scrambling like a retreating army to disassemble and pack away everything before it got drenched. The festival area began to look more and more like a battlefield. Strewn everywhere were saturated posters, soggy half-eaten food scraps, and debris spilled from overflowing trash cans. A humid fog rose from the soaking hot pavement. The crew worked in gloomy silence. The banter and laughter that had punctuated their cooperative efforts only yesterday were not to be heard.

When the tedious job was completed at last, Topher bid us a hasty farewell. He would catch an evening flight back to Europe. Julie gave me one last hug. She too was heading for the airport. My parents and the kids climbed inside their small rented RV to follow the tour bus on a three-hundred-mile drive to Memphis, site of tomorrow's marathon.

Inevitably, a healthy sampling of wetness and filth created by the recent deluge was tracked onto the bus. A dank stench now filled our cramped quarters. The windows clouded over with

After the Marathon

Given our travel requirements, my typical post-marathon routine during the Endurance 50 was not ideal for recovery. Here's what you *should* do after finishing a marathon:

• Drink plenty of water to rehydrate your body. Drink enough so that your urine is consistently clear or pale yellow in color.
• Eat a nice hearty meal containing protein to repair your muscles, as well as carbohydrate to replenish your depleted muscle fuel stores. Examples include fish with rice pilaf, a turkey wrap, and pasta with meat sauce.
• Immerse your legs in an ice bath for ten minutes to reduce swelling and muscle pain. I do this regularly at home, but it wasn't practical during the Endurance 50.
• Hit the sack early and sleep as long as necessary to wake up feeling fully rested.
• Try to run—okay, hobble—the next day for at least twenty minutes to work out the stiffness.

condensation. Everything inside our mobile locker room became damp and slimy, and the floorboards were a slippery hazard.

"Well, this is pretty," I said to English with forced levity as I stepped aboard the bus. He grunted affirmation.

After we began rolling, I felt the exhaustion come on. It was not the muscular depletion I was accustomed to feeling after a hard run but the brain-centered fatigue that one feels at the end of one's wedding day, after twelve straight hours of meeting, greeting, gabbing, smiling, solving small crises and being on stage. The marathon had taken a little out of me, but the post-race festivities had taken most of what remained. I wondered how the heck I could possibly keep this thing together all the way to New York, our final destination forty-nine days in the future.

How to Officially Run Fifty Consecutive Marathons

How is it possible to run fifty official marathons in fifty days in fifty states when most marathons take place on the weekends? Our solution was to involve the race directors of all the marathons whose sanctioned courses we chose to officially run. Sure, it required a ton of work and became a massive, painstaking undertaking, but it was the only legitimate way to accomplish the goal of running fifty marathons in fifty states in fifty days. It took us many months to get all the logistics in place, but it was the right decision.

We knew that many of the marathon course maps posted on the Internet were either incomplete or followed routes that were not passable on foot except on race day. Without the help of the race directors, we wouldn't be certain we ran their actual marathon. Anyone could question our credibility. We had gone the extra mile in every other phase of planning the Endurance 50; none of us was willing to compromise here.

From all this planning, hard work, and forethought, we now had an official starting line, a mechanism for following the sanctioned course, an official finish line, and an official race clock. Without all this in place, someone could legitimately debate the validity of the accomplishment. We had taken the extra measures to ensure we had the certification to prove each marathon. Done any other way, I couldn't have slept at night.

We also wanted potential participants to be able to sign up for the Endurance 50 marathons just as they would any other marathon. So interested runners could go to the Endurance 50 Web site and register on an Active.com page just like they would for any other running event. They were sent an official entrant's packet prior to the marathon, and they were entered in the system and cross-referenced upon sign-in at the marathon start. To all appearances, this was just like every other race.

Did we start on the right foot after all? I asked myself. The surest way to experience a disastrous marathon is to run before you're ready—before you've done the hard training that's necessary to prepare your body to go the distance. The chaos of today's post-race autograph frenzy, the unexpected brutality of packing up and leaving in a monsoon, and the dispirited looks I now saw on the faces of Koop, Hopps (now bald-headed), and Dave, our rock-and-roll tour manager, suggested we might very well have bitten off more than we could chew. Enduring forty-nine more days of this seemed highly improbable.

Moments later, I caught myself making emergency contingency plans. We could return the sponsors' money, ditch the tour bus, and finish this thing on the small scale it maybe should have started on. But I realized this vision was an idle fantasy. Forget the sponsors—how could I disappoint the dozens more Johns out there waiting to have an experience like his (minus the hurling, I hoped)? No way. The Endurance 50 would have to be all or nothing.

Quit your whining, Karno, I told myself. *It's going to take a lot more than a bumpy start to stop this expedition.*

On the long drive that night, I read an e-mail that lifted my spirits and reaffirmed my commitment to keep going, not to mention providing a good belly laugh. It was in reference to the surprise renewal of my wedding vows with Julie. It went like this:

Message to Dean Karnazes –

Dude, you suck. You've now set the bar so high that none of us will be able to rival that. My wife keeps asking me what my plans are for the next marathon. I know *exactly* what she's getting at!

Good luck Karno. Just, please, for the sake of all of us guys out here, don't pull anything like that again.

CHAPTER 2

Thank You for Your Support

Day 2
September 18, 2006
St. Jude Memphis Marathon
Memphis, Tennessee
Elevation: 778'
Weather: 78 degrees; heavy rain showers
Time: 4:19:58
Net calories burned: 6,374
Number of runners: 17

deally, on the day before you run a marathon, you do a short jog in the morning to release some pent-up energy, relax the rest of the day, eat a healthy dinner, and turn in early. On the day before I ran the re-created version of the St. Jude Memphis Marathon on Day 2 of The North Face Endurance 50, I had a predawn blood draw, ran a marathon in the morning, signed autographs for two hours, rode three hundred miles on a bus, and checked into a hotel at 1:00 AM.

Shortly after sunrise, I joined the crew back on the bus. English then drove us downtown in search of the official starting line near the corner of Fourth and Beale streets. After a while, I realized we were repeatedly circling the Memphis business district.

"There's nowhere to park." English said calmly, almost cheerfully.

The St. Jude Memphis Marathon is normally run on the first Sunday in December. Today was September 18. A Monday morning. Rush hour.

22

Dean's Routine

Each day of the Endurance 50 was scheduled to follow roughly the same time line:

5:00 AM Wake up.
6:00 AM Blood draw and urine collection (when scheduled, following research protocol).
6:30 AM Breakfast.
7:30 AM Arrive at starting line.
8:00 AM Start.
  Noon Finish (plus or minus one hour).
12:30 PM Finish Festival.
5:00 PM Wheels up.
6:00 PM Dinner on bus.
Midnight Arrive at next destination (plus or minus two hours).

Repeat 50 days.

At last we ditched the bus in a place of dubious legality and dashed blindly to the starting area across an intersection with no crosswalk. Awaiting our arrival were the seventeen runners who had signed up to run with me, race director Wain Rubenstein, and a large contingent of Memphis police officers who had just witnessed our death-defying group jaywalk (or "jayrun," as it were).

I shook Wain's hand and expressed my sincere gratitude for all the hard work he had done to make this event possible. Thanks to Wain, my new running friends and I would complete a formally sanctioned marathon this morning, with a certified course and an official race clock.

Staging marathons is a tough job. It demands long hours and with few exceptions is not especially high paying. Race directors take pride in giving most runners a great experience, and they

Sign Me Up

The number of runners in each Endurance 50 event varied considerably, from just one (the re-created Deadwood Mickelson Trail Marathon in South Dakota on Day 10) to forty-two-thousand (the live Chicago Marathon on Day 36). The eight live events were the largest, of course, because they had all of the infrastructure in place and permits lined up for mass participation. Most of the forty-two re-created marathons were capped at fifty participants, because that's the largest number we were able to obtain permits for. When support from local event organizers and officials allowed it, we were sometimes able to accommodate more runners. Other times, local authorities required us to cap the field at fewer than fifty runners.

Few of the early Endurance 50 marathons sold out. Interest steadily grew, though, and after a couple of weeks most events filled to capacity, with long waiting lists forming for some. None of us could believe it. In fact, many of the later marathons saw their share of "bandits"—non-official participants who missed the cutoff but wanted to run anyway. I had no problem with that during the re-created marathons. Many of these folks made generous donations to our charity to cover their participation.

grieve over the complaints they receive from a small number of participants who missed a turn or couldn't find their favorite sports drink flavor at an aid station. Race directors, their staffs, and their race-day volunteers are the unsung heroes of our sport.

After introductions were made, we turned our attention to the commanding officer, who gave us the game plan. His team would not close the roads entirely for 26.2 miles, as they do during the live marathon, he explained. Instead, they would create a sort of roaming road closure, using motorcycles to contain us runners in a manageable pod and sending patrol cars ahead to stop traffic as we ran through intersections.

"Can we order food?" one of the runners joked.

"Only if it's doughnuts," an officer shot back, drawing laughter.

I'd been on group runs before and was aware of at least some of the challenges this format would present. First of all, not everyone runs at the same pace—especially over such a great distance. How would the group hold together? Beyond differences in people's running pace, shoelaces come undone and need retying. Overheating occurs, and layers of clothing must be shed. Chafing arises and demands prompt attention. Also, what happens when nature calls? How welcome would the watchful eye of a police escort be then? There were bound to be more bumps in the road along the way. I just hoped these would be molehills and not mountains.

As they would at many of the daily marathons throughout the Endurance 50, Alexandria and Nicholas started us off by shouting, "On your marks . . . Get set . . . Go!" While we runners spent the next four hours sweating, the kids passed the morning by participating in homeschooling (or was it road-schooling?) under the tutelage of their grandmother, now retired from classroom teaching. They would break for lunch in time to hold up the finish line tape, hang out with us at the Finish Festival, and then usually do some sightseeing with my mom and dad while we packed and got ready to drive to the next state. All in all, not a bad routine.

Scarcely fifteen minutes after the first strides were taken of our inaugural re-created marathon, sure enough, it started raining heavily. Some of the runners had tied rain gear around their waists in anticipation of the inclement weather, but most had stashed their extra clothing in the SAG wagon that was trailing us. *SAG* stands for Support and Gear, although neither of these things was being provided at the moment, because the Toyota SUV that was serving this role was stuck in traffic well behind us. The rain had snarled intersections, and it was all the patrol officers could do to keep the runners moving along. The

When It Rains

Some runners don't like running in the rain. Others do. Including me. Running in the rain will do you no harm as long as you avoid totally saturated feet. Once your socks become soaked, your chances of getting a blister increase. Gore-Tex shoes can help keep your feet dry, up to a point. But when it's really coming down, be mindful of potential blistering, and stop, if possible, as soon as you feel a hot spot emerge. When running in the rain, you'll find it most comfortable to use breathable rain gear, such as the North Face Diad jacket, designed especially for this use. It will keep the water out without trapping your excess body heat against your skin.

SAG wagon was caught at a red light. Fortunately, its crew had a GPS system on board called "Never Lost." Unfortunately, it didn't work. After the device sent its occupants the wrong way several times, we started calling it "Never Found."

By the time the SAG wagon caught up, the damage had already been done. Most of us were soaked to the bone. Putting on rain gear at this point was useless, so no one even bothered.

Manning the vehicle were Garrett Greene, from the Squires Sports Group, and Koop, whose role in this operation seemed to be expanding by the minute—and thankfully so, because as a runner himself Koop understood exactly what I needed and when I needed it.

Garrett, on the other hand, was not a runner. He looked more like a lumberjack. A stocky and muscular figure with a laid-back demeanor and a Louisiana drawl, he was officially serving the Endurance 50 in the role of course manager, though currently he seemed more like a mobile vending machine, dispensing dozens of energy bars, bottles of fluid, and energy gels from the window of the SAG wagon as we traveled the next two blocks. As quickly as these goodies were handed out, they were snatched up by the runners and consumed. Empty packaging was then returned to the vehicle.

Back in the real world, Koop and Garrett held jobs that looked nothing like this one, yet here they were busting their tails as high-speed food and beverage servers without a hint of complaint. I felt my heart swell with gratitude for the second time this morning. *Where would we be without guys like these?* I thought.

The rain eventually lightened, the streets began drying out, the sun poked through the clouds, and the runners started sharing their stories. What I heard blew my mind.

"Where are you from?" I asked a tall guy in his early thirties who reminded me of the actor Zach Braff.

"Mexico," he said. He didn't look Mexican. Or sound Mexican.

"How long have you been in the United States?"

"No, I live in Mexico," he clarified.

"Oh. So what are you doing here?"

"Running a marathon with you."

His name was Brad, and he was indeed an American expatriate, originally from Nebraska. He explained that he had flown in from Mexico City for the express purpose of taking part in this event. He had arrived last night and would leave tonight. Over the next few miles, I learned that Brad had started running only within the past year, after he quit drinking. This was his first marathon. His dream was to create a foundation to help others use running as a tool to overcome addictions.

"That's a great idea," I said, and I meant it. There's no cure for an addictive personality. If you're going to express a compulsive tendency, it might as well be through running. As Lily Tomlin once joked, "Exercise is for people who can't handle drugs and alcohol."

The next runner I spoke with was Wally, an elementary school education director from North Carolina.

"Today's my twentieth wedding anniversary," he said.

"Congratulations! How are you going to celebrate?" I asked.

"I'm celebrating right now."

I laughed, thinking he was making a joke about his current state of suffering.

"I'm not kidding," Walter said. "My wife surprised me by signing me up and buying two round-trip tickets from Charlotte to Memphis."

I was speechless.

Another runner had taken a day off from work and driven all night to be here. Later, a big fellow named Paul, from Arkansas, told me he was planning to run three of the fifty marathons with me.

"You'll see me again in Oklahoma and Kentucky," he said.

"Wow! How long have you been planning for this?" I asked.

"Actually, I just decided to do the other two marathons now."

My jaw dropped.

Our tidy little pod began to disintegrate at mile twelve, as a couple of the first-timers found themselves struggling to hold our pace of roughly nine minutes per mile. This wound up happening at most of the subsequent events, and in the majority of cases it didn't cause major problems; Koop and Garrett did a terrific job shooting back and forth among the various splinter groups to provide needed aid.

The sun now had an unobstructed view of our progress, and the air was warming. Worse, my wet socks had softened the skin of my feet. As we shuffled past Sun Studio, where Elvis made his first recordings, I could feel a blister developing along the arch of my right foot, and I mentioned it to Koop.

"Do you want to tape it?" he asked.

"Nah. Let's just wait till we reach the finish."

Bad call. We got separated from the SAG wagon again, and that little hot spot on my foot developed into a nice baby volcano. By the time the finish line came into view, it was ready to erupt.

Aid Station Etiquette

Without the support provided by the volunteers who manage fluid stations and perform other essential duties, running events wouldn't happen. Make their jobs easier and more enjoyable by observing these points of etiquette:

• Call out what you're looking for as you approach the aid station. For example, "Water!" or "Sports drink!"
• Make eye contact with your chosen volunteer and extend your arm toward the cup being offered several paces before you reach him or her.
• Thank the volunteer who hands you your drink.
• Try not to stop or slow down in the flow of runners. Instead, pull off to the side to drink, if necessary.
• To avoid potentially spraying other runners, don't throw your cup across the way, but drop it straight down, preferably in one of the trash cans provided along the course.

I quickly forgot about my foot, however, when I saw Alexandria and Nicholas stretching the finishing tape across the road. A couple of dozen spectators lined the streets, shouting encouragement as we made our way down the final stretch.

We runners spontaneously joined hands and lifted our arms in the air as we took our last few strides together. Cameras flashed, hands clapped, bells clanged, and police sirens wailed. My kids greeted me with big hugs.

Now the second marathon began. Hopps ushered me over to the media area (or "mosh pit," as I began calling it). The television networks were given precedence. CBS was first. Then Fox. Then came a barrage of reporters from newspapers, radio stations, and magazines. After doing my best to remain coherent throughout the interviews, I staggered over to the huddle of tired runners who had been waiting patiently for me at the Finish Festival.

The Rub

A lot of people thought I would be getting lengthy rubdowns and massages during the Endurance 50. I should have been so lucky. The reality is that there just wasn't any idle time for such niceties. Upon completing a marathon, many of the runners wanted to have me sign their finisher's certificate or book, and perhaps snap a photo or two. Most were tired and sweaty, and wanted to get to a shower. I didn't think it would be fair to make them stand around for an hour waiting while I got a rubdown.

On the bus, there was simply no extra room to house another traveler. We were already cramped with our existing crew. There was no way I was going to burden those guys with another passenger. In the spirit of being a team player, I had to make sacrifices. The bodywork and massages would have to wait until Day 51.

By the time I had signed everything and talked with everyone, it was getting on into the afternoon.

"Shouldn't we be going now?" I asked Dave. After all, we had a 425-mile drive to Mississippi ahead of us.

"Yeah, yeah," he said, but there was still stuff strewn everywhere. Our Moroccan bazaar looked like the victim of an unexpected windstorm.

When I eventually climbed aboard the bus, I found Nicholas perched in the driver's seat, in the rightful place of English, who occupied the passenger's seat across from him.

"Dad, Memphis is so cool!" Nicholas gushed.

"Are you having fun?" I asked.

"We're having a blast!" he announced, then bolted for the door, giving English a high five on the way out.

"Reminds me of my kids when they were that age," English said, with a proud smile on his face.

Nicholas, of all people, seemed to have broken through English's English reserve, and we got to talking. I learned that he had been driving a rig like this across the country for the past twenty-eight years. "Don't use a map anymore," he told me. "No need."

Crew members busily filed in and out of the vehicle as we chatted away. Finally, Koop came in and shut the door. English glanced over at him and casually asked, "Are we a bus?"

Koop pointed around with his finger, taking a head count. "We're a bus," he said.

English started the ignition, and soon the buildings of Memphis were behind us, though the memories lived on within as we rumbled down the highway.

I was embarrassed to tell Koop about the blister. Not taking appropriate prophylactic measures was a rookie mistake. There shouldn't *be* a blister on my foot—not in marathon number two. I decided to just air it out and otherwise not mess with it much. With any luck, the skin would stay intact.

Every runner is familiar with the sin of knowing better—of stubbornly pushing ahead despite warnings from the more sensible parts of our minds. The desire to keep running until the task is completed or the goal achieved is so great that it overrides our better knowledge and our self-protective faculties. Here are a couple of typical scenarios:

1. On a long, hot run in the summer, you run out of sports drink with an hour to go and think, *I should stop at a convenience store and use my emergency five-dollar bill to buy another bottle.* Then you think, *Nah, I'll be fine.* Then you overheat. Recovery over the next several days is a grind, and your training schedule is disrupted.

2. In the early weeks of your marathon training, you develop a pain in your shin that gets a little worse each day. You think, *I should take a few days off.* Then you think, *I can't take a few days off. I'll get out of shape. The pain will probably go away on its own.* So you keep training, and as a result you develop a stress fracture that sidelines you for a month.

Grandmother's advice was prudent: "An ounce of prevention is worth a pound of cure." Yet every runner I know, including myself, has committed the sin of knowing better. Most people eventually learn to avoid repeating certain costly mistakes. Not me. As many miles as I've logged, I still make remedial blunders—like the one that had just turned my foot into an oozing, ticking time bomb.

It was nearing two in the morning when we reached our hotel and approaching three o'clock when I finally lay down to rest. *Two down, forty-eight to go*, I thought. My body felt like it was still running.

When I stepped outside the motel door in my running attire three hours later, I was greeted by a wall of warm, swampy air and a swarm of aggressive mosquitoes. Twenty hardy souls had signed up to run with me today, and it would be a test for all of us. We met up near the front gates of the Stennis Space Center, a sprawling NASA rocket testing facility located in a vast emptiness near the Mississippi–Louisiana boarder. We glistened with premature sweat and swatted our hands ineffectually at buzzing vermin as the thick air folded in upon us.

The Mississippi Coast Marathon is a flat, out-and-back course that travels along a quiet stretch of rural highway. And I mean flat. Its only hill is an overpass. We could nearly see the turn-around spot from the starting line. The mercury rose steadily as we ran. Waves of heat and moisture wafted skyward from the highway, blurring the horizon. Thick green foliage lined the roadway. A pungent, earthy vapor permeated the atmosphere, like a spinach salad being microwaved.

My blister began complaining almost immediately. By mile six it was shouting. At the halfway mark, it was screaming bloody murder.

Garrett and Koop met us at the turnaround holding plates of cut bananas. Reaching for a slice of banana, I stuck my finger right through its yellowy-brown skin. The sun had roasted the exterior into oblivion. The innards were syrupy brown, but I was hungry, so I slurped down the warm mess with both hands, dribbles of pudding-like extrusion running down my chin. What runner hasn't done something similar? Replenishment takes precedence over vanity.

Almost exactly one year earlier, the area where we were now running had been pummeled by Hurricane Katrina, and there were lingering signs of devastation everywhere. We passed houses and shops missing roofs and windows, felled trees, and

Knowing When to Say When

Toughness and determination are good qualities to have as a runner, but there can be too much of a good thing. Sometimes you need to be smarter than you are tough or determined. Here are four circumstances under which you should immediately stop running and "live to fight another day":

- Never try to run through more than moderate pain in a muscle, bone, or joint.
- Stop running whenever you experience dizziness, light-headedness, confusion, or blurred vision—all of which are symptoms of heat illness and severe dehydration.
- Don't try to continue training as normal when experiencing signs of overtraining syndrome, including persistent fatigue, declining performance, lasting muscle soreness, and low motivation.
- Do not attempt to run when experiencing a fever, flu-like symptoms, or other ailments, including diarrhea and food poisoning.

mangled road signs. At one point, we passed a bog that smelled of rotting animal carcasses.

"This area got hit pretty bad," said a gentleman in his late forties running next to me, who introduced himself as Jeff. Many of the runners in our group, including Jeff, lived in the area and had lost homes, businesses, and even loved ones in the storm.

"My shop was destroyed," he continued with surprising matter-of-factness. "But I was lucky. I had insurance and I was able to rebuild. A lot of other local business owners had no insurance." Unfortunately, however, many former residents had left the area, leaving Jeff with a fraction of his former customer base.

"You seem very resilient," I said.

"Do you want to know my secret?" he asked.

"I'd like to."

"Running," he said. "As funny as it sounds, it's running more than anything else that's given me the strength to get through it. No matter what else I lost, I could still run."

Through pants and puffs, another runner told me that he had recently lost eighty-five pounds. His doctor, a runner himself, had inspired him to change his life. "That's him next to you," he said. The two of them had driven all night to get here.

"Talk about going the extra mile for a patient!" I quipped.

There was a healthy crowd of supporters, local officials, and media folks awaiting our arrival at the finish line, and before I even had a chance to wipe the perspiration from my brow, a reporter jabbed a microphone at my mouth. As I answered her questions, my thoughts trailed back down the road with the few straggling runners, three of them first-timers, who were still on the course. I wanted to greet them at the finish line. Then maybe enjoy a cold margarita poolside with the whole group.

Instead, Jimmy Hopper escorted me over to the mosh pit to do several more interviews.

"Hey, Hopps, this is kind of draining," I said. There's nothing I hate more than being a complainer, but I just couldn't help myself. I was sweaty and tired, and I really just wanted to chill for a few minutes.

"Hang in there, bro," he said, handing me a bottle of water. "I feel for you." I thanked him, took a quick swig, shook my head like a wet dog, and tried to regroup for the line of reporters standing there.

By the time I heard those familiar words "Are we a bus?" I was nearly comatose. This was no time to take pity on my own sorry self, however. The crew had worked their tails off to make today happen. They had erected and then deconstructed a small city, moving thousands of pounds of equipment and supplies, and had kept twenty-one marathon runners safe and healthy in brutally hot conditions. We slumped into seats on the bus and stared at one another numbly, wondering how this could go on for forty-seven more days.

"Things have got to be tighter," Hopps said.

I looked at him in surprise. He seemed so young. When I'd first met Hopps, he had an unbridled youthful exuberance that was partly expressed in the golden locks of hair that dangled down to his shoulders. Now his head was shaved, and a new veneer of manly responsibility shaded his boyish lack of restraint.

"The process needs to be revamped," Garrett agreed. "We need better structure."

Dave nodded in apparent agreement but said nothing. As Hopps, Garrett, and Koop began to earnestly trade ideas about how to better manage the press, decrease my workload, improve the runners' post-race experience, and streamline the Finish Festival setup and breakdown procedures, I clumsily made my way to the back of the bus, struggling to maintain balance as the vehicle rumbled down the rough Southern highway. Pulling my shoe off, I saw that the blister was getting worse. It had grown wider, deeper, and more discolored. Why I hadn't immediately attended to it after the marathon today was beyond me. I knew better.

Koop was working as hard as he could to keep my body glued together, and here I was sabotaging his efforts by making a truly amateurish mistake and then exacerbating the problem by keeping it hidden due to my embarrassment. I was sure he'd be pissed, as he had every right to be, when I finally did tell him.

Past midnight I wandered to the front of the bus, expecting to find everyone asleep. Instead, I found Hopps, Garrett, and Koop still sitting around with papers spread everywhere, discussing plans and jotting down notes, their cell phones at the ready. They had taken matters into their own hands.

Just as important, despite their almost nonstop workload, they had somehow managed to collect a young lady's phone number today. Like me, they now stood at three for three.

CHAPTER 4

The Amazing Miracle Marathon Diet

Day 4
September 20, 2006
Little Rock Marathon
Little Rock, Arkansas
Elevation: 260'
Weather: 81 degrees; sunny and dry
Time: 4:14:38
Net calories burned: 12,748
Number of runners: 10

By the time we arrived in Little Rock, Arkansas, the site of our fourth marathon, dawn was fast approaching. Entering my hotel room only ninety minutes before I had to leave it again, I was faced with a simple choice: I could either catch a quick power nap or make some efforts to restore my personal hygiene, which was in a sorry state. There wasn't enough time to do both. I chose to nap.

Upon waking, I had just enough time to quickly glance at my face in the bathroom mirror before dashing out the door. What I saw wasn't pretty. I looked like the creature from the Black Lagoon. Maybe worse. Thick, dark stubble covered my chin, and hair was flying in every which direction. Oh, well. The North Face Endurance 50 wasn't a beauty pageant, after all.

Fortunately, Hopps had told me that today would be mellow. The marketing folks at The North Face hadn't been able to drum up much media interest, and only nine runners had signed up to traverse the Little Rock Marathon racecourse alongside me. I couldn't have been happier. We needed a recovery day.

Sitting in a reflective trance as Koop drove the SAG wagon toward the downtown starting area, I relished a brief moment of peace. Very brief.

"What the #?%*!" Garrett suddenly exclaimed, jarring me back to reality.

The rest of us looked at him and then followed his gaze out the front window. Parked along one side of Capitol Avenue was a long column of television vans with satellite dishes perched on top. An intimidating procession of glossy black Suburbans encircled the starting area. Men wearing dark suits and dark glasses stood on each corner, slowly turning their heads from side to side like lawn sprinklers. A large crowd of people was gathered inside the circle of government vehicles, and the side-walks were lined with passersby attracted by—and adding to— the hullabaloo.

I turned to Hopps, Garrett, and Koop, and asked, "Did any-body else not brush his teeth this morning?"

What we did not know, but would soon discover, was that the governor of Arkansas, Mike Huckabee, was waiting for us at the starting line, wearing running gear, no less.

Thanks to the many logos covering the vehicle, the SAG wagon was easily spotted by the sea of reporters, who immedi-ately surrounded the car. Still cameras clicked, television cam-eras rolled, and microphones jostled for position in front of me as reporters shot rapid-fire questions in my direction.

A man dressed in running clothes now stepped forward, politely parting the huddle of reporters, and shook my hand.

"Hi, Dean," he said. "I'm Mike Huckabee. Glad to meet you." His calm, reassuring demeanor immediately put me at ease. He asked me how I was feeling after running three marathons in three days—surprising me with his intimate knowledge of the Endurance 50 agenda—and informed me with unfeigned disappointment that he only had time to run six or seven miles with the group this morning. He then gave the press a chance to ask each of us a few questions and snap photos of us shaking hands. It was an interesting way to warm up for a marathon.

Alexandria and Nicholas officially started the marathon by shouting, "On your mark. Get set. Go!" Amid flashing lights and wailing sirens, our small group shuffled down Capitol Avenue, flanked by a squadron of police escorts and Secret Service agents.

As natural as he now seemed gliding along next to me, Governor Huckabee—turned presidential hopeful Mike Huckabee as I write this—hadn't always been a runner. In fact, he used to be 110 pounds heavier. During his first years in office, simply climbing the steps of the Capitol Building left him out of breath and sweating profusely. He secretly feared that he would be interviewed by the media at the top of the steps, and that he would be unable to respond appropriately due to his lack of breath. In 2003, his physician diagnosed the governor with adult-onset diabetes, informing him that he would not live more than ten years if he did not lose weight.

That was four marathons ago.

Mike Huckabee is living proof of the unique power of running to cure the most insidious health conditions afflicting our society today: obesity, heart disease, and a host of other weight-related maladies, including adult-onset diabetes. But while he may be the most prominent example of what I jokingly call "the amazing miracle marathon diet" at work, there are countless more examples among everyday folks. In fact, as I listened to Governor Huckabee recount his experience—not the least bit out of breath despite the fact that he was running nine-minute miles as he talked—I was reminded that I had already met several Endurance 50 participants, most of them men, who had lost large amounts of weight on the amazing miracle marathon diet.

Ease Into It

While running is one of the best means to lose weight, it's important that you ease into it if you're currently overweight and new to this form of exercise. Running puts a lot of stress on the lower extremities. If you don't give your bones and joints a chance to adapt, you could get injured. Start by walking. Once a brisk walk has become fairly easy, insert brief segments of slow running into your walks (preferably on dirt or grass). Gradually increase the duration of these running segments until you're able to comfortably run the full distance of your workout. Here's a sample four-week progression:

	MON.	TUES.	WED.	THURS.	FRI.	SAT.	SUN.
WEEK 1	Walk 20 min.	Off	Walk 20 min.	Off	Walk 9 min., jog 2 min., walk 9 min.	Off	Walk 8 min., jog 4 min., walk 8 min.
WEEK 2	Walk 25 min.	Off	Walk 7 min., jog 6 min., walk 7 min.	Off	Walk 4 min., jog 4 min., walk 4 min., jog 4 min., walk 4 min.	Off	Walk 4 min., jog 5 min., walk 4 min., jog 5 min., walk 4 min.
WEEK 3	Walk 30 min.	Off	Walk 6 min., jog 8 min., walk 6 min.	Walk 20 min.	Walk 3 min., jog 6 min., walk 3 min., jog 6 min., walk 3 min.	Off	Walk 5 min., jog 10 min., walk 5 min.
WEEK 4	Off	Walk 2 min., jog 8 min., walk 2 min., jog 8 min., walk 2 min.	Walk 30 min.	Walk 4 min., jog 12 min., walk 4 min.	Walk 4 min., jog 12 min., walk 4 min.	Walk 30 min.	Jog 20 min.

The Dean's List

Here are some of my current favorite quick race fuels that'll surely give you a lift:

- Clif Shot Bloks
- Sports Beans Energizing Jelly Beans
- Ginger People Ginger Chews
- Peet's Coffee Chocolate Covered Espresso Beans
- Sharkies Organic Energy Fruit Chews

There's something about the goal of finishing a marathon, or even a half-marathon or 10k, that enables an individual to establish exercise as a daily habit and shed excess weight. Strangely enough, those who start running with no other goal than to lose weight often do not have the same level of success. For whatever reason, people find more motivation in looking months ahead to the dream of completing an event—which, for most, will be the hardest physical challenge they have ever faced—than they find in simply trying to run three or four miles a day to lose some fat.

Intrigued by the governor, I peppered him with questions as we ran. The other runners—most of them citizens of Arkansas—also seemed content to let Huckabee do most of the talking. I was particularly interested in hearing about his state's widely celebrated recent initiative aimed at addressing childhood obesity by removing soda and unhealthy snacks from school vending machines, improving the nutritional value of school lunches, and so forth.

"Is it working?" I asked.

"The most recent data we have shows that childhood obesity levels in Arkansas have started to level off, after climbing for years," he said. "It's a start, but we have a long way to go."

"That's encouraging," I said. Mike Huckabee and I share a cause. My Karno's Kids foundation attacks the same problem his administration has chosen as a top priority by promoting physical activity and a good diet. Our mission is to inspire and motivate kids to get outside and become physically active. In fact, our official motto is "No Child Left Inside." So the next words out of Huckabee's mouth were heartening.

> QUICK TAKE: *If you're looking to shed a few pounds, try eating more protein in the morning. Studies show that consuming protein in the AM helps control appetite, preserve muscle, and increase fat loss.*

"You know, Dean, we can't legislate this country back into shape," he said. "Mandating better school nutrition and stuff like that is a step in the right direction, but the key to truly solving the problem is efforts like yours."

"Really?" I said reflexively.

"We need role models to inspire others," he said. "That's what motivates people to change their lifestyle. Kids have to want that for themselves. No law can make a kid want to eat right and exercise. But you do it every day by setting an example."

I was so gratified by the governor's compliment, I didn't think to mention that he had become a pretty good role model himself. In fact, he was currently training for his fifth marathon—the New York City Marathon—which happened to be the final stop of the Endurance 50.

Before he peeled away from the group to take care of the day's gubernatorial business, Huckabee gave me a valuable piece of advice. He had asked me what the hardest part of the Endurance 50 had been so far.

"Honestly, it's dealing with the media," I said. "I like running all night by myself; dealing with the press doesn't come naturally to me."

"Listen," he said. "I know the press can sometimes be a distraction, but don't think of it that way. Think of the media as a very powerful tool that you can leverage to help change the world in the ways I know you want to change it."

He was right. I made a silent vow to do my best to be more comfortable with the press from that day forward.

"I'll see you in the Big Apple" were Governor Mike Huckabee's last words to me.

"You've got a deal," I said, feeling that the New York City Marathon was still a lifetime away.

We were approaching the seven-mile mark when Huckabee left us, along with his security detail. The nine remaining runners now got the opportunity to share their stories. I learned that one of the two women in our group was a member of Huckabee's staff. She had been so modest that I had no clue she knew him. Another runner told me he was a physician; this was his first marathon. He had left the emergency room at one o'clock this morning and driven through the night to get here. By the time we passed the halfway mark, he was already struggling.

"I'll make it," he said, "but I can't keep up with you guys." He gently faded behind us with a few of the other runners.

The rest of the group held together impressively. We crossed the finish line shortly after noon, by which time it had turned into one of those glorious afternoons when summer blends with a hint of fall. It was warm and dry with a gentle breeze and soft sunlight that was unobstructed except by a few wispy clouds.

The Finish Festival, which had been set up smack in front of the Capitol Building, was our best yet. Alexandria and Nicholas ran about and played excitedly with the crew. Six or seven members of the governor's task force on childhood obesity were present and eagerly chatted with my kids, whom they seemed to view as models for the children of Arkansas. Nicholas asked them whether they had any soda pop or candy. Even at eight years old, he had a quick wit and mischievous sense of humor.

During the short ceremony that we performed daily during the Finish Festival on the little stage that traveled with us, a representative of the governor's office presented my dad and

Follow the Losers
According to research data, these are the top three habits of men and women who lose significant amounts of weight and keep it off permanently:

1. Daily exercise
2. Portion control
3. Behavior modification

me and with large framed certificates. She explained that they were decrees appointing us as Arkansas Travelers, or official ambassadors of the state. My dad asked if this meant we got a key to the city. He hoped so, because he'd heard there were some legendary rib joints nearby.

The crew put off dismantling the Finish Festival as long as they could, because none of us wanted this perfect afternoon to end. The sun was sinking toward the horizon when the last of the gear was being stowed back in the bus. Then our first-time marathoner, the physician who had driven all night, came into view, lumbering toward the finish line. I had just enough time to dash over and congratulate him before we drove away. It was the perfect finish to the perfect day. Little did I know what lay in store for tomorrow.

Day 5
September 21, 2006
Wichita Marathon
Wichita, Kansas
Elevation: 1,544'
Weather: 62 degrees; gale-force winds and driving rain
Time: 4:23:18
Net calories burned: 15,935
Number of runners: 22

During our long drive from Little Rock, Arkansas, to Wichita, Kansas, we heard that a major storm was in the forecast for our twenty-two-person re-creation of the Wichita Marathon the next morning. Sure enough, dawn brought rain, and wind—a Kansas specialty. By mile fourteen, a raging storm was upon us. The rain came down sideways, pelting our bodies and stinging our faces as it hit. To avoid being blinded by bullet-like liquid projectiles, we ran with our heads down, tracking off the lines in the road to keep our bearings.

The wind whipped across the open expanse of Kansas prairie land, making forward progress almost impossible for us when we ran into it and nearly blowing us off the road when we changed direction and exposed our flank to a crosswind. Pebbles from the roadway were lifted into the air and driven into our legs and lower bodies like pellets from an air gun.

One of the runners succumbed to hypothermia. Two others sought refuge inside an outhouse to escape the elements. Yet as a whole, the group showed incredible grit and mind-over-body determination. Three first-time marathoners crossed the finish line. How they were able to accomplish this remarkable triumph in conditions that tested even the most experienced runners is a question I can't begin to answer. I was just glad to have witnessed it. Inspiration is a two-way street. On this day, I was the primary beneficiary.

I was also blessed by the magic of Koop. The rain today had further exacerbated my blister, and there was no avoiding the need for treatment now. When I showed him, he used a butterfly needle (a very small-gauged hollow needle typically used in venipuncture) and drained the wound brilliantly. Then, using a thin strip of sterile gauze and some duct tape—yes, that silver adhesive tape widely used by car mechanics and industrial shop workers—he expertly patched my foot with near clinical precision.

And just like that, I never felt a thing from this day forward.

CHAPTER 5

Here Comes the Future

Day 6
September 22, 2006
Des Moines Marathon
Des Moines, Iowa
Elevation: 1,205'
Weather: 68 degrees; partly cloudy
Time: 4:06:33
Net calories burned: 19,122
Number of runners: 35

The last tune-up race I ran before starting The North Face Endurance 50 was the Leadville Trail 100—a classic one-hundred-mile footrace that follows rugged trails up and down the Rocky Mountains in the vicinity of Leadville, Colorado. It almost killed me. My legs had been thrashed from too much racing before I even started the Leadville 100, so I found myself struggling early. As I wheezed my way along the seemingly endless climb to the summit of Hope Pass, elevation 12,500 feet, I locked strides with a fit young woman who introduced herself as Jamie Donaldson. I knew of Jamie and joked that I was surprised to see her "back here with the slowpokes."

We ran the next sixty miles together, taking turns encouraging each other and, eventually, taking turns puking. There's a lot of time to talk when you run sixty miles on someone's shoulder. I told Jamie all about the Endurance 50, which was then just a few weeks from beginning. She told me she taught the sixth grade at a school near Littleton, Colorado.

"Hey, you know what?" she said. "I think it might be really cool if I created a lesson plan around the Endurance 50 for my students. We could learn a little geography, some math—maybe even throw in a bit of science."

Weird science, I thought.

Jamie was not the first runner-teacher to whom this idea had occurred. Several teachers had already contacted me about creating a lesson plan around the Endurance 50. But the potential scope of this aspect of our endeavor never crossed my mind until I met Jamie. I guess I hadn't realized just how many American schoolteachers also happen to be runners. As it turned out, hundreds of classrooms around the country—most (but not all) of them headed by teachers who run—followed the Endurance 50. The calendar of marathons that had been published in *Runner's World* was pinned up in classrooms across America. In every state we visited, there were passionate educators who saw the learning value in having their students follow the event, and who, along with their pupils, poured tremendous energy, enthusiasm, and creativity into making the most of it.

Some teachers whose schools happened to be located within driving distance of an event made their own arrangements to get their students to the site and give them an opportunity to run a short stretch with me—which added a real-life component to the lesson plan. A runner-teacher in Nevada loaded three classes onto a small fleet of school buses and rode two hours to run the last mile of the Valley of Fire Marathon with me.

Eric Baker, a seventh-grade special education teacher from Indiana, found a clever way to teach his students how to subtract with decimals (a skill they struggled with). Each day he had them subtract 26.2 miles from my fifty-state mileage total. (On Mondays, they subtracted 78.6 miles for Friday's, Saturday's, and Sunday's marathons.) By the time we reached Indiana (marathon number thirty-nine), nearly all of his pupils had mastered it.

Chris Shell, a middle school teacher in Wausau, Wisconsin, also created a math lesson around the Endurance 50 by tracking my cumulative distance, average pace, and other numbers with his classes.

As we passed through Billings in the last few miles of the Montana Marathon, we ran by Central Heights Elementary School. One of the teachers, Kris Cummings, was running the marathon with us that day. His entire fifth-grade class was waiting for us. They were wearing T-shirts with the phrase ENDURANCE IS . . . printed on the back. We all ran together to the finish line.

Along the way, Kris had explained to me that the school's fourth-, fifth-, and sixth-grade classes were following the Endurance 50 as part of a lesson plan he had designed, and that each of the students was required to write his or her interpretation of what endurance is on the back of his or her T-shirt.

At the Finish Festival, I had an opportunity to check out what some of them had come up with. I saw:

ENDURANCE IS . . . NEVER GIVING UP!

ENDURANCE IS . . . ALWAYS TRYING YOUR HARDEST.

And one little boy had written: ENDURANCE IS . . . SITTING THROUGH CLASS. At least no one could fault his honesty.

These are but a few examples of the tremendous classroom creativity I witnessed and heard about during the Endurance 50.

Although it wasn't planned so, the majority of my interactions with students and teachers involved in the Endurance 50 occurred through the Internet and e-mail. It started slowly, but grew and grew until it was very nearly out of control. During the 450-mile drive from Little Rock, Arkansas, to Wichita, Kansas, site of my fifth marathon, I had sat down at the computer to catch up on e-mails and nearly fell off my seat when I found that more than one hundred messages had accumulated in my inbox within the past twenty-four hours, many of them from teachers and students.

It took me nearly six hours to respond to all these messages. A couple of times motion sickness upset my stomach so severely that I had to close my eyes and stop breathing to keep dinner down, but I worked through it and got the job done. I could not bear the thought of letting down the teachers and students across the country who wanted to participate remotely in my adventure. I was nearly cross-eyed by the time I finished, after midnight, but if this was what it took to inspire even one child—one more steward of our nation's future—to become more active and adventurous, the effort was worthwhile.

A similar scenario had played out the previous night. As soon as the tour bus got rolling toward Des Moines, Iowa, I settled back in front of my computer to check my inbox with curious anticipation. Sure enough, the volume of e-mail messages from teachers, students, and others that I found awaiting my attention was even greater than it had been the day before. The Endurance 50 blog hosted on RunnersWorld.com had become the most visited section of their entire Web site. In the messages awaiting my response was one from my own Web master, who manages my personal site. He asked me what

Running and Sleep

Due to commitments that extended beyond running, and the travel factor, I slept little during the Endurance 50—no more than five hours a night, typically. This was not ideal. Research has shown that adequate sleep is needed to repair and refuel muscles between runs. The effects of sleep deprivation are cumulative, so that even a modest amount of sleep deprivation each night can add up to big problems over time. As few as thirty hours of cumulative sleep deprivation have been shown to reduce the cardiovascular performance of runners by more than 10 percent. If you need eight hours of sleep a night and get only seven, your running may be compromised within a month. If you want to run well, do as I say, not as I did during the Endurance 50, and get the sleep you need!

the heck was going on—the jump in traffic had blown out our server!

By the time I had answered each of the messages, we had nearly completed our 390-mile drive.

At mile ten of the Des Moines Marathon, the course makes a loop around the famous blue Drake University track. When I arrived there with the large, spirited group of nearly three dozen runners who had signed up to run with me today, we were greeted by the Drake University mascot (a bulldog named Spike) and more than fifty young kids wearing matching yellow T-shirts. *Here comes the future!* I thought, as the kids wildly broke ranks and stampeded around the track with us, cheering and throwing high fives the whole way. The smallest of the children was a towheaded boy, no more than six years old, who seemed intent on demonstrating his fabulous running form and speed to me. I was rightfully impressed and congratulated him on his magnificent stride.

"Mr. Karnazes," he said, panting, "I run like I mean it!"

We had just completed our lap when a woman standing at the exit from the track handed me one of those bright yellow T-shirts, in my size, that had been signed by all of the children who'd run a quarter mile with me. The words KIDSTRONG IOWA, INC. were silk-screened on the front. I learned later that the woman who handed me the shirt was Cindy Elsbernd, founder and president of Kidstrong Iowa.

Cindy is a veteran of multiple marathons who started this organization in response to her concerns about the childhood obesity epidemic. With two young kids of her own, these concerns began right at home. The program's concept is simple but brilliant. Participating elementary schools invite their students to take part in supervised walking and running sessions during their recess time. For every five miles a child accumulates, he or she is given a little plastic foot that can be attached to shoelaces. Kids being what they are, they get very excited about these plastic feet.

Tips for Parents of Youth Runners

- Lead by example. If you run, your kids probably will. If you tell them to run, they probably won't.
- Keep it fun by varying runs with different environments (trails, grass, tracks) and workout types (hills, sprints, easy runs, and so on).
- Celebrate every run as an accomplishment, even if it's just with a sweaty hug. (That probably means more from a parent than all the finisher's medals in the world.)
- Kids love technology. Consider incorporating it into your child's running. My kids enjoy using a GPS device that allows us to map runs in real time as we go.
- Kids are naturally competitive. Give them opportunities to compete in fun runs and such. But be sure to teach them that, win or lose, every race is a success when they give their best effort.

Children who amass a whole marathon's worth of walking or running are rewarded with one of those cool yellow T-shirts and are recognized during morning announcements at school. They also get opportunities to take part in special experiences such as running a victory lap at the Drake Relays—a major collegiate and professional track meet—and running the last mile of the Des Moines Marathon.

Cindy Elsbernd should be cloned. Several dozen of her would make a measurable impact on the health and well-being of America in the future. Who knows? Maybe Cindy *can* be cloned, in a nonliteral way, and perhaps her program can spread to other states like a chain letter.

In any case, she deserves high praise for recognizing running as a great way to fight childhood obesity and for acting on this knowledge. But I also applaud her for acting wisely. You can't get kids hooked on running just by forcing them to run. You have to allow youngsters to hook themselves on running by providing opportunities and experiences that make it rewarding and enjoyable. A simple moment such as running a lap while hundreds of spectators cheer and clap during an intermission in a big-time track meet has the power to plant a seed in a child that eventually can grow into a lifelong passion for running. Sometimes, as I have often seen, a single enjoyable running experience is enough to ignite the flame.

Parents ask me all the time whether my kids are runners, and whether I want them to be runners. Neither Alexandria nor Nicholas has inherited my love of running quite yet. I have never suggested that either of them take up running, and I never will. I just do my thing and give them opportunities to share in my running, for example, by crossing the occasional finish line with me. Only time will tell what sort of influence these experiences will have on them.

I will be thrilled, of course, if my children become runners, but I'm not so naive as to believe they won't turn out just fine if they don't. In fact, the main parenting value I see in my running is that it demonstrates the happiness a person derives from doing what he loves, whatever that may be. Above all, I want my children to follow their hearts and pursue their own individual passions, whether they include running or not.

I recall a funny thing that happened recently, however, when I was walking home from school with Alexandria. She announced to me that she wanted to take up hip-hop dancing this year and join the cross-country team.

Cross-country team! I thought. *Where the heck did that come from?*

Well, as surprised as I was, I guess I know where it came from.

CHAPTER 6

United We Run

Day 7
September 23, 2006
Lincoln Marathon
Lincoln, Nebraska
Elevation: 955'
Weather: 64 degrees; partly cloudy
Time: 4:15:34
Net calories burned: 22,309
Number of runners: 21

---

ike a lot of runners, I am an introvert by nature. Running naturally appeals to introverts because it's a solitary activity, unless you go out of your way to make it otherwise, and it has a way of dampening external stimuli, bringing your feelings and thoughts to the fore.

During my corporate years, our management team was put through a personality profile test called the Myers-Briggs Type Indicator. The first of the four parameters measured was the subject's disposition toward introversion or extroversion. When the facilitators went over my results with me, they said I had registered the highest score for introversion they had ever seen.

The Myers-Briggs test helped me understand a few things I had noticed about myself. It explained, for example, why I feel overwhelmed in large crowds, especially if I'm the focus of any attention. It also explained why running for hours by myself is so refreshing to my soul, whereas many people might find it mind numbing.

Having reflective alone time is essential to my well-being, and I am acutely aware of this fact. I certainly enjoy spending time with others and meeting new folks, but seldom am I able to pass more than a few hours in a group before my senses get overloaded and I begin eyeing the exit. That's why, in the months leading up to the start of the Endurance 50, I worried about how I would deal with being surrounded by other people constantly for seven weeks. I would have no alone time whatsoever. While I would spend more than enough time running to satisfy my body's yearning devotion to this activity, every stride would be taken in the company of at least a few fellow runners. I was facing the longest streak of non-solo running I had ever experienced. What would it do to me?

The first few days of The North Face Endurance 50 seemed to answer this question in an unexpected way. Far from draining the battery of my spirit, running with the other Endurance 50 participants charged it up. I was pleasantly surprised by the quality of people each marathon attracted, and by the special group bond that formed among us day after day.

Marathon number seven, the Lincoln Marathon in Lincoln, Nebraska, gifted me with one of the most pleasant group running experiences of my life. The preceding night was a mixed bag. On the positive side, it being a Friday night, Julie flew in from San Francisco and met us at the hotel. But while her presence lifted my spirits, it had no effect on the nagging head cold I had recently acquired, which kept me stirring half the night.

The marathon starting line was located just outside the Nebraska University Coliseum and within a mile of our hotel, so we walked there—Mom, Dad, Julie, the kids, the crew, and me. It was a mild, fresh autumn morning—perfect running weather. A very diverse group of twenty-one runners joined me. At one extreme was a small handful of first-timers, including two of the seven women among us. At the other end of the spectrum was

The Dean's List

Prolonged strenuous exercise and overexertion can lower your body's natural immunity to bugs. Here are some ways to fortify your immune system:

- *Mushrooms.* These edible fungi have been shown to boost your body's so-called natural killer cells.
- *Echinacea.* Although controversial, some studies have found that it actually does reduce the severity and duration of colds.
- *Garlic.* Not only delicious, garlic contains allicin, which has immune-enhancing properties.
- *Probiotics.* Found in yogurt, probiotics are compounds that can boost the good bacteria in your gut.

a guy who had run more than one hundred marathons. And somewhere in the middle was a pair of triathlete buddies who both worked and worked out together and planned to cover only half the distance today as a training run.

Lincoln is a charming, low-density Midwestern city with lots of big, leafy trees and cheerful middle-class neighborhoods. It's a great setting for a marathon, not least because its gently undulating landscape provides just enough up-and-down variation to keep things interesting but not so much as to make the 26.2-mile distance more difficult than it would otherwise be.

We made our way through the course at a decent clip, which was probably unsettling for the first-timers. By the halfway point, at least one runner, an athletic-looking woman in her early twenties, was struggling. Nevertheless, she refused to allow herself to become separated from the main group. She had come here to complete her first marathon and was determined to do just that. When her turn came to talk about herself, she said her name was Sarah Sherman; she was a graduate stu-

Where Runners Gather

Group runs and events are not the only environments where runners can fellowship and share camaraderie. You can also do it online. There are several running Web sites with lively forums where runners can swap stories, advice, and ideas. Here are a few:

- www.active.com
- www.runnersweb.com
- www.runnersworld.com
- www.runningtimes.com
- www.thefinalsprint.com

dent in the athletics department at the University of Nebraska. Her father happened to be Mike Sherman, the former head coach of the Green Bay Packers football team. Clearly some of his gridiron toughness had rubbed off.

Then I noticed that the two triathletes who had planned to stop at the halfway point, hadn't. Perhaps they wanted to help Sarah make it to the finish line, or perhaps they were inspired by her grit and determination, and were feeding off it, as I was.

Marathons normally don't work this way. In big events such as the real Lincoln Marathon, each participant runs his or her own race. Sure, plenty of people run in pairs or small groups, with stronger runners holding themselves back to stay with slower friends, and slower runners pushing harder so as not to weigh down their friends too much. But this situation was different. Almost our entire field of participants was clinging together, and the differences in ability levels were extreme. Some of the runners could have been literally miles up the road if they had chosen to run as hard as they could. On the other side, Sarah and some of the others probably would have been going much slower if not for the pull created by the stronger members of the group.

As much as I love to run alone, I've never lost sight of the fact that running with others motivates me to push harder than I might solo. When competing in ultramarathons, for example, the desire to catch another runner often pulls me forward, and the desire not to be overtaken frequently propels me forward with a similar energy. It's a fundamental law of racing: Our best times are better when we run together.

Nor is this phenomenon limited to competitive environments. Recently I participated in a multiday outback run in Australia that pushed me as close to the brink of surrender as any mind-over-body challenge I have ever experienced. One powerful motivator kept me from surrendering, and that was my bond with my support crew, whose members were working as hard to get me to the finish line as I was working to get myself there. The thought of letting my crew down by quitting was unbearable, so I did not quit.

The same thing happened throughout the Endurance 50. Whenever the relentless grind of running a marathon every morning, talking to reporters, posing for photos and signing things until mid afternoon, and answering e-mails and updating my blog while riding hundreds of miles on the tour bus into the night began to wear my spirit down, tempting me to raise a white flag, I thought about the immense passion and energy my crew was pouring into my dream, which had in many ways become their dream too. And this thought annihilated my white-flag fantasies every time. There was just no way I could disappoint Koop, Garrett, Hopps, and the others, not to mention my fellow runners and the thousands of people across the globe who were following our progress.

As we passed the twenty-mile mark, I began to doubt whether Sarah could continue, even with the support of the group. She was clearly in a world of hurt, running with her eyes half-closed and no longer able to say more than two or three words at a time.

But when she voiced her own doubts about finishing, the group broke into a spontaneous chant of encouragement.

"Go, Sarah! You can do it!" we shouted.

It worked. She kept running. Three miles later, however, Sarah's suffering had reached a new depth. The exertion was so great that tears began trickling down her face. The nature of our verbal support now changed from encouragement to pleading.

"Don't give up, Sarah!" said one runner. "You're almost there."

I love to interact with people when they're most exposed— when every layer of pretension and vanity has been stripped away and left strewn along the pathway. The marathon mercilessly rips off the outer layers of our defenses and leaves the raw human, vulnerable and naked. It is here you get an honest glimpse into the soul of an individual. Every insecurity and character flaw is open and on display for all the world to see. No communication is ever more real, no expression ever more honest. There is nothing left to hide behind. The marathon is the great equalizer. Every movement, every word spoken and unspoken, is radiant truth. The veil has been obliterated. These are the profound moments of human interaction that I live for.

Sarah was beautiful as she ran along, not because of her striking looks, but because of her inner strength. Her resolve and tenacity were speaking volumes about her character. But could these virtuous qualities carry her any farther?

Miraculously, she held on. The nine of us remaining together in the homestretch formed a side-by-side lineup, clasped hands, and raised our arms overhead as we crossed the finish line. Sarah doubled over and began sobbing with a mixture of joy and other emotions that are too complicated to name, but are known to everyone who has pushed his or her body beyond known limits to achieve a goal.

"This is the best day of my whole life," Sarah said after she had recovered. "Is that pathetic?"

No, Sarah, it's not pathetic. It was a great day for all of us—precisely because it had become such a memorable day for you and the others who had blasted through previous limitations to cross that finish line. We all felt the power in it.

Better Together

In a recent study, Arizona State University scientists found that the maximal weight-lifting ability of men and women improved significantly when they competed against others or lifted in the presence of others versus alone. Similar results have been observed in earlier studies involving runners. Interestingly, in a recent study involving elementary school children, only boys ran faster in a competitive race than they did in a solo time trial.

The marathon finished in the same place it had started, right outside the football stadium. The Nebraska Cornhuskers football team was scheduled to play a game there against Troy University that very night. Sarah's boyfriend, Zac Taylor, was Nebraska's star quarterback, who would lead his team to a 56–0 demolition of the opponent. They would both have something to celebrate.

When we crossed the finish line it was only 11:20 AM, still more than seven hours before kickoff, but already there were groups of students tailgating in the stadium parking lot. I couldn't even imagine the condition these kids would be in come game time. Running a marathon seemed tame compared with what they were putting their bodies through.

Because the crew had feared getting trapped in the parking lot by early arriving spectators, the Finish Festival had been set up a few blocks away. We walked over there together and went through the usual routine of interviews and handshakes. It was a bit of a comedown from the high of the magical group bonding experience we had enjoyed during the run. Despite the initiative the younger Endurance 50 crew members had taken after the Mississippi Coast Marathon on Day 3, the organization of this post-marathon festival hadn't improved much. None of us had yet thought of simple measures that could be taken to make things flow more smoothly, such as arranging the sponsors' tables in a manner that was intuitive, guiding people in a natural sequence from one to the next. Instead, tables and booths were strewn about haphazardly, confusing everyone.

World-class introvert that I am, I began to feel increasingly overwhelmed as the mingling wore on. For me, the post-marathon marathon was more straining overall than running 26.2 miles. Could I really survive another six weeks in this environment without snapping and running off into the woods to be alone? As magical as today had been, suddenly I wasn't too sure.

CHAPTER 7

The Running Clinic

Day 8
September 24, 2006
Boulder Backroads Marathon
Boulder, Colorado
Elevation: 5,200'
Weather: 61 degrees; sunny, very dry
Time: 3:46:56
Net calories burned: 25,496
Number of runners: 2,200

unning is a participatory sport, not a fan sport. For this reason, typical runners have only limited interest in sitting back and admiring elite and other well-known runners. Rather, typical runners want to learn from these folks and apply the knowledge to their own performance.

Every time I travel to running events and meet other runners, I get a lot of questions about training, nutrition, shoes, and other topics of interest to those seeking to go faster or farther. The Endurance 50 was no exception. I answered a lifetime's worth of questions from runners between St. Charles, Missouri, and New York City, many of them quite common ("How do you stay motivated?"), others more unusual ("What can I do to keep my inner thighs from chafing on long runs?").

The eight live events that I ran brought the most questions, because they involved thousands of runners instead of the handful or few dozen who kept me company during the re-created events. Indeed, for me, the live events brought a whole new meaning to the term *running clinic*. Sometimes I felt as though these events were 26.2-mile workshops on the run, and along with giving away truckloads of suggestions, I learned a lot from the other runners.

> **QUICK TAKE:** *Many runners experience uncomfortable chafing of their inner thighs on long runs. To prevent this problem, apply some lubricant into this area before you start. Bodyglide and Aquaphor are two favorites.*

The Boulder Backroads Marathon was a typical case. I ran the live event alongside twenty-two hundred other runners as marathon number eight of the Endurance 50. Since it was a live marathon and I didn't have a group to keep pace with as I did at the re-created marathons, I was able to run the race at my own natural pace. But because of the visibility surrounding the Endurance 50, dozens of runners chose to converse with me for varying lengths of time throughout. Some just wanted to encourage me in my quest. Others wanted to ask me questions. Still others wanted to run together for a few miles and talk about whatever.

Chris Carmichael, Lance Armstrong's cycling coach, who had given me lots of valuable advice in the run-up to the Endurance 50, had suggested a strategy to use in this type of situation if I grew tired of talking.

"If someone asks you a question," he said, "ask them that same question right back." This tactic would allow me to minimize my talking and conserve my breath while encouraging the other runner to really think about his or her own solution. It would prove especially helpful in Boulder, because my body was already oxygen-deprived by our high-elevation location and by the sinus infection I had picked up within the past couple of days.

"Do you run with a GPS?" one runner asked shortly after the starting horn sounded.

"Yes. Do *you* run with a GPS?" I asked, instead of elaborating on how or why I used a GPS.

"On long runs, do you prefer a backpack or a waist pack?" another runner asked.

"Backpack," I said. "Which do *you* prefer?"

Of course, I felt obligated to provide a little more substance in some of my responses. I did not want to abuse Carmichael's tactic, after all. But I was also genuinely interested in hearing others' answers to some of these questions. While I may have run a few more miles than most, I still have a lot of learning left to do. I've gained plenty of valuable new tips from my peers, whether they're more or less experienced than me. One of the things I love about running is how open most runners are to sharing ideas with one another. Another thing I love is that you never stop learning, as long as you keep an open mind and maintain a willingness to experiment.

"Don't you ever get injured?" a female runner asked me as we climbed a small hill in the latter miles of the marathon.

"Not yet," I said, rapping my knuckles on my skull. "Knock on wood."

Short Answers to the Three Questions I Hear Most Often

Q. *How do you train?*

A. I train by feel. I run as far and as fast as my body tells me to each day, though I do try to do at least two very long runs per week. Those base-building long runs are critically important to me.

Q. *What do you eat?*

A. I try to base my diet in natural, whole foods that existed hundreds of years ago (vegetables, meat, dairy) and avoid modern processed foods (fast food, packaged products, soft drinks).

Q. *How do you keep from getting injured?*

A. I do a lot of cross-training with other sports, including mountain biking and windsurfing, to strengthen all my muscle sets.

"That's incredible," she said. "How do you do it?"

"They say one of the best things you can do as a long-distance runner is to choose your parents well," I said, meaning I was lucky to have inherited favorable biomechanics for running. "It's nothing I've trained for," I admitted. "I'm one hundred percent Greek, and my dad insists we're from the same village as Phidippides. I always tell him, 'Dad, we're from Southern California; what *village* are you talking about?'" Joking aside, there's more and more research showing that common injuries are linked to stride irregularities. But it's not much easier to improve one's running biomechanics than it is to choose one's parents, so I let my questioner in on my third secret, and perhaps the only one that's useful to other runners.

"I've also done a lot of cross-training," I said. The truth of the matter is that I mountain bike, windsurf, climb, surf, and snowboard primarily for fun, not to prevent injuries. But I am certain these activities have increased my injury resistance by strengthening muscles that oppose the primary running muscles, thus enhancing the stability of my joints.

"What do you eat?" asked the next runner to pull alongside me, a mountain of a man who looked like he ought to be wearing pads and running on artificial grass. I hear this question often. Some people are very food-focused and seem to believe it is the cause of everything, for better or worse.

"Do you mean in general or when I'm running?" I asked.

"I don't know." He thought for a moment. "What did you eat for breakfast today?"

"I had a bowl of Greek-style yogurt [there is no added sugar in Greek-style yogurt] and granola with banana slices," I said. "I find it easy to digest, and it provides carbohydrates for fuel, protein for muscle integrity and recovery, and fat for satiety. I also had an apple on the drive over to the start for a little extra fuel."

"I'll have to try that," he said.

"Well, it works for me," I said. "But there's no guarantee it will work for you."

> **QUICK TAKE:** *Peel appeal. The peel of many fruits may be the most valuable part. That's because the peel contains triterpenoids, a powerful type of antioxidant. So use the whole fruit if you want maximum health benefits.*

If I could offer only one piece of advice to runners, it would be this: "Listen to everyone, follow no one." That's because each runner is unique, so there's no single training system, shoe, or breakfast that is equally effective for every athlete. I always encourage other runners to experiment during training and find what works best for them.

During my early days as an ultrarunner, a more experienced acquaintance advised me to double-knot my shoelaces to keep them from loosening. The first time I tried it, my feet swelled up, causing them to throb with constriction pressure, which happens sooner or later in every ultra. But this one happened to be a trail run that passed through a burr patch, leaving dozens of spiky little burrs clinging to my double-knotted shoelaces. I

Recommended Reading

I enjoy learning most by talking with fellow runners, but I do my share of reading as well, and I encourage you to do the same. Here are three good resources for valuable information to improve your running performance and experience:

- *The Courage to Start,* by John "The Penguin" Bingham. An inspirational and educational book for beginning runners.
- *Marathon & Beyond.* A bimonthly publication that's always packed with great articles for marathon and ultramarathon runners.
- www.injuredRunner.com. A valuable source of tips to identify and treat a number of common running injuries.

needed to loosen my shoes to relieve the pressure, but I could not untie the laces to save my life, so I wound up having to have my shoes cut off at the next aid station. I never double-knotted my laces during a wilderness trail run again (although I still do so in road races). This experience taught me to be more circumspect in applying the bits of advice I receive from other runners.

My most involved conversation during the Boulder Back-roads Marathon was with Stephen, an experienced runner of about my age who was training for the New York City Marathon. He had signed up for the half-marathon that was being held concurrently with today's marathon but wound up running all the way to the twenty-mile mark.

Stephen was very interested in learning how ultrarunners do things, so I clued him in on a new *enhancement* trend I had recently heard about.

How Do You Do It?

One of the questions I was asked most frequently was how on earth I'd be able to run fifty marathons in fifty days.

As I worked with Chris Carmichael, we theorized that the best way to recover from one marathon was not to put myself too far in debt during the previous day's marathon. We did two things to meet this objective: First, we set a baseline fitness goal of being able to run a four-hour marathon with an average heart rate of 110. We got there prior to the start of the first Endurance 50 marathon. Second, I participated in numerous ultramarathons that were much longer than 26.2 miles (see appendix A). The thinking here was that if I could run a hundred miles comfortably, I could click off a marathon without undue strain.

Would this strategy work? We would have to wait fifty days to have our answer.

"Viagra," I said.

"Viagra?"

"People swear by it, although personally I never touch the stuff. I'm Greek; I don't have to," I joked. "Apparently there's even been a study showing it improves performance at altitude."

"*Running* performance?"

"Yeah, that too," I said. We both laughed.

A few hours later, as English began to guide the tour bus toward our next destination in Casper, Wyoming, I fired up the laptop. I had been blogging most days since starting the Endurance 50. As I began to read and answer e-mails, I found that many of the messages were from runners offering cold remedies. I had complained about my sinus infection in the previous day's blog post. Some of the proposed remedies were familiar, others were intriguing, and still others were plainly off the deep end—like sleeping with a magnet attached to my nose. Conventional, unusual, or downright bizarre, however, I appreciated the gesture symbolized by every single one of them.

We are all teachers and we are all students in this sport.

CHAPTER 8

Running Wild

Day 9
September 25, 2006
Casper Marathon
Casper, Wyoming
Elevation: 5,200'
Weather: 65 degrees; very dry
Time: 3:54:12
Net calories burned: 28,683
Number of runners: 9

Recently, I participated in a rather unusual publicity event on behalf of the makers of Accelerade sports drink. I ran for twenty-four hours straight on a treadmill suspended above Times Square in New York City. It was different, to say the least. My image was displayed on those giant video screens that are attached to the sides of buildings all around Times Square. Pedestrians gawked at me from the street two stories below. They were mostly tourists from other parts of the country and world, who seemed awestruck that someone could run for twenty-four hours, let alone on a treadmill.

Reporters from major media outlets, including CNN, lobbed questions at me as I treaded the mill. Howard Stern, who happens to be a runner himself, interviewed me live on his radio show. I found it difficult to keep my balance while turning my head to engage these interviewers, and feared that I would trip and fall to the belt, which would shoot me off the back at six miles an hour. Fortunately, I stayed upright.

One thought played over and over again in my head throughout that long day and night of running nowhere: *I can't believe I'm doing this.* Fifteen years earlier I was a tiny moving part in a corporate machine and my only ambition was to become a somewhat bigger and more influential moving part in that machine. If you had told me that I would one day make a living by doing things like running for twenty-four hours on a treadmill hanging twenty feet above Times Square while TV cameras beamed my image across the world, I would have said you were crazy.

There was also a second thought that echoed repeatedly inside my skull on the treadmill: *I can't wait until this is over.* As much as I love running, I'm not a big treadmill runner. If treadmills were the only places to run, I would probably stick with windsurfing and other outdoor sports. I'm also not a big fan of running in close proximity to taxis and buses spewing diesel exhaust in the middle of a major city. One of the biggest appeals of running for me is the way it connects my body and spirit to nature—given the right environment. Times Square is not exactly that environment.

I happen to live in an urban area, but San Francisco is a good running city. In fact, it was voted the best running city in America by the readers of *Runner's World* magazine. My home is located one mile from the Presidio, a massive, lush forest park with miles of inviting running trails and clean air that is purified by the vast Pacific Ocean.

As big as it is, the Presidio is too confining for my longer outings. That's okay. When I long for some real wilderness, I can easily run there. I have a personal policy of never driving somewhere to run if I don't have to, and living where I do, I seldom have to. I do a lot of my running in the Marin Headlands, just on the other side of the Golden Gate Bridge, which is accessible from the Presidio. When I am charging along a technical singletrack trail on Mount Tamalpais, overlooking the headlands, the smell of sage thick in the fresh air, I feel as though I am five hundred miles, not five miles, from the nearest city. That's my idea of a good place to run.

Wyoming is also a great place to run. Something about the landscape there makes you feel as though you're always standing on a mountain summit. You can see so much. The high plains spread for miles around you in every direction. The sky is even more wide-open above. Snowcapped mountains mark the horizon in the seemingly unreachable distance. You certainly don't have to worry about dodging pedestrians or stopping for red lights.

The sinus infection that had nagged me the past few days was worse than ever on the morning of the Wyoming Marathon. I felt like my head was going to explode, and soon enough it did. I was riding toward the starting line on the tour bus when a powerful urge to sneeze overtook me. I dashed to the bathroom to grab a tissue, but the sneeze erupted before I got there. Two streams of thick, yellowy green snot poured down my chin. It was really gross, and I thought, *How am I going to run a marathon today?*

Nevertheless, I did. As we covered the first few miles of the Casper Marathon on Day 9 of the Endurance 50, herds of antelope bounded through the fields and across the roadway ahead of us. After winding through the hills for several miles, the course dropped down to the Platte River and followed a path along the water for much of the way. The mountain peaks in the background were still covered in snow from a storm that had passed through the area the previous weekend. The air temperature warmed to a perfect level in the mid sixties and remained bone-dry. The air had a grassy smell that reminded me of—somewhere. At first I couldn't place it. Then I remembered: Namibia! I had gone there a few years back on an exploratory running adventure, also sponsored by The North Face.

As with all runners, whenever I run in a new place of natural beauty, my five senses automatically contrast it with other places I've run. I might be running deep in the Australian outback when I happen to see a gum tree, a type of tree I often see

Natural Splendor

If you're looking to run a marathon in a beautiful natural environment, you can't go wrong with these five:

1. Valley of Fire Marathon, Overton, Nevada
2. Deadwood Mickelson Trail Marathon, Deadwood, South Dakota
3. St. George Marathon, St. George, Utah
4. Triple Lakes Trail Marathon, Greensboro, North Carolina
5. Breakers Marathon, Middleton, Rhode Island

in San Francisco's Presidio Park, and for a brief moment I forget where I am. Then I see some type of bizarre bottlebrush tree with a kangaroo standing next to it and I remember.

I have been fortunate to have run in some of the most beautiful and exotic places on earth, on all seven continents. Among the very best was Patagonia, Chile. Its towering granite spires, pristine snowdrifts, brilliant turquoise lakes, and rushing rivers are forever imprinted on my mind's eye. And my mind's nose can recall the unique scent of Patagonia anytime. I'll never forget how vastly removed from humanity I felt running in that truly wild environment, laughing aloud and hooting to myself at the splendor of it all.

Another place that deserves a spot on the list of the top ten most memorable locations I've ever run is Tavarua, a speck of an island that lies a few miles off the coast of Fiji. I went there to surf during the time when I happened to be training for my first one-hundred-mile running race. To keep in shape, I ran literally dozens of laps around that twenty-nine-acre patch of unspoiled tropical perfection. I was entertained by the sight of exotic coral reefs and frolicking dolphins, while being periodically shocked by the sight of slithering coral snakes (luckily they're slow and docile creatures, although extremely deadly). I can still taste the pure, thick, salty air and feel the crunch of the grainy coral sand beneath my feet.

I suppose such places can be enjoyed well enough while sitting or walking, but something about them makes me want to run. It's a primal urge that I find nearly impossible to resist. Running seems to enhance my body's exposure to nature. It invigorates the senses. I get more air in my lungs, cover more ground, enjoy more perspectives. My concentration seems heightened. It just feels right. Every runner knows the feeling.

Day 10
September 26, 2006
Deadwood Mickelson Trail Marathon
Deadwood, South Dakota
Elevation: 5,100'
Weather: 66 degrees, dry and breezy
Time: 3:53:34
Net calories burned: 31,870
Number of runners: 1

During the long drive from Casper, Wyoming, to Deadwood, South Dakota, I decided I would try to shave in the small sink on the bus. The road was bumpy, and the bus bounced up and down as we drove. I tried to stabilize myself by wedging my legs against the cabinet below and holding my right shoulder against the wall next to the sink. I found that if I bent my knees slightly forward, I could put more pressure on them against the cabinet to help hold my body in place.

I was just getting started when we hit a big bump in the road and I sliced my chin open with the razor. The pain caused me to reel backward. Right then we turned a sharp corner in the road and the bus lurched to the side, sending my body lurching forward again. Both of my knees smacked into the cabinet with a loud thud. For a few scary moments, I thought I might have cracked my left kneecap.

I stood there with blood dripping on the counter and floor, my knees throbbing (especially the left one), and holding on to the faucet for dear life as the bus careened and bounced down the highway. My left kneecap was bruised and tender for the next several marathons.

Happily, the next day brought a special treat that took my mind off the pain. I ran the Deadwood Mickelson Trail Marathon, which, as its name suggests, takes place entirely on dirt trails in the Black Hills of South Dakota. Even better, I completed it with just one other runner, Amy Yanni (whose friends call her Amos), a fifty-three-year-old public defender from nearby Rapid City who runs a marathon almost every weekend and appreciated the splendor of our surroundings as much as I did.

I love trail running, and the tree-lined Mickelson Trail was absolutely stunning. We spotted white-tailed deer and wild turkeys as we climbed almost a thousand feet into the hills against a stiff headwind. Naturally, because we were strangers and alone together, Amos and I did a fair bit of talking, although the conversation never seemed forced. We ran long stretches in near silence, without a hint of self-consciousness, just soaking up the experience. Amos and I could relate.

She grew up in cities—Detroit and Boston—but moved to South Dakota after finishing law school in search of a slower pace and elbow room. "I don't miss the crush of cities," she told me.

Amos was a low-key recreational runner until she developed breast cancer in 2003. After recovering from a double mastectomy, she became a little more serious about her running—actually, a lot more serious. She completed her first marathon later that year, winning her division and qualifying for Boston. In the next three years, she ran another fifty marathons, recording a personal-best time of 3:19 and being named MarathonGuide.com's Female Outstanding Runner of 2006 after posting top-three finishes in fifteen separate marathons.

Upon hearing this, I briefly considered inviting Amos to finish out the Endurance 50 with me. Possibly to carry me, if need be.

At various points along the trail, we were met by students from nearby Spearfish Middle School. They assisted Koop and

Trail-Running Tips

All runners know that running on trails is very different from running on the roads. Here are some tips for a smoother transition to the dirt:

- Try wearing gaiters (fabric coverings for the ankles and lower legs) to keep pebbles and twigs out of your shoes. You can find gaiters at most outdoor retail stores. You can also purchase trail-running shoes with integrated gaiters.
- Normal running shoes work fine on graded fire roads, but on technical singletrack, consider trail-specific running shoes.
- To reduce your risk of twisting an ankle on the trails, strengthen your quadriceps (the muscles on the front of your thigh). I do this by cross-training on a mountain bike.

Garrett with support services, and a few of them even joined in and ran alongside us for a stretch. Amos kept us moving at a brisk pace, because she had to return to work that afternoon. It was Tuesday, after all. By this time, she had sheepishly informed me that she'd signed up to run with me as a last-minute favor to race director Gerry Dunn. Apparently nobody had registered within just a few days of our scheduled arrival here, and Gerry felt it would be a personal disappointment if I had to run alone. Luckily, he knew somebody who was willing (not to mention able) to run a marathon anytime.

The fourth- and fifth-grade classes from Deadwood Elementary School ran over from school for the Finish Festival. They had a million questions. Their energy and enthusiasm for the Endurance 50 blew me away. A couple of them asked whether *they* could join me for the rest of the journey. I asked one boy what his parents would think of that. He said, "My dad's a runner. He'll understand."

I had a good laugh at that one, but it also gladdened my heart. Earlier, Amos and I had talked about the purpose of the

Endurance 50, and I had told her that a primary mission of mine was to inspire kids to become more active.

"No Child Left *Inside!*" I said, quoting the official motto of Karno's Kids. Amos smiled in appreciation of the line's reference to the federal government's "No Child Left Behind" education initiative (in which a lot of children seem to be getting left behind). A woman of liberal views, she jumped right in and took a couple of humorous jabs at the current presidential administration during our four hours together.

Although I had thought up that motto long ago, while out on a run (where I do some of my clearest thinking, actually), speaking it aloud in my current context gave me a different perspective on it. I had been thinking of the Endurance 50 mission strictly in terms of *exercise*. But as I ran along with Amos in the great American outdoors, taking a water bottle from a smiling sixth-grader at an aid station and breathing in the fresh mountain air, I fully appreciated that my mission was also to get kids—and adults, for that matter—*outside*.

"Adventure happens the moment you step out the front door," I often tell my kids.

Step outside.

Be active.

Get back to nature. Explore wild places.

To me, and many others, these are words to live—and thrive—by.

CHAPTER 9

A Woman's Touch

Day 11
September 27, 2006
Fargo Marathon
Fargo, North Dakota
Elevation: 891'
Weather: 55 degrees; overcast
Time: 4:16:22
Net calories burned: 35,057
Number of runners: 18

Upon starting the Fargo Marathon** on Day 11, I quickly discovered several born comedians in our pack of eighteen runners, who had me laughing from the first mile. The biggest crackups of the bunch were a few women representing a local running club called Women High On Running. Their apparent ringleader, Ann, wore an expectant look on her face when she told me the name of her group. I chuckled, but I could tell she was hoping for more. I wouldn't figure it out until later.

After we'd gone four or five miles, some of the runners who had no intention of going the whole way began to fall off the back of the main group. One of these runners shouted out, from a few yards behind me, "How do you get such great calves?" It was Ann.

"Let's see," I shouted back. "You run about five thousand miles a year, much of it on hills, do thousands of stair repeats, mountain bike on the side, and, I dunno, it just kind of happens."

Several other Women High On Running members ran later segments of the marathon, after Ann had finished her morning jog, and still others cheered us and provided aid (including freshly baked cookies!) along the course. A bunch of them came together at the Finish Festival, one of our rowdiest yet, which took place in the parking lot of the Fargodome. I was joking with a couple of the runners when I thought I heard Koop yelling, "Whores! Whores! Let's get a picture with the whores!"

I turned my head in the direction of these unexpected words and saw Koop, Hopps, and Garrett crowding together with Ann and several of her friends to have their photograph taken together. That's when I figured it out: Women High On Running: WHORs.

Now I laughed as Ann had initially expected me to, and quickly joined the group for another photo. At the precise moment the shutter clicked I felt someone goose my backside. I was not able to positively identify the culprit, but I have suspicions about who it was—namely, a mischievous-looking woman who must have been in her early seventies and stood there grinning at me.

QUICK TAKE: Because soy contains phytoestrogens (plant versions of the primary female sex hormone), soy is a popular food among health-conscious women. But it's a nourishing food for men and women alike: high in protein, vitamins, minerals, and antioxidants, and low in fat. To get more soy in your diet, try using one tablespoon of soy flour and one tablespoon of water instead of an egg when cooking or baking. You can also substitute a quarter cup of mashed silken tofu for an egg in almost any recipe.

Women High On Running is a loosely organized collection of approximately twenty women who share a love for running and a laughing spirit. Their core members met while training for and participating in the 2005 Fargo Marathon. Afterward, sev-

Join the Club

Joining a running club is a great way for both female and male runners to enrich their running experience. Clubs boost motivation, provide group workout opportunities and sometimes even expert coaching, and offer an excellent chance to make new friends with a common interest. To find clubs in your area, ask around at your local running specialty shop or search a nationwide list of running clubs at the Road Runners Club of America Web site (www.rrca.org/clubs).

eral of them began getting together for weekend long runs. Within a short time, they were attracting new recruits and had come up with their colorful name and created a blog that enabled them to interact outside of workouts and other physical events.

Long after the Endurance 50 had left Fargo, I sent an e-mail to Leah Swedberg, one of the WHORs (they seriously don't mind—and even delight in—being called that, or I wouldn't do it, because they'd kick my ass), and asked her about the importance of the group's being all female. I was curious to know whether she felt it nourished its members in ways that a coed group might not.

"Most of us started running as a way to accomplish something for ourselves, to get out of the house, make our way through a life evaluation stage or get a daily break away from the kids," Leah explained in her reply. "I think a lot of us run for reasons that other women can relate to, and because we are all women, I think it's less intimidating for newbies. That, coupled with the fact that women tend to put more meaning behind what a group like this means, gives us strength and a bond that makes our group unique."

Happily, Women High On Running is not a complete anomaly. Groups like it across the country deserve a lot of credit for transforming running from a boys' club into an almost perfectly gender-balanced sport within the past thirty-five years. When I was a young kid growing up in the late 1960s, women simply didn't run marathons. They weren't even allowed to. Then Kathrine Switzer shook free of the grasp of race official Jock Semple to finish the Boston Marathon in 1967, and after that, things began to change. In 2006, for the first time in history, more women than men completed marathons in the United States.

As Leah suggested to me, there are differences in the ways and reasons men and women typically get hooked on running. Men are more likely to start running after a scary doctor's appointment, buy a book on training, and take it from there. Women are more likely to get coaxed into joining a running group by friends. Initially, it's about the fellowship, not the running. But the next thing they know, they're running marathons.

There also seem to be some gender differences in the emotional rewards of running. Our society is tougher on the self-esteem of females than males, and I believe that running is the perfect self-esteem builder for girls and women. I serve on the board of Girls on the Run, a national organization aimed at developing self-esteem and camaraderie in young girls, and it really works. (Interestingly, the same organization tried to create a brother group, Boys on the Run, and it *didn't* work.) Alexandria participated in this program when she was younger, and it was one of the most fulfilling experiences of her life. I always tell her that women can do anything men can do, often better. I mean those words.

Granted, in many sports men have a decided advantage over women, but in distance running, and particularly ultradistance running, the gap is so small that it's almost invisible. It is not unheard of for a woman to be the outright winner of a fifty- or one-hundred-mile running race. For example, in 2003 Pam Reed claimed overall victory in the toughest ultramarathon of them all, Badwater, finishing fifteen minutes ahead of—me.

My friends had a field day with that one, which was only to be expected, but what surprised me was that the media did too. They tried to manufacture some big rivalry between Pam and me. Well, there *is* a rivalry, but it's no different from my friendly rivalry with any male competitor. Yet the press tried to paint me as a chauvinistic ogre who loses sleep for weeks after losing to a woman.

Pam and I have had the last laugh, however. Whenever I see her at an event, we trade insults and talk smack, ridiculing the notion that we hate each other by acting as though we do. In fact, I saw Pam twice during the Endurance 50—in Boulder, Colorado (where she finished fourteen seconds ahead of me—argh!), and again in Green Bay, Wisconsin. And what did we do both times? We went running together, just like anyone else.

Day 12
September 28, 2006
Montana Marathon
Billings, Montana
Elevation: 3,648'
Weather: 71 degrees; clear
Time: 3:56:44
Net calories burned: 38,244
Number of runners: 14

We arrived in Billings the evening before the Montana Marathon. My mom and dad, Alexandria, Nicholas, and I were walking along the quiet streets of downtown after most of the local businesses had closed, looking through the windows of Western-wear shops, when we rounded the corner and came upon a bustling Greek restaurant, of all things. We walked in the door automatically, without a word of discussion. The scents and commotion naturally drew us in.

The scene inside was chaotic, which is typical of Greek restaurants. The waitress had a million orders going at once and was constantly yelling back at the cooks in Greek. When our food finally arrived, it was gloriously prepared, authentically home-style Greek fare, fresh and exquisitely flavorful. There was tiropitakia (cheese pastries), dolmas (stuffed grape leaves),

A roadside mural along the highway to New Mexico. (photo courtesy of Journeyfilm LLC)

Julie and I renewing our wedding vows at the start of the Lewis & Clark Marathon, in St. Charles, Missouri, at marathon number one. (photo courtesy of Journeyfilm LLC)

My kids, Nicholas and Alexandria, holding finishing tape during their lunch break from "road school" in Memphis, Tennessee.

Heading toward the finish line in Little Rock, Arkansas. You can see Governor Huckabee's office in the background. (photo courtesy of Journeyfilm LLC)

Running with the officers through McConnell Air Force Base during a wicked storm at the Wichita Marathon in Kansas. (photo © Corey Rich/Aurora Photos)

Fired-up kids who ran the last mile of the marathon with me. (photo courtesy of Journeyfilm LLC)

The streets of San Francisco at the marathon on
October 3, 2006. (photo © Corey Rich/Aurora Photos)

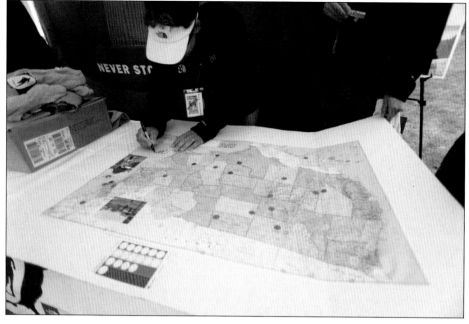

Signing a school map for fifth graders.

Life on the road, with crew members Garrett, taking a power nap, and Hopps, working on logistics. (photo courtesy of Journeyfilm LLC)

A gnawed-off moose leg along the trail in Alaska. (photo © Corey Rich/Aurora Photos)

Pushing David Ames across the
Golden Gate Bridge, surrounded
by our lifelong friends.

Girl Power!
Four happy
marathon finishers.
(photo © Corey Rich/
Aurora Photos)

*The marathon in Hawaii was among the prettiest, and the hottest.
(photo © Corey Rich/Aurora Photos)*

The Arizona heat, a day after our Hawaii marathon, topped the thermometer at 104 degrees Fahrenheit. (photo © Corey Rich/Aurora Photos)

An ice soak from a rooftop cooler along the route of the Desert Classic Marathon in Arizona. (photo © Corey Rich/Aurora Photos)

Riding the Marshall University bison mascot vehicle in Huntington, West Virginia.

Finish of the Boston marathon, number twenty-nine.

Stunning New England scenery in New Hampshire. (photo: JustinCash.com)

The Finish Festival, after I fell during the Georgia Marathon in Atlanta.

Among the 250 runners in New Jersey was Larry the Lighthouse, lighting our way.

Signing a book for a young runner. (photo © Corey Rich/Aurora Photos)

The fearless crew. From left to right: Omar; Alexandria; Les; Julie; Koop; me; my father, Nick; my son, Nick; my mom, Fran; Hopps; Robin; Billy; JB; and Garrett.

Stopping at a school along the run home in Aviston, Illinois.

So long for now.
Until we run again.

moussaka, octopus, lots of fresh vegetables, and, of course, homemade baklava for dessert.

My parents and I wondered aloud how they were able to get all the fresh, specialized Greek ingredients to prepare such a tasty meal all the way out here in Billings, Montana—not exactly a hotbed of Greek American culture. Nonetheless, we were certainly glad they could!

> **QUICK TAKE:** *Greeks use lots of cinnamon and spices in their recipes. Cinnamon has been shown to improve insulin sensitivity. Keep a shaker handy and sprinkle liberally on the foods you eat.*

Day 13
September 29, 2006
City of Trees Marathon
Boise, Idaho
Elevation: 2,659'
Weather: 75 degrees; clear
Time: 4:08:51
Net calories burned: 41,431
Number of runners: 18

The North Face Endurance 50 was a completely male phenomenon through its first twelve days. But on Day 13 the testosterone was tempered; we got a woman's touch. It was a little awkward at first, but in the long run our endeavor was greatly strengthened by it, much as the sport of running as a whole has been energized, balanced, and enlivened by its recent feminization. I would say the same holds true in business and, dare I say, politics.

It happened after the Montana Marathon on Day 12. On the long drive from Billings to Boise, Idaho, Hopps pulled me aside. "Karno, we need to talk," he said.

"Sure, Hopps, what's up?" I detected a note of seriousness in his tone.

"Dave is no longer with us."

"No longer with us? Is he dead?" I tried to joke. Dave had mysteriously vanished while I was running the Montana Marathon, and now he wasn't on the bus.

"It just wasn't working out," Hopps said. "I think he's actually relieved. I'm not sure he ever felt comfortable in his role."

"So what are we going to do now? Don't we need a tour manager?" I asked.

"We've hired a replacement. Her name's Robin Culver. She's a close friend of mine."

"Is she good?"

"The best there is."

"Okay, Hopps, I trust you," I said. There was a moment's pause. "Does she know she'll be the only woman aboard?"

"Oh, man! That didn't even cross my mind. I never mentioned it to her."

"Oh, well," I said. "I guess we'll find out just how good she is at dealing with the unexpected in a hurry."

I met Robin the following morning, before the City of Trees Marathon in Boise, Idaho. The context was a round-table meeting of the entire Endurance 50 crew on the tour bus. We'd never had round-table meetings before. That was the first change.

Robin had the energy of a supernova packed into her muscular body. She talked faster than my ears could listen, had multiple lists going on several notepads concurrently, and even typed on her laptop as she asked questions. And boy did she ask questions. She had so many questions that she sometimes interrupted herself to ask a second question if the first one didn't come out quickly enough.

She wanted to know all about my routine. "So after the marathons, are you getting rubdowns and massages?" she asked.

"I'd like to," I said, "but there's just no time. I tried to talk Koop into doing it on the bus, but I couldn't get any lovin' out of the man."

It was a cheeky answer, but I sensed already that Robin knew how to be one of the guys even as she brought a dis-

For Women Only

Some women prefer not to exercise in the company of sweaty men—at least not all the time—hence the success of the Curves fitness center franchise. If you're one of these women, you might want to try a women's marathon. There are a couple of them in the United States. The Nike Women's Marathon takes place in San Francisco in October, and the More Marathon, for women over age forty, takes place in New York City in March.

tinctly female influence to the team. And I liked the fact that she listened so keenly. It was clear she had no intention of forcing any preconceived ideas or favored methods on our operation, but would instead work with what we had to achieve our goals. Robin was sure to lead changes in how the Endurance 50 functioned, and I couldn't wait to see their impact.

As I formed my first impression of Robin in this meeting, I found myself thinking back to my days as a windsurfing instructor in college. While working in this capacity, I was surprised to observe that women typically gained competence on the board faster than men did, despite typically having less raw muscle power. The reason, I discerned eventually, was that men tried to outmuscle the wind—a hopeless impossibility for even the strongest—whereas women allowed the wind to guide them, relying on balance instead of brawn.

The City of Trees Marathon in Boise, Idaho, our thirteenth marathon and Robin's first, went incredibly smoothly. It was remarkable; everything flowed perfectly. Was it Robin's influence, a woman's touch, that made the difference? Could it last? I certainly hoped so.

CHAPTER 10

Fun Runs

Day 14
September 30, 2006
Seafair Marathon
Seattle, Washington
Elevation: 50'
Weather: 58 degrees; overcast
Time: 4:07:52
Net calories burned: 44,618
Number of runners: 48

Running is not fun. It's too hard to be fun. Even the most devoted runners would not describe the experience of performing a typical workout—let alone competing in a race—as *fun*. I love running as much as anyone on earth, but I am no more inclined to describe the running experience as "fun" than any other runner, unless I'm with other people, in which case the fun isn't about the running, but the people.

I'm not saying that running doesn't feel good. It *does* feel good, in the way that any form of hard work feels good to those who have a taste for it. Running feels good to me the way writing feels good to a writer and operating feels good to a surgeon. A skilled surgeon does not smile his way through a tricky operation. He knits his brows, grunts terse instructions, and is exhausted afterward. Likewise, even the most passionate writer dreads sitting down in front of a blank computer screen some days. But a skilled surgeon wouldn't trade his post-operative exhaustion for anything, nor would any passionate writer give up her dread of the blank screen, because the surgeon *is* a surgeon, and the writer's a writer.

As challenging as it is, the overall operating experience just feels right to the surgeon—like an expression of who he really is. And the writer feels the same way about writing.

And runners feel the same way about running. A hard run leaves you exhausted and glad to be done with it. Some days you dread even starting a run. But the overall running experience just feels right, like an expression of who you really are.

When I was in college, a world-renowned psychologist named Mihaly Csikszentmihalyi (pronounced *me-hi chick-sent-me-hi*) from Claremont Graduate College visited a class I was taking and talked about a theory called flow, which he had developed. Flow, he said, is a state of total absorption in a challenging activity—an enjoyable but serious state of absolute immersion in some goal-directed task. It's usually experienced when you're testing your limits in a favorite skill, which could be anything—delivering a speech, making a sales pitch, playing a video game, cooking, you name it. Flow is what athletes are referring to when they talk about being in the zone. It's somewhat different from fun, in most cases, because it entails hard work. In lots of ways, it's better than fun.

At the time I heard this lecture, I wasn't running, but this concept of flow resonated with my experiences in other activities, such as surfing. When I started running several years later, I began to experience flow at a whole new level, however. Surfing felt great, but it was also fun. Running was not fun, yet on my best days, it felt perfect.

A Mug of Stamina

Caffeine has been shown to enhance running performance. It does so partly by stimulating the central nervous system in ways that make exercise feel easier. A cup of joe allows an athlete to run harder with equal effort. Careful, though. Caffeine is a diuretic and can cause dehydration.

One of these days was the day I ran the 2006 Vermont Trail 100. Everything about it was wrong. I flew in from California the day before and was already fatigued and jet-lagged from the trip when the starting gun went off. The weather was hot and humid, the trail a muddy stew from recent rain. Horseflies ate me alive the whole way through. I should have had a terrible day, but instead it was magical. My body felt infused with superhuman endurance. One hundred miles was not far enough. I wanted to continue around the entire earth. After ninety miles of running I actually increased my pace, because I had so much left in the tank. I made a wrong turn and had to backtrack at one point, which is usually a spirit-killing disaster in an ultramarathon, but I couldn't have cared less. I won the race by nearly half an hour. I had won other grueling competitions before, but never with such an effortless feeling.

Running teaches you that there's a difference between working hard and feeling bad. Consumer culture tries to teach us otherwise. How many television commercials talk about "making life easier"? If everything you knew about life came from TV, your goal would be to live the easiest, most comfortable and unchallenging life you possibly could. You would believe that the only good feelings are sensual pleasures such as the taste of a good soft drink and the fun of driving an expensive car and lying on the beach.

But it's just not true. Challenging and testing your mind and body, even to the point of exhaustion, failure, and breakdown, can feel as wonderful as anything else life has to offer. I suppose the enjoyment of hard work is more of an acquired taste than the taste for pleasure and fun, but once you've acquired it, you're blessed with more ways to feel good, and life is better. Harder *and* better.

A greater number of people signed up to run with me at the Seafair Marathon in Seattle, Washington, on Day 14, than had signed up for any preceding event. Not surprisingly, then, it was the most entertaining run in the entire first two weeks of our cross-country adventure. Forty-eight people started with me, and I got a chance to meet and chat with each of them. A contingent of women from Team In Training, the Leukemia & Lymphoma Society's national fund-raising/marathon-training program, ran in pink mini skirts. Koop took music requests in the SAG wagon and played them loud over some external speakers he and Garrett had mounted on the roof, sending waves of energy into an already energized group. A young woman with long blond pigtails ran in a T-shirt that read I DO ALL MY OWN STUNTS, a motto that was a perfect match for her effervescent personality, I soon discovered.

One of the most memorable participants was a woman named Kris Allen, a thirty-seven-year-old mother of four, who struck me as the consummate "hip mom." She told me she had started running five or six years earlier as a convenient way to improve her health and get leaner, but had since fallen in love with the activity. I asked her what it was about running that appealed to her so much.

"Running is *my* time," she said. "It's one of the rare things I do just for me. The rest of my day is completely devoted to my kids and husband. Running lets me leave everyone else behind and recharge my batteries."

That's another thing about running that makes it different from activities that are intrinsically fun: It makes you feel good, or at least better, not just while you do it, but for the rest of the day.

"My kids can always tell when I need a run," Kris said. "If they see that I'm acting kind of cranky, they'll say, 'You haven't run yet today, have you, Mom?'"

Words to Run By

While running a race in Portugal, I noticed that spectators along the course kept shouting the same phrase over and over: *"Quem corre por gosto, não cansa."* Afterward I asked someone to tell me what it meant. "Who runs for pleasure never gets tired," I was told. How true!

How to Run with Flow

The flow state is special. You can't achieve it every time you run. But there are certain things you can do to facilitate it. Here are some of them:

- Run with a specific goal—for instance, by going for a certain amount of time, though with no particular distance in mind.
- Eliminate distractions, such as listening to music while you run.
- Race only when you're fit and ready to race. (Flow starts with the body being capable and rested.)
- Believe in your ability to achieve your goals and push all doubts and fears out of your head.
- Be in the moment. Don't think about what's still ahead. Just take it one step at a time.

About halfway through the Seafair Marathon, I got to meet Kris's kids. They were standing alongside the course and cheering for us. I stopped briefly to chat with all four of them. I could see from just the few moments I spent with them that they knew they had one hip mom.

As we resumed running, I looked around at my fellow runners and marveled at what I saw. Every single one of them was engaged in a conversation with at least one other person. The group was broken into clusters of two to four men and women, all of them swapping stories, smiling, and laughing. If I hadn't been wearing a heart rate monitor and sweating, I would have thought I was at a summer cookout.

As much as I enjoy the flow of running one hundred miles as fast as I can, I'll be the first to admit that there's something to be said for this kind of fun.

Kris and the others motored through the last few miles, and we all locked hands and crossed the finish line together. But Kris didn't stop. She kept right on going until she arrived at her car, got in, and zoomed away to host a birthday party. "Her time" was over.

Only later did I find out that this event had been Kris's first marathon. What's more, she had decided to do it only a few days earlier, and her longest training run had been thirteen miles—merely half the distance she ran with me.

Upon receiving this information, I found myself wondering why so many people like Kris are drawn to marathons and other such challenges these days. I can't help thinking that the phenomenon is in part a largely unconscious backlash against comfort culture and the easy life. Heated seats and online shopping and robot vacuum cleaners have created a void that we're all sensing. Our modern comforts and conveniences have accumulated to the point that they have stopped making us feel better and started making us feel worse. Some primal instinct lurking deep inside is trying to tell us that what is needed is a good, hard sweat—some struggle in our lives; some physical challenge.

Kris says she does not plan to do a second marathon. She claims it's because she was spoiled by the first one. Most marathons aren't as much fun as our romp through Seattle was—in fact, they're sometimes not fun at all. She says that it can't get any better, so why bother. She maintains that she is content. But I have my doubts. My sense is that a fire has been ignited.

My hunch seems to be correct. Last I heard, Kris was training for a long-distance triathlon.

CHAPTER 11

Man and Mystique

Day 15
October 1, 2006
Portland Marathon
Portland, Oregon
Elevation: 872'
Weather: 70 degrees; clear
Time: 3:44:12
Net calories burned: 47,805
Number of runners: 9,200

Portland is one of my favorite cities to run in. Not only is it scenic, but the mystique and lore of running in Oregon are unparalleled. The headquarters of Nike, Inc., is located just down the road in Beaverton, and the University of Oregon is in nearby Eugene. Two of my early heroes in the sport were Bill Bowerman, who co-founded Nike in 1964 and coached track and cross-country at Oregon from 1956 to 1970, and Steve Prefontaine, who not only rewrote the record book as a runner at Oregon but, more important, ran with an unbridled passion that incited others to be the best that they could be.

I learned about these two legends during the short first chapter in my running career, which started in my freshman year of high school and ended—in my freshman year of high school. My mom bought me a pair of Nike Waffle Racers to compete in. This shoe was so named because of the waffle-textured tread pattern on its outsole. Bill Bowerman had invented it—literally with the aid of a waffle iron—and it was considered revolutionary at the time due to its combination of light weight and traction. I just thought my Waffle Racers were super-cool. When I wore them, I could imagine myself as one of Bowerman's "Men of Oregon," a team of giants running their hearts out to make a legend proud.

The greatest giant of all was Prefontaine, who was killed tragically in a car accident at age twenty-four, just one year before I started running competitively in high school. When a man of greatness dies too young, his mystique is suddenly elevated to a higher level, and Pre's legend was never more intoxicating for a young runner than when I became one. Memories of his astonishingly courageous run in the 1972 Olympics, where he finished fourth in the 5,000 meters after just about killing himself to win, were still etched in the minds of every American runner.

The thing I liked about Prefontaine was that he ran because he loved to run. He almost didn't even care about winning. It was the *effort* to win that he lived for. "Most people run a race to see who's the fastest," he said. "I run a race to see who has the most guts."

My first running coach had the same attitude. Benner Cummings was a wise man of the old school who believed that success in running had little to do with speed or efficiency and everything to do with sheer determination and a pure love of running. "Don't run with your legs," he once told me. "Run with your heart." I never forgot that.

When I ran for Benner Cummings, I was only fourteen years old—young enough to view him as a sort of hero. As we become adults, we lose the ability to idolize the people we see every day. We become too perceptive and fault-focused. We develop an eagle eye for shortcomings in those who are familiar to us. But kids still have the ability to view the best people in their daily lives with the same uncritical admiration they feel toward their favorite heroes from the arts, sports, or history.

So Benner Cummings seemed larger than life to me. I knew he was eccentric, almost a caricature of his own personality, but

Running Tips from Bill Bowerman

The great Bill Bowerman was as innovative and influential a running coach as he was a shoe designer. Here are four running tips based on his proven methods:

1. Obey the hard–easy rule. You'll build fitness faster if you do three hard runs and three easy runs per week (for example) than if you do six moderate runs.
2. Practice rational goal setting. Set goals that you are *confident* you can attain, but aren't *certain* you can attain.
3. Treat yourself as an experiment of one. Don't blindly copy the way others train. Try new workouts and methods often; keep those that work for you and discard the rest.
4. Train at your goal pace. If there's a certain time you want to achieve in a race (such as a four-hour marathon), figure out the pace you need to sustain to achieve it (in this case 9:09 per mile) and include workouts at this pace as a regular part of your training.

to me there was a poetic near perfection in the way he was. Everything he said was so *Benner*—and so true. He made me want to run hard for him, the way the men of Oregon ran hard for Bowerman. In fact, as much awe as the name *Bill Bowerman* inspired in me, Benner Cummings meant more. Bowerman was like a mythological figure; Benner was as real as they came.

At fourteen I was still very much a child, and Benner was, as far as I could tell, perfect in every way. An everyday hero, touchable, accessible, and melodiously comfortable being himself. A philosopher named José Ortega y Gasset stated that heroism is the courage to be oneself. Above all, Benner had the courage to be Benner. And, in being so, he helped me realize that by following my dreams, by listening to my heart—whatever direction that might take me—I too could be my own hero, to myself, if nobody else.

Benner entered my life in high school. My dad was my hero from the day I was born. And he remains my hero today. His best character quality is freedom in the expression of his emotions. He's typically Greek in his strong, almost violent passions. One minute he's weeping with sympathy while reading a tragic newspaper story. The next he's laughing and doing a traditional Greek dance, perhaps for no better reason than because he realized he was taking life too seriously.

I had to learn to fully embrace this quality in my dad. My essential nature is more inclined toward Prefontaine's calculated determination than my dad's expressiveness. I guess you could say some of our Greek heritage was lost on my generation. We've become more American. People are very driven and business-like in this country, and unlike my dad I fell right into that way of being. My dad never really found a career that he embraced. Instead, he embraced life. Work was secondary, just something that needed to be done to provide for the family. When I was in my twenties, I had a completely different attitude. Work, for me, became everything. Making money was the key to happiness. Why didn't my dad understand this fundamental truth of the universe?

But as I worked myself into exhaustion in my early adulthood, I started to question what was so wrong with the happy zeal for life that my dad had modeled for me from the day I was born. I always appreciated this aspect of his character, but I did not truly embrace it until I was well into my adult years, when I realized my unbalanced drive and blind determination had led me down a path of life that did not make me happy. I had become too narrowly focused on the American dream of making money and climbing the corporate ladder. Luckily, I rediscovered running on my thirtieth birthday, and it brought meaning to my life as work never had.

Running as Play

One of the things I enjoyed most about running for Benner Cummings was that he made workouts seem like play. My favorite Benner workout consisted of running along the beach and repeatedly sprinting away from incoming waves to avoid getting wet. It was an incredible workout, but we didn't realize how hard it was until after we had completed it. You can mix effective training with play by doing what the Swedes call *fartlek* workouts, meaning "speed play." During a regular training run, randomly pick out landmarks ahead of you and run hard until you reach them. Go completely by feel. Hold your sprint until you reach your mark. It'll mix up your workouts and help build fitness quickly.

My dad has been by my side through it all. We've experienced some great highs, and some horrendous failures and devastating lows. He has always encouraged me to keep moving forward no matter how badly I failed. "It's not how many times you fall down that matters," he once told me. "It's how many times you get back up."

One of the questions I am asked most often by other runners is who my greatest heroes in the sport are. Ann Trason and Tim Twietmeyer certainly come to mind. Both are incredible athletes. Ann won many of the ultras she entered over the period of more than a decade. Tim was nearly as dominant, winning five Western States titles between 1991 and 1998 and amassing twenty-five Western States silver buckles over the course of his career.

After becoming an ultrarunner, I quickly came to admire Ann and Tim as much as the rest of the ultra-running community did. And because it's such a small community, we soon became acquainted. Both of them happened to live in Northern California, not far from me. Over the years, I've become fairly close with Tim. We've enjoyed many epic runs together, and through these experiences I have come to admire him even more than I did before I knew him. Tim's passion for running is immense. He simply can't get enough of it. That's why he still runs Western States every summer, even after twenty-five years. Tim runs the way my dad lives. I am eternally grateful to him, because he showed me that it's possible to run with calculated determination *and* for sheer joy. A runner doesn't have to choose one or the other.

While heroes and role models can help us make small steps forward in the never-ending journey of becoming our true selves, they can only take us so far. Once you pass a certain point in the journey, you have to stop becoming more like the people you admire and start becoming your own unique self.

I reached this crossroads after a few years of "traditional" ultrarunning. As much as I enjoyed taking part in structured events like the Western States 100, they were no longer enough for me. I felt a deep yearning to go even farther, to break free from the wildly loose confines of periodic course markers, sporadic aid stations, and occasional support found in most ultramarathons, and to try something really over-the-top. So I started doing my own thing. I ran a 199-mile, twelve-person relay race alone as a team of one. I'd sometimes run unsupported through the mountains for days. Sure, it was extreme, and it was unusual, but it was me, and it made me happy. It was what I loved to do, my way of following my heart. That's probably why I'm still at it.

Although the Endurance 50 blossomed out of my love of running and my deep internal yearning for ongoing exploration, the seed had been planted many years ago. For that, I must thank Mr. Bowerman, and Pre. Ann and Tim. And, of course, Benner and dear ol' Dad. Without them, I wouldn't be me.

CHAPTER 12

If It Stinks, Eat It

Day 16
October 2, 2006
Mayor's Midnight Sun Marathon
Anchorage, Alaska
Elevation: 135'
Weather: 41 degrees; cold and overcast
Time: 4:27:18
Net calories burned: 50,992
Number of runners: 18

eventeen miles into the Mayor's Midnight Sun Marathon (so called because it's normally run at the height of summer, when it's still light at midnight) in Anchorage, Alaska, our group of nineteen runners (eighteen plus me) emerged from a dirt trail onto a paved road. Standing there on the roadside waiting for us was a pizza delivery dude. I blinked my eyes a few times to make sure he was real. Sure enough, someone had phoned ahead and ordered pizza.

My personal policy is not to eat pizza on runs of fewer than fifty miles, but rules are meant to be broken, are they not? The group tore into the pizza like vultures competing for roadkill. Within seconds the delivery guy was left holding a warm, empty box. The pizza was Hawaiian-style—my favorite—with big chunks of pineapple half immersed in the gooey cheese surface. It was as hot as if it had just left the oven. We voraciously filled our stomachs with every last crumb, eating as we ran.

I was a little surprised to find that I had any appetite, given what I had just seen. A few miles back on the trail, just beyond the halfway point, our group had come upon the severed leg of a moose. Just the leg. Nothing else.

"Oh man," I said to the local runner next to me. "What did that?"

He gave me one of those looks, like: *Do I really need to tell you?*

One of the runners, a swarthy Alaskan, stopped and picked up the leg. I turned back to see him brandishing the bloody appendage like a cutlass as he ran along. Shuddering, I picked up my pace to stay ahead of him. Misinterpreting my actions as an invitation to play some bizarre grown-up version of tag, the man started chasing me. I accelerated to a full sprint. So did he. I kept running full-tilt until my pursuer got the message that I wasn't frolicking, I was terrified, and he hurled the leg into the brush.

To improve your running times, speed work is a necessary evil, though not something I'm particularly motivated to do. Needless to say, I got in some pretty good speed work at that point.

Half an hour later, when the pizza came, my biological needs trumped my lingering horror, fortunately, and I was able to wolf down two slices with gusto.

Thanks to a couple of passages in my first book, I have become known to some people as "that pizza-eating runner." Whoever called ahead for the roadside pizza in Anchorage probably intended it, in part, as a nod to this notoriety. But in truth, I eat lots of things besides pizza when I run. Just recently I tried kung pao shrimp, having discovered a Chinese restaurant willing to deliver to a street corner instead of a street address. I slurped it down right out of the box as I ran. (The trick to eating pizza on the run is to order thin-crust, request that it not be sliced, roll the whole thing up, and chow it like a giant burrito.) The kung pao shrimp experiment was a success. It stayed down and provided the energy surge I needed. The only downside, typical of Chinese food, was that I was hungry an hour later.

> *QUICK TAKE:* As a substitute for pasta, try kombu noodles. They are
> made from a sea vegetable and contain no flour. They have a much
> lower glycemic index than regular pasta, so they provide more
> lasting energy.

My eating habits on the run and my everyday diet are very different. When wearing street clothes, I rarely eat pizza or anything else containing white flour or gobs of cheese. Given the extreme energy demands of ultra-endurance running, however, all my strict everyday nutrition rules are largely tossed out the window when I'm on my feet for more than sixty or seventy miles. When you're burning six to seven hundred calories an hour, and you're moving forward for thirty, sometimes forty or fifty hours straight, you need a fast and convenient energy supply. That occasionally means junk food. Fruits and vegetables take up way too much valuable space in your stomach for the number of calories they provide. A slice of pizza contains seventy-three calories per ounce, an apple just fourteen. Two slices of pizza can fuel an hour of exercise. It would take twelve apples to do the same.

There is nothing magical about my everyday rules for healthy eating. I do the same things many other careful eaters do. The foods that I try to eat in the greatest abundance are fresh fruits and vegetables and lean meats and seafood. I moderate my consumption of starchy grains and do my best to ensure that those I do consume are whole grains such as oats, whole wheat, and brown rice. The foods and drinks I work hardest to avoid are those containing high-fructose corn syrup and other refined sugars (such as soft drinks), trans fats (such as french fries), and hydrogenated oils (such as most processed, packaged baked goods). In short, I try to eat only foods that existed in caveman times, and to steer clear of those that did not.

Perhaps the most unusual feature of my diet is not *what* I eat but *when* I eat. Instead of three big meals a day, I eat six or

First Things First

If I could recommend only one dietary change to improve your health, it would be to reduce your consumption of refined sugars. Although fat—and especially saturated fat—has typically received the most blame for causing America's weight problem, increasing evidence suggests that sugar might be the true culprit. For example, the rate of obesity is more than three times greater in our country than in France. Yet the French actually eat more fat than we do (42 percent of calories versus 37 percent)—and more saturated fat as well.

The one glaring difference between the American and French diets is the amount of sugar in each. We get more than 17 percent of our daily calories from sugars added to foods, whereas the French get only 10 percent. So if you want to improve your diet and overall energy level, the very first thing you should do is cut out sugar. Learn to scrutinize the labels of the packaged foods you eat. If it contains more than ten grams of "sugars" per serving, don't eat it.

seven small ones containing only four or five hundred calories each. I find that taking in frequent, small doses of energy gives my body and mind a steady flow of energy throughout the day, whereas the three-big-meals approach results in excessive energy spikes followed by annoying energy crashes.

In addition to limiting the size of my meals, I try to include a good balance of carbohydrates, fats, and protein in each meal. Many endurance athletes gorge on carbohydrates, which are the primary energy source for vigorous exercise, but I believe that healthy fats and lean proteins are no less important. Fats are also a great energy source—especially for moderate-intensity, prolonged exercise—and strengthen the immune system, support brain health, and help the body recover from exercise. Meanwhile, protein is critical for muscle tissue repair and re-

The Dean's List

Along with the artificial sweeteners Splenda (sucralose), Nutra-sweet (aspartame), and Sweet'N Low (saccharin), there are many all-natural sugar substitute alternatives to choose from, including:

- SlimSweet (lo han)
- Xylosweet (xylitol)
- SweetLeaf (stevia)
- Sun Crystals (erythritol)

building between workouts. Whereas some runners get as much as 70 percent of their daily calories from carbohydrates, I get only 40 percent, plus 30 percent each from fat and protein.

A few years ago, I plugged my typical day's meals into a software program that nutritionists use to analyze their clients' diets, which confirmed that I was eating the proportions of macronutrients I thought I was eating. Since then, I've been able to guide my eating choices by feel. I don't count calories, keep food journals, or even weigh myself. And when I feel like indulging in a treat (I have a weakness for chocolate-covered espresso beans—

The Dean's List

If it stinks, eat it. Cruciferous vegetables have a number of health benefits, including reducing the risk of some forms of cancer, and are packed with nutrients. Don't fret about the odor; it is the valuable sulfur-containing compounds in cruciferous vegetables that give them their pungent aroma. Here are some excellent sources:

- Broccoli
- Cabbage
- Brussels sprouts
- Cauliflower
- Watercress

The "Neanderthal" Diet

*Diets come and go. This one's been around
for thousands of years.*

The premise is straightforward. When trying to decide what
to eat and what not to eat, use this simple filter: Would a Neanderthal man have had access to this food? The rationale for
asking this question is simple: The foods that early humans ate
are those that our bodies were designed to eat. Could Neanderthal man have eaten pasta? Nope. Ice cream? Unh-unh.
White bread? No way. Fruit? Sure, find a tree. Vegetables? You
bet; he'd pull 'em right from the ground. Fish and lean meat?
Definitely. If Neanderthal man could catch it, he could eat it.
And back in the Neanderthal days, it was all organic, so try to
go organic whenever possible as well.

It takes some discipline to eat in this primitive way, but you'll
be amazed by how much better you feel when you do. Long
live Neanderthal man!

okay, it's more of a vice than a weakness), I partake with limited
discretion. In other words, I'm not fanatical; I'm human.

There are those whose ultrastrict dietary regimens make my
careful habits look like "anything goes" by comparison. The
legendary triathlete Dave Scott is one such person. For many
years, Dave followed a vegetarian diet. He later decided to re-
introduce meat to his diet, but he skipped over hamburgers and
bacon in favor of fish, chicken, and turkey, and his diet remains
primarily plant-based. There's no denying the fact that this strict
diet works for him—his results, which include six Hawaii
Ironman victories, speak for themselves. I'm not sure I could
get by on a largely plant-based diet, however, or would have
the willpower to stick to it. What works best for one person
doesn't always work best for another. Dave customized his diet
over the years. When I went through a similar process of re-

fining my diet based on what seemed to make me feel and perform better, I arrived at a different destination. I use my upper body a lot for sports other than running, and have found that I crave animal proteins—principally fish—to keep my shoulders, chest, and arms strong.

I grew up eating a mixture of traditional American fare and traditional Greek cuisine, because that's what my mother cooked. Today Greek food is considered a "Mediterranean diet," and Mediterranean diets are hip because medical research has found they are associated with reduced risk of metabolic diseases compared with other Western diets. But as a Greek American boy growing up in the 1960s and '70s, I did not think of stuffed grape leaves, grilled octopus, and tomato and cucumber salads as health food; they were just food.

The first time I became responsible for managing my own nutrition was when I went on a surfing safari to Baja, Mexico, with some friends as a teenager. Our budget was tight, and one of us came up with the bright idea of tossing a case of Pop-Tarts into the car so we wouldn't have to pay for any food during our time south of the border. My buddies and I ate nothing but Pop-Tarts for two weeks. On the first day, we thought we had died and gone to heaven—no mothers around to prevent us from devouring sugar-filled treats four or five times a day! By the final day our trip had become a living hell. I would have gladly traded our last remaining Pop-Tarts for anything else: brussels sprouts, beets, you name it. I have not eaten another Pop-Tart since.

Toward the end of high school, I started to become more interested in nutrition, both as a general field of knowledge and as a lifestyle factor that I could manipulate to improve the way my body felt and performed. Traditionally, young men and women gleefully allow their diets to degenerate when they leave home for college, trading Mom's cooking for pizza, beer, and fatty cafeteria food. My mom's cooking was as wholesome as anyone's, but the quality of my diet actually might have improved in my college years, because I wanted to get the most

Marathon Fuel

You don't need solid food to fuel your way through a standard marathon. Sports drinks such as Accelerade, energy gels, and other ergogenic aids including Clif Shot Bloks can provide all the energy you need in the most convenient and fast-acting form available.

out of my body and I clearly got more out of it when I loaded up on vegetables and lean protein and kept the pizza and beer consumption within limits—by college standards, anyway.

Nothing has changed over the years. Whenever I lapse and eat foods that are best reserved for long runs when I'm not, in fact, on a long run, I pay a price of lethargy and muddled thinking. Acquaintances who see how I eat often tell me, "You're so disciplined." But it's not discipline that causes me to consistently choose salad over french fries. It's something closer to hedonism. I feel lousy and perform poorly after I eat french fries. I feel good and perform well after I eat nutritious foods. How much discipline do I really need to do the thing that makes me feel and perform better? Not much. The choices come easily, as do the miles when I stick to a wholesome diet.

A cold drizzle plagued us for the last hour of the Mayor's Midnight Marathon, which finished on the West High School track. The sky had an ominous, threatening appearance, and the rain clouds were building rapidly. Suddenly, as we entered the track for the last quarter mile, the sky parted and a beam of light came shining down upon us. The mountain range in the background, whose towering peaks were covered in snow, glowed brightly in the sun. It looked like we were in an Ansel Adams landscape photo. Five minutes later, the clouds closed in and rain began to pour down heavily upon us.

The cold rain, however, could not wash away my warm memory of this enchanting day.

CHAPTER 13

Running for Others

Day 17
October 3, 2006
San Francisco Marathon
San Francisco, California
Elevation: 29'
Weather: 70 degrees; partly cloudy
Tme: 4:08:22
Net calories burned: 54,179
Number of runners: 50

O n a Sunday morning roughly fifteen years ago, I went surfing at San Francisco's Ocean Beach. Also enjoying the waves that day was an athletic-looking man who appeared to be about my age. When two surfers meet for the first time on their boards, their conversation always begins with a few comments about the waves, and this case was no exception.

He introduced himself as David Ames and told me he worked as an attorney. I read him instantly as a man with a huge appetite for life—the kind of person I have always been drawn to. David must have liked something about me too, because when I told him I was a runner he invited me to run with him sometime.

David was not an ultrarunner, but he was very strong at shorter distances. Fast. He pushed me hard the first time we ran together, and he continued to challenge me in each of our many subsequent runs. After a few years, however, David began to lose his edge. Without going any faster, suddenly I was the one pushing him. Although he was approaching his fortieth birthday, forty's not very old for someone who takes care of himself the way David did. His lifestyle hadn't changed, so he thought perhaps he had the flu or a lingering cold. Something that would eventually pass.

Then, while surfing in Cabo San Lucas, Mexico, in the early winter of 2002, David suffered the terrifying experience of not being able to muster the strength to stand up on his board—something he'd done in the past as easily as he tied his shoes. His chest and arms were now too weak to push his body upright. Soon thereafter he was diagnosed with amyotrophic lateral sclerosis (ALS), better known as Lou Gehrig's disease, a degenerative condition that affects the brain's motor neurons, slowly robbing the patient of the ability to move—and eventually to eat and breathe. It's a horrible disease for anyone to experience, but especially so for a gifted and passionate athlete who places the highest value on the active use of his limbs.

David has faced his disease with fortitude, courage, and dignity. Determined to fight ALS tooth and nail when traditional therapies failed him, he relocated to South America to seek alternative treatments. In the many times I have seen David since his diagnosis, he has shown no anger or self-pity, but remains free-spirited and outward-looking. After setting up a part-time residence in Brazil, he founded an organization called Heaven's Helpers, which provided assistance to people who are confined to wheelchairs, as David himself has been for the past few years.

In 2005, during a visit to his home in the San Francisco Bay Area, David called me up and asked if I wanted to run with him again, like old times. I met him at his house in Corte Madera and pushed him for twenty-five miles. It was his best workout in a long time, he told me afterward, half joking, half serious.

As The North Face Endurance 50 approached its seventeenth day, on which I was scheduled to run the San Francisco Marathon with a full-capacity group of fifty runners, I found myself thinking more and more about David. I traded some e-mails with his sister and was able to set up a special event-within-an-event that meant a lot to me.

The San Francisco Marathon racecourse has a number of scenic sections, but none is more breathtaking than the double crossing of the Golden Gate Bridge. At mile six, we merged onto the bridge heading northbound, out of the city. There's a small parking area just over the north end where motorists can stop and enjoy the view. Awaiting us there was David, who sat smiling in a heavy metal wheelchair. He was surrounded by a small entourage of family, friends, and handlers, including our own Garrett Greene, whose strength had been called upon to help get David down a flight of steps. I grabbed the handles of David's conveyance and began pushing, as I had pushed him for twenty-five miles a year ago and as he had pushed me—in another sense—during so many unforgettable runs that had taken place in a past life, as it now seemed.

Grabbing hold of the handles on the back of his wheelchair, I powered him from the north end of the Golden Gate Bridge across to the south end, joking that, just like old times, I was trailing be-hind him. We bid farewell on the south end of the bridge and David was once again absorbed back into his loyal entourage.

During the remaining sixteen miles of the event, I had the pleasure of sharing stories and laughing with many of the other runners, and I finished feeling satisfied that each of them had gotten something out of the experience. It was important to me that all of the Endurance 50 participants walked away from the finish line feeling proud and inspired, and on that day the hap-piness and appreciation I saw in David's face as we glided over the bridge impacted us all. Marathon number seventeen was our biggest yet, with fifty energized official runners and perhaps another fifty "bandits" who joined in along the way. It was a brilliant tribute to one great man who may never run again with his legs, but whose spirit will continue to run in each of us who was touched by the experience that day.

Ways to Run for Others

There are lots of ways your running can benefit other people. Here are a few:

- Join Team In Training (www.teamintraining.com).
- Ask your friends and co-workers to pledge a dollar per mile for your next marathon, then send the grand total to your favorite charity.
- Participate in races that benefit charities (as most do).
- Volunteer for Girls on the Run (www.girlsontherun.org) or one of the many other great youth running programs.

There is something special and almost unexplainable about running for others. It has become quite a phenomenon in recent years. Individuals and organizations all around the world are choosing to raise money for and awareness of causes and to honor and commemorate people and events by running. Of all the ways to raise money, build awareness, honor deserving people, and commemorate important events, why running? I can't explain it. All I know is that it has power, and it works for both the recipient and the giver.

You could say that the tradition of running for others goes all the way back to Phidippides, the messenger of ancient Greece who, according to legend, ran from the battlefield of Marathon to Sparta in an effort to recruit the Spartans to help his badly outnumbered countrymen and then, from the battlefield to Athens to bring word of the victory. If anything qualifies as running for others, that did.

The modern tradition of running for others may not be as dramatic, though it is every bit as noble. More than a billion dollars has been raised by runners for causes ranging from diabetes to childhood organ donation to improving the world's clean water supply. The recipients are grateful for this show of support and funding, and the runners benefit from knowing they are helping others through their efforts. It is a model in which truly everybody wins.

My personal history of running for others dates back to 1994, not long after I met David Ames, when my friend Heather Shannon asked me to join a new organization called Team In Training.

"What's it all about?" I asked her.

"It's a program of the Leukemia Society," she said. "We provide free coaching and, group workouts, and handle the travel and logistics to run a marathon for anyone who's willing to help us raise money. People who sign up collect donations from family, friends, co-workers, and businesses."

I signed up, raised a few thousand dollars, and ran the Honolulu Marathon with some other first-generation members of what has become one of the most innovative, successful, and celebrated fund-raising programs ever created. Team In Training has raised more than seven hundred million dollars for the Leukemia & Lymphoma Society, as it's now called. More than three hundred thousand walkers, runners, cyclists, and triathletes have participated in the program. In fact, Team In Training has become so huge that it has helped fuel the tremendous growth in marathon and triathlon participation over the past decade.

Team In Training succeeded for a reason. Its early participants became involved because they wanted to run a marathon for those who couldn't. Committing to months of dedicated training in the hope of completing a grueling physical endeavor was their way of showing support and compassion for those in need. From the outside, it might not seem entirely logical, but it's the way the human heart functions. I think that's why Team In Training took off.

A few years after I completed the Honolulu Marathon as a member of Team In Training, I met Jeff Shapiro, a medical doctor who, in his spare time, directed an annual 199-mile relay running race that started in Calistoga and ended in Santa Cruz. When I told Jeff I wanted to run the entire distance not as part of a twelve-person relay team but alone, his first thought was that I was crazy. I even joked with him that I didn't have eleven friends left at this point. Still, I could tell he thought I was nuts. But then he saw an opportunity.

Jeff told me he was deeply involved in efforts to raise public awareness of the desperate need for organ donors for critically ill children. He suggested that I dedicate the colossal challenge I was planning to a little girl he knew of who had liver disease and would soon die without a donor. Recalling my satisfying

How to Raise Money for Your Cause

We all have different causes that are important to us. To raise money outside an existing program (like Team In Training) requires a slightly different approach. Here is a suggested format to follow:

- Register with one of the online donation sites. Active.com is one of my favorites. It's free for the fund-raiser and allows potential contributors to make secure online donations.
- You can customize this site to explain your cause and the event you're planning to participate in. Some people build elaborate sites—including pictures, graphs, charts, and maps—while others take a very simple approach.
- Once you've developed the site to your liking, send a message to all your contacts explaining what you're doing and why you're doing it. Be sure to always include a link to your fund-raising page.
- Active.com has a variety of online tools that allow you to measure the activity of your fund-raising campaign, including the amount of traffic to your site and the amount of money raised.
- At the end of each month, Active.com will send your charity a check. They take one dollar out of each donation as a processing fee.
- Be sure to always thank your donors. You are a hero, and so are they!

Team In Training experience, I embraced the idea immediately and asked everyone I knew to donate a dollar per mile—or whatever they could afford—to help save this child's life.

That 199-mile run (which ended up being 200 miles, because I made a wrong turn and added a mile) was the hardest challenge I had yet faced. In fact, I might not have completed it if not for the commitment I had made to save a life. Quitting on my own behalf would have been one thing, but quitting on little Elizabeth Woods and her family was unthinkable. The fact that I was running for "Libby" made this one-man relay far more meaningful than it would have been had I run it only for myself, and as a result I dug deeper than I had ever done before.

The payoff made all of the suffering worthwhile. Not only did I get a big show of gratitude from Libby's family at the finish line, but a week later she received a new organ. The whole experience was so rewarding that I repeated it several times, with variations, to help save other children.

After finishing the San Francisco Marathon on Day 17 of the Endurance 50, I was approached by a representative of the Fleet Feet running store in Stockton, California, who handed me a check for $2,620—$100 for each mile our group had just run—made out to Karno's Kids, the foundation I created to support getting kids outside and active.

As I accepted the check, I felt the strength of my enthusiasm for the next thirty-three days, states, and marathons suddenly double. There's just something about running for others that makes running by yourself all the more worthwhile.

CHAPTER 14

Trains, Planes, and Running Shoes

Day 18
October 4, 2006
Maui Marathon
Maui, Hawaii
Elevation: 52'
Weather: 88 degrees; partly cloudy, humid
Time: 4:26:40
Net calories burned: 57,366
Number of runners: 8

During one of our late-night drives from state to state, I opened an e-mail from Kazuhiko Sakashita, a Japanese runner I did not know, who informed me that he had made a last-minute change to his wedding plans. Instead of staying home and going through with a large, traditional ceremony he had planned with his bride-to-be, he was going to whisk her away to Maui, exchange vows with her on the beach without witnesses, and run the Maui Marathon with me and a handful of other runners.

Initially, I thought it might be a joke. But after rereading the message, I realized the man's intentions were sincere. My gut reaction was to try to talk him out of it, though he was a perfect stranger to me, and I figured he had his reasons. Actually, he stated his reasons, or at least one of them, in his message: He wanted to prove himself worthy of his new wife. It sounded thoroughly Japanese to me, and I respected that.

I met Kazuhiko at the starting line of the Maui Marathon on Day 18. He was quiet, serious, and earnest. I worried about how the groom would fare this morning. The air temperature was already in the seventies and rising, and heavy with moisture. The conditions were not optimal for marathon running, and would be especially tough on those who had traveled long distances from milder climates, and most especially on travelers who had been married the previous day.

Since there were only nine of us, I had plenty of opportunity to converse with Kazuhiko. His English wasn't perfect, but it was good enough for him to explain that his wife was not exactly pleased about having to scrap her elaborate wedding plans only to fly off to Hawaii for an elopement on the beach so that he could run a marathon. *Gee whiz*, I thought. *Imagine that.*

"So did you get much sleep last night?" I asked Kazuhiko with a wink and a smile. After all, it was his honeymoon night. He stared at me blankly for a moment before he caught my insinuation.

"Oh!" he said. "Yes, I sleep full night to be strong for marathon today. I save honeymoon for tonight." Of all the sacrifices other runners had reported making for the sake of participating in the Endurance 50, this had to rank among the greatest.

The Maui Marathon bisects the island, and after running across the landmass with only limited views of the water, we reached the coast. We climbed up a winding road, gaining elevation but still not getting a very good view of the water. We passed through a natural volcanic canyon in the road, and when we emerged on the far side, the view was amazing. The trade winds had subsided, and the sea sparkled a radiant blue below us. We could see the outline of the reef through the crystal-clear, calm water; it looked like a brilliant aquarium. From this vista, the neighboring island of Molokai rested docilely in the background.

With more than ten miles still left to go in the marathon, Kazuhiko began to struggle, as we all did, yet he refused to drop off the pace. The heat and humidity were brutal. His condition deteriorated steadily for the remainder of the run. He groaned and wheezed, eventually beginning to weave like a drunken sailor. I was amazed by his determination and sheer willpower. The group did their best to encourage him and keep him hydrated.

"It's okay to walk a bit," I told him, genuinely concerned about his well-being.

"No, I will finish," he grunted.

The final few steps were quite dramatic. Kazuhiko courageously hung with the group, despite dehydration and cramping. He crumpled to the ground the moment he crossed the line and lay there in a delirium of pain and relief. His new wife dashed to him in alarm. Oblivious to the slimy layer of sweat that coated him, she held his limp head and torso and wept. The whole proving-himself-worthy thing now made perfect sense.

Eventually, Kazuhiko was able to stand and thank me, as did his bride, Miho. *"Domo arigato,"* she said with a bow. He had proven himself worthy not only in her eyes, but in mine too, and in those of everyone who had witnessed his bold effort.

The crew and I had to leave hastily for the airport to catch a flight to Phoenix, our next stop, and poor happy Kazuhiko appeared to be locked up in full-body cramps as we pulled away. I wasn't sure how much honeymooning was left in the poor guy for tonight.

Kazuhiko wasn't the only runner who had come from overseas to experience the Endurance 50 in Maui. Another gentleman had flown all the way from Milan, Italy. Throughout the Endurance 50, I was amazed by how far people were willing to travel to join me in running a low-key marathon, often in an out-of-the-way place in the middle of the week.

But perhaps I shouldn't have been so surprised. Running and travel go well together. Marathons and other running events make

Tips to Prevent Jet Leg

Flying across time zones can throw your internal body clock out of kilter and cause you to feel extremely fatigued for anywhere from a couple of days to a week. Not only is it an unpleasant experience, but it also hampers your ability to run. Use these tips to limit its effects:

- Expose yourself to as much sunlight as possible before departing.
- If you want to rest, try taking melatonin before you fly. Melatonin is a natural hormone that regulates the body's circadian rhythms and is available over the counter at most pharmacies.
- Alternatively, try a homeopathic remedy called No Jet Leg. The main active ingredient is an herbal extract called arnica. It's worked very well for me.
- Avoid drinking alcohol or caffeinated beverages during the flight. Drink plenty of water.
- If you can sleep on planes, do. Forcing yourself to stay awake with the idea that this will make it easier to sleep more soundly later on never seems to work. Sleep at every opportunity.
- When you're awake, get up and walk about the aircraft frequently.
- Change your watch to the local time zone of your destination on takeoff.

excellent centerpieces for cross-country or international adventures. And these trips are just about the only ones where you return home weighing less than you did when you left!

Through many runs on all seven continents, I have learned a few tricks to help avoid the pitfalls so often encountered in this type of travel. The first bit of guidance I would give to any runner considering traveling across time zones to race is to arrive at least one day per time zone crossed before the event takes place.

Quite apart from the jet-lag factor, flying just takes a lot out of you, and your body needs time to recuperate and adjust.

It's also prudent to learn as much as you can about a far-away event before you commit to it. For example, some marathons may not be appropriate for first-timers. While the idea of running a marathon in Big Sur, California, might sound enticing, the Big Sur Marathon course is hilly enough to humble even the most experienced marathoner. I myself once made the classic mistake of inadequate research before running the Leadville 100. I knew it wasn't as hilly as some of the other hundred-milers I'd done. What I'd failed to consider—or perhaps repressed—was the fact that the race begins at *10,500 feet of elevation.* I should have arrived a week early to adjust to the altitude. Instead, I showed up the day before the race and suffered miserably.

It's the small things that often make the biggest difference when you're traveling to a running event. One of the small things that make a big difference for me is wearing comfortable, loose-fitting clothes on the plane and even during long drives. I am less prone to sweat, and I feel less constricted. Some of my friends, like Ironman champion Chris Lieto, swear by compression tights to help minimize flight-related swelling. I encourage you to try different approaches to see what works best for you.

Enjoying new and exotic foods can be one of the great pleasures of traveling, but it's best to stick with familiar fare from trustworthy sources in the days before a race. If you really want to play it safe, reserve a hotel room with a kitchenette, buy ingredients from a grocery store or market, and prepare your own pre-race dinner.

Assuming you eat a fairly healthy diet at home, it's also a good idea to maintain your usual dietary standards as well as possible while traveling—at least until you've completed your event! It used to be nearly impossible to find wholesome food choices in airports, but nowadays you can always find salads and fresh fruit. When making your flight reservation, consider

Tips for Traveling Abroad to Marathons

Marathon tourism is a huge phenomenon. Each year, thousands of runners cross borders to combine marathon participation with foreign adventure. Getting the most out of marathon tourism, though, requires a little planning. Here are some tips:

- Thoroughly research the marathon you're considering signing up for before you commit to it. The best way to do this is by logging onto MarathonGuide.com, where you can read reviews of virtually every marathon on the planet posted by past participants. These reviews will help you pick an event that provides a good experience for most and will help you make specific preparations to ensure you avoid problems that past participants have encountered.

- Make all your arrangements—including flight and hotel bookings, visa acquisition, and event registration—as far in advance as you can. This will spare you a lot of energy-sapping stress in the final weeks and days before you depart.

- If you're traveling with family, try to involve them in your race in certain ways, so they won't feel it's taking away from their vacation. Buy each of them something at the race expo, have your kids make signs that read GO, DAD/MOM!, and create a fun and easy spectator plan for the family. Make them feel like an important part of the team, as they rightfully are!

- If you want to combine your running with tourism, save the tourism for *after* the marathon. You don't want to spoil your race by walking your legs to death, eating the wrong dinner, or picking up a cold or flu beforehand. You'll also be less preoccupied with the upcoming race when you're out touring. Better to be basking in the glow of a runner's high than stressing about an upcoming event.

- Be careful about the food you eat. I once ate a kebab from a street vendor in New York City the day before a twenty-four-hour race. I won't clutter your mind with the details of my suffering, but needless to say, I spent about as much time running for the bathroom as I did running on the racecourse.

Pack Your Snacks

A good way to ensure that you have wholesome food available to eat when hunger strikes you during your travels is to pack and carry your own healthy snacks. Here are a few of my favorites:

- Energy bars
- Dried fruit
- Trail mix
- Salmon jerky
- Hard fruit (apples, pears)

requesting a vegetarian meal, even if you eat meat: Vegetarian meals usually contain more nutrient-dense foods and less fat.

Having said all of this, I should also emphasize that it's important not to be too much of a perfectionist once things get under way. Travel rarely goes perfectly. You'll have more fun if you don't stress yourself out trying to prevent every possible mishap and just roll with those mishaps that inevitably do occur. Hope for the best, but anticipate the worst, I always say.

Take a cue from Kazuhiko Sakashito, who probably would have suffered less if he hadn't gotten married the day before the Maui Marathon, but would plan it the same way if he could do it all over again. How do I know? Because I received an e-mail message from him a couple of days after we ran together. In it, Kazuhiko stated that it was a great honor to run with me and the other "magnificent runners," and that he will forever cherish the memory of crossing the finish line hand in hand with the group and with the kids who came out to run alongside us. He said the pain of ruptured blisters didn't matter. Our "moment of misery," as he put it, was like a dream.

CHAPTER 15

The Heat Is On

Day 19
October 5, 2006
Desert Classic Marathon
Phoenix, Arizona
Elevation: 1,227'
Weather: 103 degrees; partly cloudy, roasting
Time: 4:45:16
Net calories burned: 60,553
Number of runners: 46

---

slept little throughout the Endurance 50, but on the night before the Desert Classic Marathon on Day 19, the situation became critical. Our flight from Maui landed in Phoenix after midnight. We had flown directly from the finish in Hawaii and I hadn't had time to shower, so I was still covered in sweat and road grime. Worse, I had slept only a few hours during the prior night's flight to Hawaii from San Francisco.

When we landed in Phoenix, a crew member's wife was waiting. Jennifer and JB Benna lived in the area, and she had thoughtfully baked fresh peanut butter cookies for us. It was really hot outside, even though it was in the middle of the night, and after eating a warm, gooey peanut butter cookie, I crashed. It was all I could do to keep my eyes open to get in the cab that would deliver us to the hotel. I kept doing the tired traveler's head bob on the drive, nodding off and then waking up with a start as my chin dropped. When we got to the hotel, we found no receptionist; the place was deserted. We looked all around for someone, to no avail. Finally, I lay down on the carpet inside the lobby. Naturally, I had just fallen asleep when the receptionist showed up and I had to get back up. Quickly, in fact, as she said there could be scorpions on the floor. It seemed like sleep would never come that night.

The Desert Classic Marathon takes place on the first Sunday in February each year. February is not exactly peak marathon season in most parts of the country, but in Phoenix it's the best time to run. The average high temperature in early February is in the upper sixties.

We ran our forty-six-person re-creation of the Desert Classic Marathon on October 5. The average high temperature is ninety degrees at that time of year, and triple-digit mercury readings are not unusual. After suffering through a muggy eighty-eight-degree marathon in Hawaii, I was hoping we would luck out and find a cold front awaiting us in the desert, but instead Arizona bumped it up a notch. The temperature ranged between 90 degrees at the start of our marathon and 103 at the end. The air was bone-dry, with a slight tailwind on the way out and an almost nonexistent headwind on the return. Perfect conditions for sitting in a pool all day. Not so great for running.

> **QUICK TAKE:** *Staying hydrated is important not only for performance when running but also for basic health every day. To stay properly hydrated throughout the day, get in the habit of carrying a water bottle with you wherever you go. Drink enough so that your urine remains pale yellow or clear in color.*

Many runners believe that cool conditions are ideal for marathon running, but research has shown that relatively *cold* weather is even more conducive to running faster times. Recently, researchers from the US Army Research Institute of Environmental Medicine gathered many years' worth of race results and weather data from six major North American marathons and performed statistical analyses to determine the effect of air temperature on finishing times among runners at various levels of performance.

The results showed a clear trend toward faster times at colder temperatures. For example, the finishing times of male race winners were closest to the course record (only 1.7 percent slower than the very best time on each course) when the air temperature was between thirty-four and fifty degrees. The finishing times of the top male runners were 2.5 percent slower than the course record, however, when the temperature was between fifty-one and fifty-nine degrees. And at temperatures exceeding sixty, finishing times fell off even more dramatically.

The ideal marathon temperature, according to these analyses, was a bone-chilling forty-one degrees. Think about that when you sign up for your next marathon!

Most marathons are held in the spring and fall, when the weather is typically neither cold nor hot but cool. Interestingly, however, most ultramarathons are held in the summer. I suppose the people who manage these events figure that if you're going to run extreme distances, you might as well toss in extreme heat. The Badwater Ultramarathon, with its 135-mile total distance and its cumulative elevation gain of nineteen thousand feet, would be hard enough if it were held in February, but instead it takes place in the middle of July, when Death Valley temperatures can reach 130 degrees!

If I hadn't finished Badwater six times myself (after collapsing at the halfway mark in my first attempt), I might not believe a human being could be capable of running so far in such extreme heat, but with adequate training, a calculated pace, and constant fluid intake, it can be done. In fact, biologists say that when it comes to running long distances in the heat, human beings are better designed than almost any other species on earth. We have many times more sweat glands than most other animals, allowing us to dissipate excess heat from the core to the surface of our bodies at a high rate. Our paucity

Tips for Heat Acclimation

Whenever you relocate from a temperate environment to a hot one (with air temperatures exceeding eighty-five degrees), it's best not to immediately resume your normal training routine. Instead, give your body a chance to acclimate to the new conditions. Here's how to do it:

1. On the first day, run lightly or do not run at all. Either way, spend some time outside in the afternoon heat.
2. The next day, go for a shorter-than-usual run at a slower-than-normal pace.
3. Gradually increase the duration and intensity of your runs each subsequent day until you're doing your normal workouts by the sixth or seventh day. Research has shown that it takes that long for the body to fully acclimate.

of hair allows us to enjoy the cooling effect that comes with the evaporation of sweat into the atmosphere.

Humans also have a remarkable ability to adapt to running in the heat. After two weeks of heat training, runners exhibit a markedly increased sweating capacity, greater blood volume, reduced salt concentration in their sweat, and other changes that enable them to run substantially faster and farther without overheating.

Runners seldom experience heat illness, as many other animals would if they attempted to run far in very hot environments, because the human body has built-in mechanisms to prevent it. Your subconscious brain is able to sense your core body temperature and knows the upper limit that can be allowed before organ and tissue damage occur. As your core body temperature approaches this limit during running, you will begin to experience feelings of discomfort and fatigue and your pace will drop involuntarily. These symptoms typically emerge before you're in any real danger of bodily injury—thus preventing you from harming yourself.

Hydration Guidelines for Runners

Consuming fluid during your workouts and races will help you run stronger and may help you avoid overheating. Here are a few simple guidelines to follow:

- Consume fluid during all runs lasting an hour or more, and during runs of any duration in very hot weather (eighty-five degrees or higher). This will improve your performance by limiting the amount of dehydration you experience during your workouts.
- Carry your fluid in a squeeze bottle, such as those used by cyclists, and keep the bottle in a fluid belt; or use a hydration pack with an internal bladder for storing liquid (such as a CamelBak). Both items can be purchased at most running specialty shops or ordered online. My personal favorite is the North Face Gulper.
- Know how much fluid you will need for a long run before you start, and create a plan to ensure you have access to enough. If you will need more fluid than your hydration system will hold, put a five-dollar bill in your pocket and buy a bottle of liquid from a convenience store midway through your route, or return home for a refill.
- For the best results, use a sports drink instead of water. Sports drinks hydrate better than water because they replace sodium and other minerals that are lost in sweat, whereas water does not.
- Drink small amounts frequently: roughly four to eight ounces every ten to fifteen minutes. Your stomach empties faster when it's fuller. Drinking frequently helps keep your stomach consistently fuller.
- The exact amount of fluid you need depends on your weight, your running pace, and how long you run. So try to listen to your body and tune in to your individual hydration needs.

- Don't force yourself to drink more than you're comfortable consuming. This can lead to gastrointestinal stress or, in extreme cases, a dangerous dilution of the blood known as hyponatremia, or water intoxication.
- Drink one or two glasses of water after completing your run as well. Even when you drink appropriately during a run, by the time you finish you may be somewhat dehydrated without even knowing it.

Many runners believe that overheating is caused primarily by dehydration, but in most cases it's not. Dehydration can make overheating more likely, but the main cause of overheating is the accumulation of heat produced by working muscles. So the most effective way to prevent overheating is to slow your pace.

The body's primary cooling mechanism while running in the heat is perspiration. The higher your sweat rate, the more heat you can transfer from the core of your body to the environment. Improving your fitness level also improves your sweat response. The fittest runners tend to have the greatest sweating capacity and therefore have the greatest ability to regulate their body temperature while running.

Another way to enhance your sweat rate is to drink fluids while you run. As you become progressively dehydrated during a run, your blood volume decreases, and as your blood volume decreases, so does your sweat rate. Drinking while you run keeps your blood volume and sweat rate from falling as quickly. Exercise scientists used to believe that drinking during exercise in the heat kept the body temperature lower, but recent studies using high-tech sensors that athletes actually ingest before racing have shown otherwise. Whether they drink or not, runners unconsciously adjust their pace to keep their core body temperature below the safety limit. It follows that by allowing your body to dissipate more heat through sweating, drinking on the run allows your muscles to work harder (in other words, it allows you to run faster) while maintaining a safe body temperature. Put succinctly, drink plenty because sweat rules!

In the triple-digit heat of the Desert Classic Marathon, the Endurance 50 support crew understood the importance of keeping the runners well hydrated. Over the course of the run, Koop, Garrett, Hopps, and Robin worked tirelessly to keep everyone safe. We even brought in reinforcements from headquarters: namely, Jim Anderson, of the Squires Sports Group,

The Ideal Sports Drink

Not all sports drinks are the same. I recommend that you choose one with the following characteristics:

- *Six to eight percent carbohydrate (fourteen to nineteen grams per eight-ounce serving).* Drinks with higher level of carbohydrates will not be absorbed as quickly and may cause gastrointestinal distress (nausea, stomach bloating, and sometimes also vomiting or diarrhea).
- *At least 120 milligrams of sodium per eight-ounce serving.* You need this amount of sodium to maintain proper fluid balance in your body. Also, sodium aids the absorption of fluid, so it doesn't slosh around in your stomach.
- *At least two types of carbohydrates.* Different types of carbohydrates are metabolized through different pathways. Therefore, sports drinks containing multiple carbohydrate sources are able to deliver energy to the muscles faster than sports drinks with an equal total amount of just one type of carbohydrate. Look for some combination of glucose, sucrose, dextrose, maltodextrin, and fructose.
- *Not too much fructose.* Avoid sports drinks whose labels list fructose or high-fructose corn syrup as their first ingredient. Too much fructose can cause GI distress during exercise.

and his family, whom he recruited to lend a hand because of the extreme heat. Together, they doled out ninety gallons of liquid and burned through more than a hundred pounds of ice in an effort to keep us all cool and hydrated.

At the midpoint of the run, I began experiencing mild vertigo from the heat and lack of sleep. It shook me to the core. I'd felt this way before during other long races over the years, and I realized that I was entering a dangerous spiral, because my mind just wasn't operating clearly on the fewer than six combined hours of sleep I'd gotten over the past two days. Thankfully, I still had enough wits left to know what to do.

"Koop," I muttered in the general direction of the SAG wagon. "Badwater tactics."

Koop had been with me during my sixth Badwater Ultramarathon this past summer and knew precisely what I was talking about. When I reached the SAG wagon the next time around, he had hoisted the cooler on top of the vehicle's roof and instructed me to stand under it. Shocking as it was, he dumped the icy contents over my head.

Instantly, I was revived. Most important, my mental acuity jumped up a couple of dozen points and I was able to think clearly once again. Feeling my core temperature cooling was reassuring, and I now realized how close to the edge I'd gotten.

"Keep an eye on me, will ya?" I said to Koop. "I was losing it back there."

Over the course of the next ten miles, he repeated the ice shower routine three more times. Our finishing time in the Desert Classic Marathon was the second lowest of the entire Endurance 50. All of us—including five first-timers—made it the whole way, though it was a slog. Still, it beat passing out on the roadside and being carted off to the ER, that's for sure.

When we got to the finish, I hopped directly into the large cooler filled with drinks. I didn't care that there were a bunch of sports beverages and bottles of water floating next to me; I needed an ice bath, so in I went.

It would have been nice to take more post-marathon ice baths during the Endurance 50, as I firmly believe in the benefits of doing so: They not only cool you down but also reduce muscle pain and inflammation. Still, it just wasn't possible most of the time. It was a matter of trying to wrap things up as tightly as possible at the Finish Festival so we could get on the road for the next state. The trade-off for delaying our departure for an ice bath would have been fewer hours of sleep for everyone. The Endurance 50 had become a team event, and I felt like we were all integrally dependent on one another to perform at our peak. To me, this meant, among other things, that I needed to give the crew adequate time to rest and recuperate. I could sacrifice some niceties—like post-race ice baths—for the good of the team.

I dunked my head under one last time and headed into the bus soaking wet. English was sitting in the driver's seat looking at a weather report.

"Okay, wheels up shortly," I said to him. "Where we off to next?"

"Valley of Fire."

Maybe I should have stayed in that cooler longer.

Day 20
October 6, 2006
Valley of Fire Marathon
Overton, Nevada
Elevation: 1,868'
Weather: 78 degrees; partly cloudy
Time: 4:06:55
Net calories burned: 63,740
Number of runners: 35

After running in hundred-degree temperatures the previous day, I did not consider the section of Nevada known as the "Valley of Fire" to be the most appealing destination for my next marathon. I would have preferred the Valley of Blustery Winds or even the Valley of Ice. Anything but Fire. However, names can be deceiving. The high temperature in the Valley of Fire Marathon was more than twenty degrees cooler than it had been in Phoenix. Granted, seventy-eight degrees isn't exactly the ideal temperature for marathon running either. But after yesterday, it felt perfect.

My good friend Ferg Hawke had come out to run with me. When the first rays of sunlight hit the red sandstone valley, it looked as if its walls were on fire. The last time Ferg and I had run together, that fire could have been real. We'd competed in the Badwater Ultramarathon, in temperatures that crested 120 degrees and melted the soles of the shoes of those who weren't careful.

"This feels pretty comfortable to me," Ferg commented as we ran through the Valley of Fire, admiring the beautifully sculpted arches and burning rock walls. "Remember our last run?"

"Nah, I don't remember that one; I was too delirious to remember much of anything," I said, only half jokingly.

We swapped war stories about Badwater, laughing with the others in the group about the qualities it takes to complete the 135-mile desert crossing, principally a limited IQ. The miles came easy today—all things are relative, including heat—and the splendor of the landscape and the good company had an uplifting effect, mellowing the edge that yesterday had taken on.

We finished the marathon forty minutes faster than we'd finished the Desert Classic, on a much tougher and hillier course. The cooler temperatures had certainly played a part, but the camaraderie had a greater role. As we said good-bye to the other runners and bid farewell to the hundreds of schoolkids who'd come out to run the last mile with us, I found myself glad to be traveling northward—our next stop was Utah—and to be one day deeper into autumn. As I settled back in my seat and watched the setting sun light the dusk sky ablaze, all I kept thinking was one thing: *Bring on fall!*

CHAPTER 16

Running High

Day 21
October 7, 2006
St. George Marathon
St. George, Utah
Elevation: 2,940'
Weather: 68 degrees; clear
Time: 3:20:04
Net calories burned: 66,927
Number of runners: 5,100

ran three and a half marathons at altitude over the course of the Endurance 50. A marathon is generally considered to be "at altitude" if it takes place above five thousand feet (roughly a mile) of elevation. The Boulder Backroads Marathon, the Casper Marathon, and the New Mexico Marathon were each a mile high. The St. George Marathon in Utah started at 5,240 feet and ended at 2,680 feet, so half of it was at altitude.

The five-thousand-foot dividing line is not arbitrary. Above this level, the thin-air factor begins to have a measurable effect on running performance. If you've ever run or done any type of vigorous exercise within a short time after arriving at altitude, you probably recall what this effect feels like. At five to seven thousand feet it can be pronounced. When running within this elevation range, initially you might feel as though you haven't run for ten days and your fitness has gone two steps backward.

Above seven thousand feet, the effect becomes considerably more noticeable. You feel as though you are trying to run while breathing underwater. Your lungs just can't get enough oxygen. At eight thousand feet, the barometric pressure is 25 percent lower than it is at sea level. This means you get 25 percent less oxygen per breath than at sea level. That's a difference you can't fail to notice.

The most extreme high-altitude running experience I've had was when I ran the John Muir Trail a few years back. I crossed over mountain passes exceeding thirteen thousand feet of elevation. I was reduced to a near crawl at these high points. It was humbling.

> **QUICK TAKE:** *Get there early. New evidence shows that acclimatization begins after just a few high-altitude hours, when a chemical trigger in the body called HIF-1 alpha activates genes that help you adapt to heights.*

Many elite runners seek out high-altitude locations for training camps or even permanent residence. If you aren't familiar with the phenomenon of altitude training, you might wonder why runners would deliberately train in an environment where it's hard to breathe. The answer, of course, is that over time the human body adapts to living at altitude in ways that improve sea-level running performance. Within a few weeks of relocating from sea level to a high altitude, runners exhibit a number of beneficial physiological changes. Foremost among them is increased production of erythropoietin (EPO), the protein that regulates red blood cell production. Red blood cells transport oxygen to the muscles. Thus, higher EPO levels enable runners to consume oxygen at a higher rate when running, partially counteracting the effects of high altitude.

Being born and raised at high altitude has been shown to be more beneficial than relocating to the mountains later in life. No wonder some of the world's greatest runners hail from high-altitude locations. A hugely disproportionate number of the best distance runners come from the Rift Valley in Kenya at altitudes ranging from five to ten thousand feet. America's best young marathon runner, Ryan Hall, is also a child of the heights. He grew up in Big Bear, California: elevation seven thousand feet.

The Dean's List

Acute mountain sickness (AMS) can strike endurance athletes at altitudes as low as sixty-three hundred feet. Signs of
AMS include loss of appetite, a strong headache accompanied
by nausea, ringing in the ears, loss of breath, and dizziness.
Here are some products that can help:

- Diamox, a prescription drug
- *Ginkgo biloba,* an over-the-counter herbal remedy that's
  shown mixed results in studies
- Ginger—preferably raw, if you can tolerate it

There is one disadvantage to training at high altitude, however. Because it isn't possible to run as fast at altitude as at sea
level, runners who always train at the heights miss out on some
of the benefits that come from running at faster speeds. This
limitation has led to a philosophy called "live high, train low."
The most basic way to practice this approach is to live at high
altitude and drive down to lower-lying locations for some workouts. Top running coach Greg McMillan, who's based in Albuquerque, uses this tactic with his runners.

The fanciest way to live high and train low is to sleep in an
altitude simulation tent or live in a hypobaric house. A hypobaric house is an entire house that is mechanically depressur-
ized to simulate the thin air of high altitude. Nike converted a
house in Eugene, Oregon, into an altitude house for several
members of a Nike-sponsored running team, who live there. As
long as the runners spend at least ten hours per day in the
house, their bodies undergo the same VO_2-max-boosting physiological changes that they would experience if they lived at ten
thousand feet. Yet they can walk right out the door and train at
sea level. Hey, we Americans need every (legal) advantage we
can get to compete with those Kenyans!

Shortcuts to the Mountains

If you're very serious about improving your running performance and you have seven to ten grand burning a hole in your pocket, you can get the benefits of living at altitude by sleeping in an altitude (or "hypoxic") tent. Leading brands are Hypoxico (www.hypoxico.com) and Colorado Altitude Training (www .altitudetraining.com). Using one should improve your personal-best race times by 2 to 4 percent.

A cheaper alternative that could yield roughly half as much improvement is to spend five minutes a day breathing through a straw. This simple exercise strengthens the breathing muscles so they don't fatigue as quickly during high-intensity running.

The International Amateur Athletics Union, the world governing body of track and field, actually has considered banning altitude tents and houses. Some feel this ban would be too strict, because these devices accomplish nothing that can't be duplicated by living on a mountain. Another, existing ban that I very much favor is the prohibition of blood doping, or using drugs such as artificial EPO and blood transfusions to thicken the blood, thus simulating some effects of living at altitude. If you ask me, those who go for such shady practices are cheating themselves more than anyone else. The point is not to win at all costs but to become the best that *you* can be through dedication, commitment, and sacrifice, not through needle injections.

I have never been the least bit tempted to try blood doping. It probably wouldn't help me, anyway. In ultramarathons, the rate of oxygen consumption is relatively low, so boosting your body's capacity to consume oxygen through doping offers less advantage than it does in shorter, faster races. Other factors are more limiting in ultramarathons—including pain tolerance and raw endurance—and that's the way I like it. No amount of EPO will help you there.

Day 22
October 8, 2006
New Mexico Marathon
Albuquerque, New Mexico
Elevation: 5,217'
Weather: 67 degrees; cloudy
Time: 4:09:58
Net calories burned: 70,114
Number of runners: 30

Altitude and hills go hand in hand. You have to climb mountains to reach altitude, so when you run at altitude, you're bound to encounter some killer hills.

The New Mexico Marathon took place at altitude and included a few challenging hills. We started at fifty-seven hundred feet and climbed to sixty-one hundred feet by mile eight. The next eighteen miles brought us down more than a thousand feet. If you think that sounds like an escalator ride, though, think again. Running downhill for long stretches can be just as tough as running uphill. While running uphill stresses the heart and lungs more, running downhill is harder on the muscles, because they have to act as brakes to keep you from tumbling. After running downhill for eighteen miles, your thighs feel as though they have been tenderized by mallets for three hours.

We were rewarded for our suffering with some delightful sights. The New Mexico Marathon starts and finishes in historic Old Town Albuquerque. The adobe architecture of the pueblo-style buildings was stunning. Grandest of them all was the high-walled San Felipe Church, which towered above an immaculate grassy plaza dating back to the city's birth in 1706. I saw lots of amazing architecture, representing a plethora of styles, during the Endurance 50, but nothing topped the clean-lined, earthy structures of Old Town Albuquerque, elevation 5,217 feet.

Some runners love hills. Other runners dread them. I'm in the former group. I don't know if it's because hill running is one of my strengths, or because I love the feeling of accomplishment that comes with reaching the top of a hill (or, better yet, a mountain). Whatever the reason, I find myself wearing a smile every time the road or trail turns upward.

Love them or hate them, I encourage you to incorporate some hill running into your training, if possible. Not only will it lessen your dread of hills, supposing you have such a dread, but it will also make you a stronger all-around runner. There are various ways to incorporate hills into your training. The simplest is to choose hilly routes for some of your longer runs. Doing a ten-mile run on a hilly route can provide the same fitness benefits as a twelve- or thirteen-mile run on a flat course, with less pounding.

When I do hilly long runs, I sometimes try to "coast" up the hills; other times I attack them. Wearing a heart rate monitor can help you coast up hills effectively. The idea is to keep your heart rate from increasing by more than ten beats per minute as you transition from level ground to an upward slope. This will teach you to run hills relaxed and to conserve energy. Attacking the hills—by which I mean running up at a hard but manageable effort—provides all the benefits that come with cranking up the intensity of running.

Another great way to incorporate hills into your training is with hill repetitions. A session of hill repetitions is a lot like a set of speed intervals at the track, except with less speed and more

Steep Hill Sprints

In recent years, steep hill sprints have become popular in the elite ranks of distance running. Of course, they're beneficial for runners of every level. To do them, find the steepest hill around and sprint up it at maximum effort for just ten to twelve seconds. Walk back down and repeat a few more times. Try to work up to six to eight reps per outing. Steep hill sprints help build a more powerful stride, and also reduce injury risk by strengthening the running muscles.

Going Downhill

Some runners actually prefer running up steep hills to running down them, because running down steep hills can be rather scary, especially on technical singletrack trails. You fear losing control and twisting an ankle, or worse. Plus, it can be rather hard on the knees. The key to overcoming this fear and discomfort is to learn how to run downhill properly. Instead of leaning back and landing on your heels, tilt your entire body forward from the ankles and land on your midfoot. You will run faster this way, and with more control and less shock to your knees.

gravitational resistance. All you do is warm up and then run hard up a stretch of hill, jog back down, and repeat. Most runners do relatively short hill repetitions of a couple hundred meters. As an ultrarunner, I like to do longer hill repetitions with 250 to 300 feet of elevation gain over a quarter mile or so.

Choose a manageable number of repetitions to perform (start with just two or three), and run each at a pace that's within 10 percent of the fastest pace you can sustain through the last repetition. Time yourself to make sure you aren't slowing down significantly in the latter repetitions. If you are, then begin the workout with a little more restraint the next time you do it so you're able to finish at close to the same pace.

Hill repetitions are hard, but once you get used to them they can become quite exhilarating. At least *I* think so. But my very favorite type of hill workout is mountain runs. Find the longest hill available (hopefully at least a mile) and simply run straight to the top, turn around, and charge back down. It's the best bang-for-your-buck workout I know. The first half builds strength and endurance; the second half increases durability and technique. That about covers it.

I have nothing against Nebraska, but I'm glad I live in a place with a little more topographic variation. I'd spend a lot of time running up the Cornhuskers Memorial Stadium stairs if I lived in the heartland!

CHAPTER 17

You Never Forget Your First

Day 23
October 9, 2006
Route 66 Marathon
Tulsa, Oklahoma
Elevation: 626'
Weather: 74 degrees; clear
Time: 4:17:36
Net calories burned: 73,301
Number of runners: 44

The youngest event in the **Endurance 50** was the Route 66 Marathon in Tulsa, Oklahoma. It was a first-time event. In fact, it was even younger than that. We ran it on Monday, October 9, almost six weeks before its official inauguration on November 19. Our forty-four-person tour of the course was like a dress rehearsal for the new race's opening night.

Race director Chris Lieberman seemed glad to have the opportunity to practice for the real thing, and took advantage of it by making the experience more like the real thing than we had any right to expect. He provided excellent runner support throughout the marathon and brought the Tulsa Police Department out in full force to guide us safely through the busy streets to the finish line.

Fittingly, a large number of first-time marathoners participated in this first-time marathon. At the starting line, I asked all of the newbies present to raise their hands. Eight arms shot up.

Half of the runners attached to these arms explained that they planned to run only halfway, though. I had heard this one many times over the past twenty-two marathons, and had been amazed by how many folks who intended to drop out at the midway point went on to complete the entire 26.2 miles. Sure enough, all four of today's would-be half-marathoners wound up running the full distance.

In the first few days of the Endurance 50, I was surprised to see such large numbers of first-timers coming out. I had expected our events to draw mostly veterans who were confident of being able to finish a marathon. I'm not sure I would have wanted to do an Endurance 50 event as my first marathon. When you run a regular marathon as your first, you can fail more or less in private. You're running alone, and if you falter, no one will notice. But in the Endurance 50 marathons, we ran as a small group. Falling off the back of this group and perhaps eventually climbing into the SAG wagon would draw more attention than it would in a larger event. In a sense, the stakes were higher.

Then again, so were the rewards. The Endurance 50 had an unequaled support system. Cheering spectators on the side of a marathon course can offer some encouragement, but a slap on the back from a fellow runner struggling alongside you during the Endurance 50 offered a whole different level of inspiration. Looking back, I see that the Endurance 50 was actually an ideal format for first-time marathoners.

I'm glad that first-timers became such an integral part of the Endurance 50, because watching runners complete their first marathon is a truly uplifting experience for me. Crossing a marathon finish line for the first time is a life-changing moment. In doing it, you prove something to yourself that can never be taken away. You walk away with hard, experiential evidence that you are strong, resilient, and gutsy. It's one thing to *suppose* you have what it takes to run a marathon; it's quite another to *know* it, because you've done it. First marathons are immensely

Race Day Tips for Your First Marathon

- *Arrive early.* Get to the race an hour beforehand to allow time to park, make a pit stop, and reach the starting line without feeling rushed.
- *Don't experiment.* Don't do anything on race day that you haven't done on your long runs, whether it's wearing different shoes or eating a different breakfast beforehand.
- *Layer your clothing.* You'll often find yourself much colder at the race start than you'll be once you get moving. Wear layers of clothing that you don't mind parting ways with along the course. A disposable painter's jacket is inexpensive and recyclable.
- *Pace yourself.* Before the race, choose a pace that you're confident you can maintain and stick to it no matter how good you feel.

challenging, even for the most naturally gifted runners. Twenty-six point two miles is just a long way to go, no matter who you are. Anytime you're able to take on and overcome a challenge of such proportions, you come away with benefits—in the form of confidence, self-respect, and fearlessness—that never fade.

Even if the process of training for a marathon weren't extremely health promoting, I would still encourage everyone to run at least one marathon simply for its powerful effects on the mind and spirit. After all, don't we spend enough of our lives doubting ourselves, thinking we're not good enough, not strong enough, not made of the right stuff? The marathon gives you an opportunity to tackle these doubts head-on. It has a way of deconstructing your very essence, stripping away all your protective barriers, and exposing your inner soul. The marathon tells you it will hurt you, that it will leave you demoralized and defeated in a lifeless heap on the roadside. It says it can't be done—not by you. *Ha!* it taunts you. *In your dreams!*

So you train hard. You dedicate yourself wholeheartedly, you sacrifice, and you overcome countless smaller challenges along the way. You pour everything you've got into it. But you know the marathon will ask for even more. In the dark recesses of your mind, a gloomy voice is saying, *You can't.* You do your best to ignore this self-doubt, but the voice doesn't go away.

On the morning of your first marathon, the voice of doubt multiplies, becoming a full chorus. By mile twenty this chorus is screaming so loudly, it's all you can hear. Your sore and weary muscles beg you to stop. You *must* stop. But you don't stop. This time, you ignore the voice of doubt, you tune out the naysayers who tell you you're not good enough, and you listen only to the passion in your heart. This burning desire tells you to keep moving forward, to continue putting one foot boldly in front of the other, and somewhere you find the will to do so.

Courage comes in many forms. Today you discover the courage to keep trying, to not give up, no matter how dire things become. And dire they do become. At the twenty-five-mile mark, you can barely see the course any longer—your vision falters as your mind teeters on the edge of consciousness.

And then, suddenly, the finish line looms before you like a dream. A lump builds in your throat as you cover those final few steps. Now you are finally able to answer back to that nagging voice with a resounding *Oh, yes I can!*

You burst across the finish line filled with pride, forever liberated from the prison of self-doubt and self-imposed limitations that have held you captive. You have learned more about yourself in the past 26.2 miles than on any other single day in your life. Even if you can't walk afterward, you have never been so free. A marathon finish is more than just something you earn; a marathon finisher is someone you become.

As you are being helped away from the finish line, wrapped in a flimsy Mylar blanket, barely able to raise your head, you are at peace. No future struggle, doubts, or failure can wipe away what you accomplished today. You have done what few will ever do—what you thought you could never do—and it is the most glorious, unforgettable awakening. You are a marathoner, and you will wear this distinction not on your lapel, but in your heart, for the rest of your life.

During the long drive that night to Dallas, I couldn't rest. Walking up to the front of the bus near midnight, I could see two legs jutting out from one of the bench seats, a half-eaten slice of pizza on the table and a half-drunk bottle of beer in the cup holder. It was Garrett, lying flat on his back in the seat sleeping, his arm draped across his face. Koop was on the other side, sitting upright with his arms folded across his chest and his head tilted back and on the headrest, facing straight toward the ceiling. He snored and gurgled a little with each inhalation. Hopps was curled up sideways sleeping on the floor. Gear and equipment were strewn everywhere. It didn't smell very good.

Sitting politely at the table across from Garrett was Robin, doing her nails.

"Robin?" I said. "What are you doing?"

"Oh, my nails are getting kinda thrashed carting all that stuff around during the day, so I thought I'd redo them," she answered matter-of-factly.

I went on to have a heart-to-heart conversation with her, explaining that I was sorry to have initially been skeptical of her ability to fulfill the role she was put in and transform our chaotic team into one that was smoothly run, moving without hiccups from one event to the next. Clearly, since coming on board, she had earned the respect and admiration of the entire crew, myself included.

"Thanks," she interrupted. "Now, could you grab me a paper towel?"

"Huh?" I stared at her.

"I got a little smudge mark on the table. They're in the cupboard above Koop."

And so our heart-to-heart conversation ended, just like that. We went on to joke about the scene in the bus looking more like an infirmary than a marathon tour while she continued with her nails. The bus rumbled along into the night, and I knew right then and there that we had hired the exact right person for the job.

Day 24
October 10, 2006
Dallas White Rock Marathon
Dallas, Texas
Elevation: 438'
Weather: 68 degrees; stormy
Time: 4:12:20
Net calories burned: 76,488
Number of runners: 75

The Dallas White Rock Marathon featured our largest field of participants to date, and the largest number of first-timers. We were originally limited to fifty runners, but these slots were filled quickly and a waiting list of twice as many runners then formed. We persuaded the Dallas authorities to let us accept a few more participants, and they graciously increased our limit to seventy-five. Actually, many of the Dallas authorities were runners themselves, so it was an easy sell. Of these seventy-five runners we obtained permits for, more than twenty had never run a marathon before.

> **QUICK TAKE:** *Many first-time marathoners cross the finish line with sore, chafed nipples from four or five hours of friction against their running top. Being wet from rain compounds the issue. To avoid this often unforeseen problem, tape your nipples before the marathon. Regular Band-Aids will work, though a product called Nip-Guards offers the best protection.*

This was not a good day for a first marathon. Mother Nature compounded the challenge of covering the distance with deaf-

Runabout

The legendary running coach Jeff Galloway has probably trained more first-time marathoners than anyone. Jeff is a hero of mine and teaches a unique training system that includes regular, brief walking breaks. He's also among the few running coaches who encourage runners training for a marathon to do training runs exceeding 26.2 miles in distance (including the walking breaks). Beginners who follow this advice report that the walking breaks make these "overdistance" workouts perfectly manageable (provided they do them toward the end of the training process, when they're already pretty fit) and that they're great confidence builders.

I recommend a slight modification to Jeff's approach that I simply call runabout. Inspired by the Australian Aboriginal practice of walkabout, it works like this: After you've put in some good training and built a fairly high level of baseline fitness, pick a weekend morning to set out the door with a running pack containing a credit card, a cell phone, and some fluid and snacks—maybe also a map or a GPS if you want to get really sophisticated. Choose a direction (say, north) and start running. Keep running until you feel like taking a break. You can jog, walk, or hike—just try to stay on your feet. When you're ready for some more running, go for it. If you see a Starbucks and feel like a latte, stop and grab one. Stick a straw in it and drink as you run.

Try to make a complete day of it. Don't worry about how many miles you actually run. Focus on staying on your feet and on moving forward one way or another, whether it's by running, hiking, or walking, for six to eight hours. Mostly, have fun. Not only will you get a great workout and build confidence for an upcoming marathon, but a runabout is also just an interesting way to spend a day.

(Continued)

(Runabout, continued)

Personally, I particularly enjoy starting before sunrise and finishing after sunset. Rarely in our modern society do we spend
an entire day outside, and there's just something enchanting
about watching a day go by from the exterior of a building
rather than locked inside. There's lots to be learned from those
Aboriginals, Starbucks notwithstanding.

ening thunder and terrifyingly close-by lightning strikes, as well
as a heavy downpour that thoroughly soaked the group. By
midmorning, the temperatures had begun to warm, though not
enough to dry our clothes—just enough to make them stick to
us uncomfortably.

I ran alongside a first-timer who was laboring to get the job
done. "I think we've got a couple of steep climbs coming up,"
I commented, remembering the elevation profile of the course
that I'd briefly checked out on the way to the start this morning.
I have an aversion to nasty surprises in running events, so
throughout the Endurance 50 I made an effort to study course
profiles online before the start of each marathon, and to catch a
weather report. On this particular course profile, I recalled
seeing two pronounced spikes around the twenty-mile mark.

"You mean the Dolly Partons?" he asked.

"The what?" I said, stunned.

He laughed. "It's okay," he replied. "That's what those two
peaks are known as."

They say everything is bigger in Texas. I laughed with the
others as we plodded our way up the Dolly Partons. The discomfort of being wet and exhausted gave way to a jovial second
wind. Please allow me to retract what I said earlier: Maybe this
wasn't such a bad day for a first marathon after all.

CHAPTER 18

Baby Steps

Day 25
October 11, 2006
Baton Rouge Beach Marathon
Baton Rouge, Louisiana
Elevation: 61'
Weather: 87 degrees; humid
Time: 3:59:27
Net calories burned: 79,675
Number of runners: 28

In preparing to embark on any endurance endeavor—be it a marathon or a two-hundred-mile run—it's helpful to set realistic expectations. Don't kid yourself. Accept the fact that you will encounter low points—often devastating lows when you feel you can't go on. No matter how well you prepare, you will likely encounter moments when you doubt your ability to succeed, or perhaps even to take another step. It's not a lot different from life. The most important element is to remember that such setbacks will inevitably occur. They always do. If you're honest with yourself beforehand, you will have an easier time dealing with these low points.

When I hit a low point, I use a technique that I simply call "baby steps." Let me tell you a little story that I think illustrates this concept. The first time I attempted to run 200 miles nonstop, I hit a point at mile 168 where I couldn't take another step. I'd been running for some forty straight hours: I was completely spent and in tremendous pain. It hit me in the middle of the second sleepless night, and I sat down on the curbside, unutter-ably depressed that I'd fallen short of my goal.

I sat there, wallowing in my grief, knowing that covering another thirty-two miles was a complete impossibility. I could barely lower my bottom to the ground, let alone run another marathon plus a 10k. I wanted to scream in defeat, but I didn't have enough energy.

Instead, I decided to block out the fact that there were still thirty-two miles left to cover. The thought was too daunting to consider. I broke that bigger, seemingly impossible, goal into smaller, more manageable, micro-goals: baby steps, if you will.

Just stand up and run to that bush ten yards up the road, I told myself. *Don't think about the mileage still ahead. Be in the moment; put one foot in front of the other to the best of your ability. Take baby steps.*

Once I reached that bush, I celebrated the accomplishment. *Okay,* I said to myself. *You made it!* Then I set my sights on a traffic signal twenty yards up the road. *Just take baby steps,* I kept repeating.

After reaching the traffic signal, I set my sights on a bend fifty yards up the road. After that, I chose another marker, and then another, celebrating every milestone as I reached it. I stayed in the moment, just putting one foot in front of the other, not thinking about the mileage still left in front of me.

Some eight hours later, I crossed the finish line. How? By taking baby steps.

I used the same approach to get through the Endurance 50. Whenever I found myself looking too far ahead—considering all the running that still lay in front of me—my stomach felt queasy and my heart sank. The math was terribly intimidating. The world's top professional marathoners typically run 110 to 130 miles per week for a few weeks at the height of their training. The Endur-ance 50 would require me to run 183 miles per week for seven consecutive weeks, plus a day.

Contemplating such numbers made my confidence plummet, so I trained myself not to look too far ahead. Instead, I celebrated each completed marathon as a baby step toward my final destination and looked no farther ahead than the next one—the next baby step. Would I be able to finish all fifty? I had no idea. I thought that I had trained and prepared adequately, but this was largely a step into the unknown. Every morning, I awoke with the same commitment: *"Today* I will do the best that I can. *Today* I will try my hardest."

One way to use baby steps that comes naturally to many runners is dividing marathons and other challenging runs into equal halves and focusing on reaching the halfway point until that point is reached. Only then do they think about the finish line. If making it all the way to the finish line or the end point of a run is too daunting to think about, making it just to the halfway mark usually isn't. There's something magical about the midpoint. Once you pass it, you know you have covered more distance than remains in front of you. Every mile you run now

Small Goals

Setting short-term goals is an effective way to use baby steps to build confidence and morale as you train for a marathon or other event. Here are examples of short-term goals you might use for yourself in training for a marathon:

- Run six days next week.
- Run forty miles next week.
- Increase my running by five miles per week for the next four weeks.
- Complete a half-marathon.
- Run 150 miles next month.
- Complete my first twenty-miler.

makes the total distance behind you two miles greater than the total remaining distance in front of you. Your confidence gets a boost. Now you can focus on the finish line.

In my freshman year of college, I registered for an ancient history class. On the first day, the professor handed out a syllabus that listed all the required reading and writing for the semester. I couldn't believe how much he was asking us to do—and I expressed my exasperation.

"This workload is overwhelming," I said. "It seems impossible to do all this in one semester."

"Don't look at it that way," the professor replied. "Just try to get an A every day." What he meant was that I should not think about the entire semester's workload but only the small part of it that I needed to complete each day, and complete it to the best of my ability.

I took his advice to heart, and it worked. Instead of stressing myself out by thinking about the total workload, I focused entirely on getting an A on that small portion that had to get done today. Sure enough, when the semester ended, I had read everything the syllabus asked me to read and written everything the syllabus asked me to write.

The same strategy will work for you in running. Suppose you're training for a marathon and you struggle to complete your first twelve-mile training run. *This is a calamity!* you think.

The 10 Percent Rule

Trying to take big steps in the process of building your training for a marathon or other event is never a good idea. Increasing your running mileage too quickly may result in an injury such as a pulled muscle or shin splints. To avoid these problems, obey the 10 percent rule: Increase your running mileage by no more than 10 percent per week. So if you ran twenty miles last week, run no more than twenty-two this week.

How am I supposed to run a whole marathon in ten weeks if I can barely run twelve miles today?

Don't look at it that way. Instead, consider that twelve-mile run—difficult though it was—as just one more step on the path toward eventually being able to run twice as far. Remind yourself that it's a mile or two farther than you ran last weekend, and if you want to look ahead, don't look any farther ahead than next weekend's thirteen-mile run.

The Endurance 50 presented the closest thing to a formal training schedule that I have ever used. Because I participate in so many races and events throughout the year, I don't follow a structured training schedule. Normally, I have no clue how far I will run tomorrow, let alone seven weeks from tomorrow. But when I toed the starting line for the Lewis & Clark Marathon on Day 1 of the Endurance 50, I knew exactly how far I would run each day for the next seven weeks plus. In some ways, though, the Endurance 50 was more like a fifty-day race than a fifty-day training plan. A good training schedule is designed to ease you into your workout regimen and become gradually more challenging as your body adapts to the workouts you've done. In races, you're thrown in over your head from the first step, and you just hang on from there.

I approached the Endurance 50 in much the same way I approach a race, which is to say I did my very best to exist completely in the moment. I tried not to think about our final marathon in New York City, or how many marathons I had left to run before I got there. Sometimes I slipped up and started counting, and whenever I did I felt anxious, so my slips became fewer and fewer as I went along. In fact, I became so focused on the moment that I completely failed to observe one of the most significant milestones in any endurance test.

I was hanging around at the Finish Festival after completing the Baton Rouge Marathon with a terrific group of runners—including a twelve-year-old who went the full distance—when I got a call from my wife.

"Congratulations!" she said.

"Thanks," I said. "What for?"

"Twenty-five down, twenty-five to go. You're halfway there!"

I stood in silence for a moment as I tried to mentally confirm Julie's statement. Was yesterday's marathon in Dallas number twenty-four? It was.

"I guess you're right," I said. The crew and I celebrated by climbing aboard the tour bus and driving five hundred miles to Huntsville, Alabama, for number twenty-six.

CHAPTER 19

What's My Motivation?

Day 26
October 12, 2006
Rocket City Marathon
Huntsville, Alabama
Elevation: 607'
Weather: 68 degrees; partly cloudy
Time: 4:15:27
Net calories burned: 82,862
Number of runners: 32

Prying myself out of bed at sunrise on Day 26 was not easy. The previous night's drive from Baton Rouge, Louisiana, to Huntsville, Alabama, had been long and exhausting. My sleep had been brief and shallow. Yet the drive was no longer and no more arduous than many of the preceding drives our crew had endured together; nor had I gotten less sleep than usual.

So why was it so hard to throw back the bedcovers on the morning of Day 26? Probably because it was the morning of Day 26—the first day of the second half of my fifty-marathon challenge. I had been plowing forward for a long time already, and I still had a long way to go. My level of motivation had been very high in the early days, when my body felt fresh and the whole experience was novel. I knew that my motivation would surely rise again as I got closer to New York. But right now I seemed to be suffering from a mild case of the halfway blahs.

It is human nature to struggle for motivation at such moments. When you begin a major challenge, your body and mind feel charged and ready. Later, when you near the end of a big challenge, you are pulled along by the drive to achieve your goal, or to just get the darn thing over with (which can be as powerful a motivator as any). The middle part of a big challenge is the part where morale tends to flag, because the challenge is no longer new, and physical and mental fatigue have begun to set in, yet the goal remains far off—too far for its magnetic draw to have any effect.

The best way I know to overcome low motivation for running is to get back in touch with the source of my passion to run. Motivation and passion are somewhat different. Passion is an overwhelming love for the experience of a favorite activity. Motivation is a drive to engage in an activity based on some reward the activity offers beyond the simple enjoyment of the experience itself. When you have great passion for running, or anything else, you don't need any extra motivation. But motivation without passion can only take you so far.

Nonrunners become runners by developing a passion for running. But runners often take their running in directions that distance them from the source of their passion. Trading the simple joy of running for a focus on competition is the classic scenario. I seldom feel burned out on running. When I do, it's usually when I devote an extended period of time to training for a specific event. I start to view my runs not as adventures but simply as exercises necessary to achieve my race goal. While I am highly motivated to reap the benefits of my workouts and attain my race goal, I steadily lose my passion for running; once the passion ebbs beyond a certain point, the motivation soon follows, and I enter a state of burnout.

I've learned to pull myself out of such stale patches by shifting my focus away from the big event and back to the activity of running itself. Sometimes I jump into another event spontaneously just for the fun of it, even though doing so might throw my preparations for the bigger event off track, because by following my heart I'm bound to reawaken my passion for running, regardless of how I perform in any race. I just don't like pinning the rewards of running on the results of a race. I like running to be its own reward.

That being said, there is no question that setting event goals can be a powerful motivator for runners, and it has had a positive effect on my morale in the past. Looking forward to a specific event goal has a way of making each individual training run more meaningful, and that extra layer of meaning keeps the motivation level high. However, goals only have this effect when they are appropriate, and when they are viewed with the proper perspective. For example, if you set a goal to run a marathon as a way to impress others, it probably won't keep you motivated. Goals have to come from the heart. They must represent achievements that you desire for yourself. And if you place too much importance on any goal, then it won't keep you motivated. If achieving a certain finishing time in your next marathon becomes the only thing about your running that matters to you, then you may not enjoy the process of training for that marathon. Sure, achieving a goal can be rewarding, but it's the journey—not reaching the destination—that brings true fulfillment.

Another trick I use to ward off and overcome running burnout is *not* running. I think it's a mistake to assume that *motivation* is always the problem when you feel unmotivated to run. Sometimes *running* is the problem. Who says you have to love running every day, just because you love running in general? While running is by far my favorite outdoor activity, there are many others that I also enjoy, including mountain biking and surfing. I have never lost my enthusiasm for outdoor activity altogether. So whenever I get a little bored with running, I do something else. In fact, I often do something besides running even when my passion for running is high, and I believe that doing so helps keep it high.

Mind Games

All runners occasionally find themselves dreading a planned run. Overcoming this dread and having a good run anyway can be as easy as using one of the following motivational mind games:

- Change your route to something unfamiliar.
- Buy new running shoes or clothes for your run.
- Find a friend to run with.
- Take your dog with you (or, for a real adventure, take a neighbor's dog).
- Tell yourself you'll just run for fifteen minutes. (You'll almost certainly wind up running longer!)
- Drive somewhere cool to run—the beach, a nice park.
- Change your pace: Do something short and fast.

Breaking routine was not an option to maintain my motivation level during the Endurance 50, however. Every run was totally scripted. I had committed to run precisely the same distance at more or less the same pace for fifty consecutive days. Each route was also predetermined. Because each marathon took place in a different state, the Endurance 50 did have some built-in variety that kept things very interesting. Nevertheless, now that I was about halfway through, my spirit began to yearn for some unscripted, spontaneous running—a yearning I could do nothing to satisfy for a few more weeks.

In fact, on the morning of the Rocket City Marathon, my spirit yearned not so much for unscripted running as to sleep in and maybe take a day off. That changed, though, when I arrived at the starting line. Upon seeing the other runners standing on a street corner near the starting line, psyched to run, my spirits lifted immediately. While the Endurance 50 was routine to me by now, it was fresh and exciting to these folks—as it was to each new group of runners I met throughout my human-powered tour of America—and their enthusiasm was infectious. In this particular circumstance, it was the people that kept me motivated to run the next marathon rather than any factor intrinsic to the running experience itself. So be it. When it comes to motivation, I say get it wherever you can.

> **QUICK TAKE:** *It's hard to find motivation to run when you don't have the energy to run. Dietary fiber is a good friend to runners, because it slows the absorption of food calories and helps provide a more steady, lasting supply of energy to the body. There are two types of fiber: soluble and insoluble. Soluble fiber dissolves in water to form a gel-like material and can help lower blood cholesterol and glucose levels, while insoluble increases the movement of material through your digestive system. Soluble fiber sources include oats, beans, apples, peas, and citrus fruits. Insoluble fiber sources include bran, nuts, many vegetables, and whole wheat flour. Aim to consume at least twenty-five total grams of fiber daily.*

I do quite a lot of motivational speaking for corporations and other groups. The job of a motivational speaker is, of course, to motivate people. The irony is that I don't believe one person really can motivate another person. Pep talks may have a short-term effect that causes participants to leave the seminar room with a spring in their step and big plans in their head, but it seldom lasts. Real motivation always comes from within. You must choose to be motivated. The most that others can do is help you make this choice by serving as inspirational examples of great passion. And that's all I try to do in my motivational talks. I simply tell folks about my great passion for running and the incredible journey this passion has opened for me. There is no need for me to translate this message from the domain of running to the domain of business or whatever else when I speak before nonrunning groups. People are pretty adept at doing this for themselves.

The key to keeping your passion for running strong over the long haul is to ensure that it remains a journey and never becomes routine. Lots of runners, myself included, use running to test and redefine various physical and mental limits, which brings endless fulfillment. Others pursue intellectual development through running, learning ever more about the art and science of effective training, how nutrition affects performance, and so forth. The possibilities are endless. The only wrong move is to miss out on *all* of them and make running something it's not: boring. Because the simple act of putting one foot in front of the other and moving forward at an accelerated rate can be one of life's greatest—and simplest—pleasures.

Day 27
October 13, 2006
Healthy Huntington Marathon
Huntington, West Virginia
Elevation: 600'
Weather: 50 degrees; clear
Time: 4:09:17
Net calories burned: 86,049
Number of runners: 18

The morning of the Healthy Huntington Marathon in Huntington, West Virginia, was among the coldest mornings I had yet faced in the Endurance 50. The temperature was in the low forties when I left my hotel. It was now October 13—mid autumn—and it felt like it.

Runners often lose some of their motivation to train in the fall, as the days grow colder and shorter. It can be hard to face that first blast of frosty air when you step outside. Cold and inclement weather is just one of several external factors that sometimes make it a battle to get out the door and complete a planned run. A busy day at work that leaves you mentally exhausted and physically flat may also do it, or the challenges of business travel, or emotional stressors such as a recent disagreement with your spouse.

I face these motivation killers just like every other runner. My way of dealing with them is very simple. Psychologists call it projection. Nonpsychologists might call it laying a guilt trip on yourself! I simply think about how much better I will surely feel after running, and I ask myself, *Do you really want to pass that up?* Over the course of the past fifteen years, I have run more than five thousand times. Not once have I ever felt worse after finishing a run than I did before I started. I always feel better after a run. My knowledge of this fact is a great motivator. Whenever I find myself tempted to skip a run for a dubious reason such as bad weather, I just remind myself of that wonderful post-run feeling, and moments later I am out the door. Give it a try. If you're anything like me, you'll be pleased with the results.

As it had at yesterday's marathon in Alabama, my motivation level got another big boost, despite the morning chill, when I arrived at the starting line of the Healthy Huntington Marathon and found eighteen beaming runners ready to bust out 26.2. The finish of this race is at the southern goal line of the school's forty-thousand-seat football stadium. Matthew McConaughey had just been there filming his movie *We Are Marshall*, about the tragic loss of the school's football team in a 1970 plane crash, so there was lots of buzz and emotion in the air.

After our group had entered the stadium and completed a stirring trek across the field to the southern goal line, Bob Marcum, the university athletic director, presented me with an official Marshall Bison football jersey. My last name was on the back, and I was assigned the number 27 to correspond with today's marathon of the fifty. Then Marcum announced that Governor Joe Manchin had just signed a proclamation declaring this day, October 13, Move Your Feet Day in West Virginia, to commemorate our marathon and to promote healthy, active living within the state each year.

The Three-Day Countdown

Motivation and smart training alone do not guarantee successful race performances. What you do in the final three days before a race can make the difference between achieving your goal and falling short. The following table provides some suggested preparations for the final three days before a competition.

COUNTDOWN	SLEEP	RUNNING	NUTRITION
72 hours in advance	Sleep and wake at same hours as race day. Get at least your normal night's sleep, if not slightly more. Adjust your bedtime to accommodate this extra sleep, not your rising time.	Low-impact, easy run, 45 minutes–1 hour.	Consume at minimum 1 gram of protein and 2 grams of carbs per pound of body weight.
48 hours in advance	Try to go to sleep at least half an hour earlier than the night prior.	Low-impact, easy run, 30–45 minutes.	Reduce fiber intake, both soluble and insoluble. Reduce or eliminate dairy intake.
24 hours in advance	Try to go to sleep at least 1 hour earlier than the night prior.	2-mile walk/jog.	Eat only low-fiber foods. No dairy.

This was, of course, a great honor to all of us involved in the Endurance 50. For my son, Nicholas, though, the greatest gift was yet to come. As if I hadn't already received enough rewards, I was lastly presented with a football signed by the entire Bison team. When I put the ball down to shake Mr. Marcum's hand, Nicholas quickly snatched it and started kicking it around the field. One of the staff grabbed him and explained that this was a commemorative trophy, not something to be booted about. Being the gentleman that he is, Mr. Marcum quickly summoned a new football and gave it to Nicholas, who thanked him and then immediately resumed his shenanigans on the field. As Plato said, "Of all the animals, the boy is the most unmanageable."

My daughter, Alexandria, meanwhile, was up to some mischief of her own. She had been inside the employee section of the stadium to use the restroom and had come across an interesting find. "Pssst," she whispered to me. She gathered up the family and snuck us in the back door she'd just exited. Inside was the school mascot, a massive woolly bison, mounted on a Harley.

"Hop on!" she ordered. "We gotta get a picture of this."

It must have been something they drive around during games to rally the fans and spectators. We climbed on top of the bison, took a quick snapshot, and then Alexandria said, "Quick, let's get out of here before they arrest us."

We hightailed it back to the field. *Boy, if Governor Manchin could see me now*, I thought as we dashed out. Well, if nothing else, I guess we were *moving our feet*. Running a marathon, escaping the law—it's all movement of a sort.

So, to all you West Virginians—athletes and outlaws alike—when October 13 rolls around, start movin' those feet of yours. If ya don't, there could be a bison-toting hog comin' after ya. And a kid with a football driving it.

CHAPTER 20

A Full Recovery

Day 28
October 14, 2006
United Technologies Hartford Marathon
Hartford, Connecticut
Elevation: 161'
Weather: 59 degrees; clear
Time: 3:29:28
Net calories burned: 89,236
Number of runners: 7,600

The **Hartford Marathon,** which I ran on Day 28 in Hartford, Connecticut, was a live event. As in the other live marathons of the Endurance 50, I ran this one at my natural pace, since I didn't have a group to pace with. I crossed the finish line in a little less than three and a half hours, or roughly thirty minutes faster than the typical re-created marathon run with a group.

When I woke up the following morning, my legs felt better than they had in several days. This came as no surprise. Over the preceding four weeks I had noticed an interesting pattern: My faster live marathons took less out of me than my slower group events. Maybe it was because I spent less time on my feet when I ran faster. Or maybe it was because I ran more efficiently at my natural pace. Whatever the cause, the effect was noticeable.

The ability to recover quickly from hard running is probably my greatest strength as a runner. I'm certainly not the fastest guy around, but like the Timex GPS system I wore throughout the Endurance 50, I can take a licking and keep on ticking.

I discovered that I was unusual in this regard after running the Western States 100 one year. The finish area looked like a battlefield triage center, with some runners laid out on gurneys, others receiving IVs, and none looking particularly well. But I felt fine. I had run as hard as I could and felt that I'd left everything I had out on the course, but after chitchatting near the finish line for a few minutes, I was almost ready for more. Instead, I drove home to go windsurfing.

Throughout the Endurance 50, my body held up surprisingly well against the brutal running schedule. I felt sore, beat-up, and wiped out some days, and I caught a few colds, but that was the worst of it. The objective data that Koop gathered from my blood and urine samples confirmed my feelings. Failure to recover properly can result in chronic dehydration, accumulating muscle damage, systemic inflammation, depressed immune function, and changes in hormone levels. If I were getting in over my head with the Endurance 50, one or more of these signs would have manifested sooner or later, and they didn't. My body fluid samples were analyzed for markers of each of these signs of incomplete recovery, and almost all of them stayed within the normal range throughout the Endurance 50.

> **QUICK TAKE:** *A convenient way to monitor your recovery status is to take your pulse first thing each morning. A pulse rate that is above normal suggests that your body is still working to recover from a recent workout and may require additional rest.*

I suppose the final conclusion of Koop's study of my body's response to the Endurance 50, which he performed on behalf of Carmichael Training Systems, had to be this: The human body is a remarkably adaptive instrument. With proper training and nourishment, there's no telling what we are capable of achieving.

Recovery is one of the most important aspects of running, and one that runners often struggle with. Even those running far less than a marathon a day generally have to make special efforts to ensure that they recover adequately between runs. In the short term (from day to day), inadequate recovery causes muscle soreness, fatigue, and poor performance. When a runner consistently trains too much and/or rests too little for a week or more, the ultimate result can be an injury or illness.

The best way to avoid overtraining is to train smart. The hard–easy rule, for instance, involves alternating more challenging runs with gentler runs from day to day. It's also a good idea to vary how hard you train from week to week. Once every two to four weeks, you should reduce your running mileage by 20 to 30 percent to facilitate recovery and prepare your body for another batch of harder workouts. Like the hard–easy rule, planned recovery weeks allow you to train harder when you mean to train hard, yet also recover from your hard training more fully than when your training load is less varied.

You may need to experiment to find the frequency of planned recovery weeks that works best for you. A good place to start is with a three-week cycle with a 20 to 30 percent reduced training load in the recovery week, as in this example:

Week 1. 25 miles (three hard runs)
Week 2. 28 miles (three hard runs)
Week 3. 20 miles (two hard runs)

One helpful way to monitor your recovery is to grade your workouts. By grading your workouts, you can measure how much you're getting out of them and adjust your training appropriately when it's not enough.

After completing each run, give it a grade in your training log: for example, great, good, fair, or bad. Three consecutive bad days indicate that you aren't getting enough recovery to perform adequately in workouts and should rest or take it easy for a day or two. A full week without any good or great workouts indicates the same.

There are a few other measures you can practice to promote post-workout recovery. After an especially hard workout or race, taking a brief cold bath may limit the tissue swelling that accompanies and often exacerbates muscle damage, enabling your leg muscles to heal faster. While scientific studies of ice baths and other cold therapies have not confirmed these benefits, many top-level runners swear they work, and I tend to agree.

The recovery method that has the most scientific support is eating properly. When you complete a hard run, you have many damaged muscle fibers in your legs, you are at least slightly dehydrated, and your muscles are low in glycogen fuel. Nutrition is

Eating for Recovery

Studies have shown that, to maximize your post-run recovery, you need to consume protein, carbohydrate, and fluid within an hour after each run. Here are some especially good post-workout snacks, meals, and supplements.

RECOVERY NUTRITION OPTION	WHY
Smoothie with whey protein powder	Appealing after exercise; rapidly absorbed form of recovery nutrition.
Tuna wrap and whole apple or pear	Ideal ratio of carbohydrate to protein.
Low-fat milk	Studies have shown that milk is an especially effective form of post-exercise nutrition for recovery.
Energy bar with water	Convenient and well formulated for post-exercise recovery.
Recovery drink mix or sports drink (such as Accelerade)	Patented 4:1 ratio of carbs to protein has been shown to extend endurance, speed muscle recovery, and enhance rehydration. It's also convenient and easy to consume even when you're not hungry.

Nature's Recovery Secrets

According to the US Department of Agriculture, the following twenty foods are excellent sources of antioxidants—nature's recovery potion: small red beans (also called Mexican red beans), blueberries, red kidney beans, pinto beans, kiwi fruit, cranberries, artichokes, blackberries, prunes, raspberries, strawberries, Red Delicious apples, Granny Smith apples, pecans, sweet cherries, black plums, broccoli, black beans, plums, Gala apples.

required to correct all of these physiological imbalances. You need protein to repair and rebuild your muscles, liquid to rehydrate, and carbohydrate to replenish your muscle fuel supplies.

Research has shown that athletes who consume these nutrients within the first hour after a workout recover faster and perform better in their next workout than athletes who wait more than an hour to eat. It doesn't have to be a big meal. A modest-size snack or a recovery supplement with carbs and protein, plus water, will do.

Maintaining a diet that's rich in antioxidants and omega-3 fats will also help your muscles recover faster after runs. Large amounts of free radicals are released from damaged muscle cells through the inflammation process after runs. These free radicals cause additional tissue damage, which may explain why you may feel sorer one or two days after a hard run than you do immediately afterward. Fruits and vegetables are full of antioxidants your body can use to neutralize free radicals and help limit post-run muscle damage. Omega-3 fats aid in the production of anti-inflammatory compounds that boost the muscle repair process between runs. Good sources of omega-3 fats are salmon, flaxseeds, and fish oil supplements.

One final measure that is very important for recovery is sleep. The majority of muscle tissue repair happens during sleep. Since I normally sleep just four to five hours a night, I rely on fresh, healthy foods to take up some of the slack. During

The Dean's List

Some nondrug alternatives for treating muscle strain and soreness include:

- *Arnica Montana*
- MSM (methylsulfonylmethane)
- C3 Complex (turmeric root)
- BioAstin

the Endurance 50, I sometimes only got two or three hours of shut-eye. Rest was a luxury that would have to wait until after I finished—*if* I finished. Until then, my motto was "Bring on the broccoli, wild salmon, and raspberries!"

CHAPTER 21

The Next Level

Day 29
October 15, 2006
Boston Marathon
Boston, Massachusetts
Elevation: 66'
Weather: 58 degrees; partly cloudy
Time: 3:59:27
Net calories burned: 92,423
Number of runners: 50 (filled to capacity, or so I thought)

The **he Boston Marathon** was out of control, but in a good way. We started in the town of Hopkinton, due west of the city, with fifty runners, our official limit. These folks had come from as far away as Israel to take part. No sooner had we gotten under way, however, than unofficial runners began adding themselves to our number. By the time our group reached the halfway mark in the Wellesley Hills, where the Wellesley University cross-country team jumped in, our group had swelled to more than double its original size. As long as the police didn't mind, I certainly didn't.

I have a hypothesis about why the Endurance 50 version of the Boston Marathon generated such enthusiastic participation. Without a doubt, it happened partly because the Boston Marathon is the oldest continuously run marathon in the world, with a mystique and an appeal unlike any other. (The first Boston Marathon was held in 1897, and was only 24.5 miles in distance.) Another factor was the simple fact that the Boston area

Reaching Higher

How fast can I run a marathon? What should my next marathon time goal be? These are questions that many runners ask themselves after they complete their first marathon and decide they wish to improve their time in subsequent events. Of course, the most basic way to set a new goal is to simply aim to beat your first marathon time by one second or more. But many runners feel that, with accumulated experience and better training, they can aim higher. How high, though? Boston?

Another way to set a new marathon time goal is to base it on your performance in a shorter race. As you train for your next marathon, enter one or more 5k, 10k, or half-marathon tune-up races. Your finishing times in these can give you a sense of how fast you will be able to run your next marathon. How? A number of running experts have created race performance equivalence tables and calculators that show how runners of any given talent and training level can expect to perform at other race distances based on a recent performance at one distance.

One of the better of such calculators can be found at www .runnersworld.com. Just enter your time for a recent shorter race and see what your equivalent marathon time would be. This is no guarantee, but it could be one helpful guideline to use in the goal-setting process.

is a terrific and popular place to run. Yet the main reason so many runners got so excited about marathon number twenty-nine of the Endurance 50, I believe, is that the Boston Marathon is normally held in April, while the Endurance 50 re-creation was run in mid-autumn, when the foliage has exploded into glorious, fiery colors, bringing the entire race route to life as never before.

Other major marathons, such as the Chicago Marathon and the New York City Marathon, are open to all comers. If you can afford the entry fee and you sign up before they sell out, you can run these marathons no matter how slow you are and regardless of whether you have ever run a marathon before. Boston is different. To run the Boston Marathon, you must first achieve a gender- and age-specific qualifying time in another marathon. Therefore, the Boston Marathon is out of reach for many runners and completely closed to first-timers.

Our group covered the course in a respectable sub-four-hour time. While many of the runners in our group had previously completed the Boston Marathon, the newbies were thrilled to be running this legendary course as their first marathon. And even the multiple Boston finishers were enchanted by this unique Hopkinton-to-Boston mid-autumn experience.

While the primary goal for first-time marathon runners is just to reach the finish line, most second-timers aim for something higher—to beat their first marathon time, to eclipse a round-number finishing time (such as four hours), or to qualify for Boston. It's a natural progression. By no means is it necessary to try to run faster in your second marathon than you did in your first to have a thoroughly satisfying experience, but a lot of runners find that raising the bar adds a new level of excitement to the training and racing process.

Improving your best marathon time requires raising the level of your training. Here are several ways to do it:

- *Run longer, earlier.* Most first-time marathon runners complete no more than one or two twenty-mile training runs. They gradually increase the distance of their long runs from week to week for many weeks until they are able to cross the twenty-mile threshold two or three weeks before race day. This approach is perfectly adequate if your goal is just to finish, but if you're gunning for a challenging time goal, you need to build more than the minimal amount of endurance required to complete the race; you need a surplus. To achieve this endurance surplus, do your first twenty-mile training run at least six weeks before race day, and do at least three total long runs of twenty to twenty-four miles.

- *Practice your goal pace.* Every marathon goal time is associated with an average pace. For example, the pace required to achieve the Boston Marathon qualifying time for women aged eighteen to thirty-four (3:40) is 8:23 per mile. It is important that your body be well adapted to running at your goal pace before you attempt to sustain it for 26.2 miles in a race.

  A simple and effective way to gain efficiency at your goal pace is to do a few goal-pace long runs during the latter half of the training process. For example, seven weeks before your marathon you might replace your typical slow long run with a workout consisting of a four-mile easy warm-up followed by eight miles at your goal marathon pace. Two weeks later, repeat the workout, but add two more miles of goal-pace running. Finally, three weeks before your marathon, do a sixteen-mile long run with twelve miles of goal-pace running.

- *Build speed.* Another tried-and-true means of improving marathon performance is to regularly do workouts involving running speeds that are significantly faster than marathon pace. Such workouts increase the body's capacity to consume oxygen during running, so that you can sustain faster running speeds more comfortably. There are two specific types of workouts that I recommend for speed building: interval runs and tempo runs.

  An interval run features relatively short segments of faster running separated by slow recovery jogs. For example, after warming up with a mile or two of easy jogging, run a mile at your 10k race pace, or the fastest pace you feel you could sustain for six miles. Jog a quarter mile and then run another fast mile. After completing a second recovery jog and a third fast mile, cool down with another mile or two of easy running. Repeat the workout a week later, adding a fourth fast mile. Build up to six fast miles over the next few weeks. By the end of this process, you will feel much better able to sustain faster running speeds comfortably.

- A tempo run consists of a single, longer block of fast running sandwiched between a warm-up and a cool-down. The appropriate pace for tempo running is comfortably hard—that is, the fastest pace you can sustain without beginning to struggle. Start with a tempo run consisting of ten minutes of tempo running between a ten-minute warm-up and a ten-minute cool-down. Repeat the workout every seven to ten days, adding a few more minutes of tempo running each time you do it. Build up to approximately thirty minutes of tempo running between your warm-up and cool-down. The more tempo workouts you do, the easier your somewhat slower marathon goal pace will feel.

Five Great Boston Marathon Qualifying Events

Choosing the right marathon event will improve your chances of achieving a Boston Marathon qualifying time. The best qualifying events feature flat courses, cool and dry weather (most years), and large fields with plenty of competitors who run as fast as you hope to, or faster. Here are five marathons that meet these criteria:

1. Bay State Marathon, Lowell, Massachusetts (October)
2. California International Marathon, Sacramento, California (December)
3. Chicago Marathon, Chicago, Illinois (October)
4. Grandma's Marathon, Duluth, Minnesota (June)
5. Mercedes Marathon, Birmingham, Alabama (February)

For a complete list of Boston Marathon qualifying races, go to www.baa.org.

The pride of qualifying to compete within a selective group of runners is not the only attraction of the Boston Marathon. This classic event also features a number of great traditions that make it unique and special. Our re-created Boston Marathon had some of the same jovialities that the live event is renowned for. Runners had journeyed from Texas, California, Florida, Canada, and even Israel, and the group was serenaded by many cheering spectators along the way. A couple of Wellesley College girls even offered "free kisses," as on race day, and several of the younger lads in our group partook, as did some of the not-so-younger lads.

When we rounded the final corner and headed down Boylston Street, we were treated to the sight of the actual Boston Marathon finishing line, which had been painted across the street especially for us that day. As we took our final few steps, people lining both sides of the road cheered, police sirens wailed, and noisemakers clanked. We runners joined hands together and broke through the finishing tape as a united group. It was a glorious and emotional moment. One runner turned to me and said it was his best Boston ever.

"How many times have you run Boston?" I asked.

"That was my twenty-fifth."

"Wow," I marveled.

"And the best thing about today," he went on, "is that I got a Wellesley kiss. So I'm twenty-five for twenty-five there too."

I chuckled.

"That's the only reason I keep doing this race." He winked at me.

What was it I was saying earlier about motivation coming in many forms? For this fellow, obviously, motivation came in the form of two lips.

As I've mentioned before, when it comes to motivation, I say get it wherever you can.

CHAPTER 22

Breaking Down

Day 30
October 16, 2006
Breakers Marathon
Aquidneck Island, Rhode Island
Elevation: 98'
Weather: 60 degrees; crystal clear
Time: 4:14:12
Net calories burned: 95,610
Number of runners: 28

More than a few Endurance 50 participants started their marathons with lingering minor injuries from training, or developed minor injuries on the course. One of the most memorable cases was that of a jet pilot who ran the Breakers Marathon with me and twenty-seven others on Aquidneck Island, Rhode Island. Years earlier, Jonathan had suffered a knee injury that had healed well enough to allow him to run every day but still caused him pain when he pushed it. He had never run a marathon before, so after completing thirteen miles with us, Jonathan was definitely pushing it.

At fifteen miles, still feeling okay, he stopped briefly to heed nature's call. When he tried to resume running, his knee locked up and ignited with intense pain. Devastated but undeterred, Jonathan began walking in a stiff-legged manner, doing his best to ignore the pain in his left knee. With four miles left to go, he began to doubt whether he would finish after all. Just then, a runner who had completed the Hartford Marathon two days earlier pulled alongside Jonathan in his vehicle, introduced himself as Paul, and asked whether Jonathan needed a ride. Paul had driven to Rhode Island expressly to provide additional support, if needed. Jonathan declined the offered lift, and instead accepted a subsequent offer of improvised medical treatment.

Paul pulled out a roll of duct tape and created a makeshift brace around Jonathan's aching joint. The additional support reduced the pain just enough to allow him to walk the last four miles—and run the last twenty-five yards to complete his first marathon. Paul's generosity and Jonathan's determination were especially noteworthy examples of the spirit evinced by Endurance 50 participants in every state across the country.

The knee is the most common site of injury in runners. In fact, running-related knee injuries are so common that doctors informally classify this type of injury as "runner's knee" (much as tennis players have "tennis elbow" and swimmers have "swimmer's shoulder"). The technical name for runner's knee is *patellofemoral pain syndrome*. The main symptom is pain underneath the kneecap that is mild, at first, and felt only during running, but tends to become more severe and to linger longer after runs, until eventually running is impossible. Its primary cause is instability at the knee joint during the impact phase of the stride, which causes damaging friction in the tissues between the kneecap and lower leg bones.

QUICK TAKE: *Runners tend to develop a lot of tight spots in their muscles that cause stiffness and can lead to injuries. One way to work out these tight spots is with a therapeutic foam roller. By rolling your legs across one of these tools at various angles for just five minutes a day, you may notice a big boost in your mobility.*

Runner's knee is considered to be an overuse injury, as are many other types of common running injuries. As the term suggests, overuse injuries involve the gradual breakdown of body

It Starts with the Shoes

Improper footwear contributes to many injuries. Wearing the appropriate type of running shoe for your foot can help prevent such occurrences. Generally, runners with flat arches may benefit from a motion-control or stability shoe, with extra stability features to manage overpronation of the foot. Runners with normal arches typically fare best with a neutral shoe. And those with high arches most often require a running shoe with extra flexibility.

These are guiding principles, not definitive rules. The "best" shoe is the one that works best for you. My recommendation is never to skimp when it comes to finding your ideal running shoe. In my experience, running specialty stores are the best retailers to purchase running shoes from, as most of the sales staff are passionate runners themselves and understand how to match a runner's foot and running style with the ideal type of shoe.

I have neutral biomechanics, but I log a ton of miles, so I wear extra-durable shoes designed for runners with normal arches, such as the North Face Arnuva 50 Boa.

tissues resulting from repetitive motion over the course of days, weeks, months, or even years. These injuries are quite different from so-called acute injuries such as ankle sprains.

Beginning runners suffer the most overuse injuries per hour of training, because their bones, muscles, and connective tissues are not yet well adapted to the new activity. When taking up running, or when starting over after a layoff, ramp up conservatively, beginning with gentle, manageable workouts and increasing their duration and/or intensity gradually over the course of many weeks as your body adapts.

Even the fittest runners can put themselves at risk of injury by making abrupt changes in their training—specifically, by suddenly increasing the duration, frequency, or intensity of workouts. For example, competitive runners often become injured when they abruptly introduce challenging speed workouts into their program after having done only moderate-intensity training recently.

No matter your fitness level, proceed watchfully when making changes that increase the challenge level of your training, whether it's adding high-intensity runs, increasing the duration of your longest runs, or adding one or more training sessions to your weekly schedule.

Errors in running technique can also contribute to running injuries. In runners, the most common injury-inducing technique flaw is heel striking, or landing heel-first rather than on the mid-

Strengthening Your Lower Abdominal Muscles

Here are two good exercises to strengthen your lower abdominal muscles and improve your core stability when running.

Lower Abdominal Squeeze

Lie faceup with your arms relaxed at your sides and your legs extended straight toward the ceiling, heels together. Now contract the muscles of your lower abdomen and, by doing so, try to lift your heels ever so slightly toward the ceiling. (This is a very small movement.) Hold the contraction for one second, then relax for one second. Repeat the exercise until you feel a nice burning sensation in the targeted muscles.

Stick Crunch

Lie faceup on the floor and draw your knees toward your chest. Hold a short stick, rope, or rolled-up towel between your hands (about fifteen inches apart) with your arms extended straight toward your toes. Try to reach the stick past your feet by contracting your abdominal muscles and pulling your chest toward your knees and your knees toward your chest (curling into a ball). Pause briefly with the stick on the far side of your feet and then relax. Repeat twelve to twenty times.

foot. Heel striking tends to cause a very sudden spike in impact forces that shoots straight up the legs, concentrating in susceptible joints such as the knees and hips. By contrast, landing on the midfoot allows the body to better absorb impact force in the foot, ankle, and lower leg, so that less force reaches the knee, hip, and pelvis. I also believe it's very helpful to strengthen your lower abdominal muscles. Runners who cannot activate these muscles properly are unable to maintain proper stability in the pelvis, hips, and knees during running. As a result, their pelvis goes into a forward tilt and they get an arch in their low back. This places extra stress on both the hamstrings and knees.

While it takes time and patience, training yourself to switch from a stride with a heel-first landing to one with a midfoot landing is possible. The easiest way is to practice angling your whole body slightly forward as you run, as though you're always running down a subtle hill. This will force you to make ground contact with your foot more in line with your body's center of gravity—rather than out ahead of it—and at a more neutral angle, instead of toes-up.

I believe the human body was made to move and that we can all enjoy miles of injury-free running if we get into shape and then simply allow our body to do what it was designed to do. We were naturally made to run. Now, sitting behind a desk all day staring at a computer screen: *That's* the unnatural state we need to correct.

Day 31
October 17, 2006
Portland Marathon
Portland, Maine
Elevation: 350'
Weather: 57 degrees; cloudy
Time: 4:12:37
Net calories burned: 98,797
Number of runners: 23

I woke up on the morning of Day 31 with full-body aches. The cold that had ebbed and flowed inside me throughout the Endurance 50 had taken a turn for the worse during the night. If I hadn't been obligated to run a marathon in Portland, Maine, on this morning, I would have bailed and taken a day off. The last thing you feel like doing when you've got a raging cold is going for a run. In my current endeavor, however, the show had to go on. Rest was not an option. Endurance never sleeps.

It has been fairly well documented that prolonged, high-intensity activity (competing in Ironman triathlons and ultramarathons, for instance, or extreme mountain climbing) can temporarily suppress the immune system. Some of the folks I had talked to about my cold during the Endurance 50 had theorized that this was precisely what was happening to me. I didn't buy into it, however. I had another theory—one that was much more verifiable.

We'd been crisscrossing the country at the beginning of cold and flu season, meeting thousands of people along the way. Intensifying this already heightened level of exposure to bugs, I'd been shaking hands with and hugging hundreds of sweaty runners, putting finger foods—like energy bars and fruit—directly into my mouth, and blowing my nose with the back of my hand. Gross, I know, especially after shaking dozens of other hands. There was just so much going on, however, that after a point I threw every basic precautionary measure to the wind. It was no use trying to remain hermetically sealed.

> QUICK TAKE: *Carbohydrate provides fuel for the immune system. While the mechanism of action responsible for this is not fully understood, research has shown that consuming carbohydrate (for example, in a sports drink) while running reduces the suppressive effect of intense, prolonged exercise on the immune system.*

One way to avoid colds is to refrain from touching your nasal tissue, a primary vector for germ transmission. Here I was shaking multiple hands—a primary carrier of germs—and then wiping my nose directly with the back of my hand, effectively swabbing the most vulnerable area of my body with millions of rhinoviruses from across the country. More than weakening my immune system through physical strain, I was infecting and re-infecting myself daily.

The minor colds I suffered from throughout the fifty days, however, were really just that: minor colds. I can't remember the last time I was laid out flat from a cold or flu. I'm sure it's been more than a decade since I was unable to get out of bed because of an illness. How do I prevent major colds and flus? In a couple of ways. First, I drink lots of water throughout the day. When I say *lots,* I mean three to four liters. I carry a water bottle with me all day long as a reminder, and constantly fill it. Second, I drink warm tea (ginger maté being my favorite) at the first symptoms of a cold to help loosen up phlegm. Yep, I'm talking about that nasty stuff that comes out of your nose when you're not feeling well.

Of course, running loosens up phlegm as well. Do I run when I have a cold? Yes, I do. Okay, go ahead and scold me—shame, shame—but I think the notion that you should avoid running when you're sick (unless a high fever is present) is an old wives' tale that's been perpetuated throughout the years without much validity. The one thing I am always cautious about, however, is blowing snot out one nostril while using my knuckle to clamp the other (commonly referred to by runners as the farmer's blow). Doing so can blast infected mucus back into the sinuses and ear canal. Better to carry a tissue and wipe when necessary. It will gross out the folks around you a lot less too.

Goo streaming down your chin is one thing; muscle and joint aches and pains are an entirely different concern. Learning when not to run through pain in your muscles, bones, or joints is an important way to prevent injuries. While I might not have had the choice to obey this rule on Day 31 of the Endurance 50,

Correcting Muscle Imbalances

One of the most effective ways to prevent running injuries is to regularly perform exercises that strengthen important stabilizing muscles. Here are three such exercises. I recommend that you try to do them every other day.

Single-Leg Squat

This exercise strengthens the stabilizing muscles of the hips. Stand on your right foot with your left knee slightly bent and your left foot elevated an inch or two above the floor. Bend your right knee and at the same time bend forward at the waist until your chest touches your knee. Use your arms and your elevated left leg for balance. Return to the start position. Do ten to twelve repetitions and then repeat with your left foot planted.

Side Step-Up

This exercise strengthens the stabilizing muscles of the hips. Stand with your side next to a twelve- to eighteen-inch platform (such as a weight bench or tall aerobics step). Place your right foot on the platform; keep your left one on the floor (your right knee is bent and your left leg is straight). Shift your weight onto your right leg and stand on that leg, lifting your entire body twelve to eighteen inches. Pause briefly with your left foot unsupported in the air next to your right foot, then bend your knee again and slowly lower your left foot back to the floor.

Cook Hip Lift

This strengthens the lower abdominal muscles. Lie faceup with your legs sharply bent. Place your left foot flat on the floor and draw the right leg up against your torso, keeping the knee sharply bent, holding it in place with pressure from your hands. Now contract the hamstrings and buttocks of your left leg to lift your butt off the floor two or three inches. Concentrate hard on keeping your deep abs contracted and your pelvis neutral. Hold this position for five seconds and relax. Repeat five times, then switch legs.

you always have the choice in your normal training runs. How do you know when to stop? It really comes down to experience and common sense. Experience gives you deeper insight into determining how far is too far. Common sense allows you to apply this insight to prevent injuries by telling you, *There's a real problem here. Stop running.*

Having to take time off from running to manage pain is disappointing and frustrating, though sometimes needed. To minimize the temptation to continue running despite pain, I suggest you find an alternative form of aerobic exercise that you can do pain-free and rely on to maintain fitness whenever running seems ill advised. Bicycling, using indoor cardio machines, in line skating, and pool running are all potential options.

Condition your body as well as possible, and closely scrutinize aches and discomfort to determine whether a temporary reprieve from running is needed. It's a fine line we runners toe, forcing us to carefully listen to our bodies. Someday there'll be a cure for pain; that's the day I throw my shoes away.

CHAPTER 23

The Long Run

Day 32
October 18, 2006
New Hampshire Marathon
Bristol, New Hampshire
Elevation: 466'
Weather: 60 degrees; cloudy
Time: 4:14:13
Net calories burned: 101,984 (cracked 100K!)
Number of runners: 5
                    (filled to capacity; we could only obtain 5 permits)

Many of the challenges I'd face during the Endurance 50 were foreseeable: the need for accelerated muscle recovery, the ability to withstand exhaustion from the long miles of driving, and missing Julie, whom I primarily saw on weekends. One hardship that surprised me, however, was how much I missed home cooking. While we were able to grab some tasty local culinary favorites in various states—the salmon jerky in Alaska was unbelievable, and the pickle okra in Texas was to die for—and while Koop did a fine job of supplying me with fresh salads on the bus every night, there's just nothing quite like a nice home-cooked meal to nourish your body and rejuvenate your soul. Though by the time we arrived at our accommodations in Bristol, New Hampshire, on the eve of Day 32, finding such a meal was the last thing I ever imagined.

The entire town had already closed for the evening. I was burned out, my lingering cold symptoms showed no signs of abating, and it looked like there would be no choice except eating another cold meal on the bus. But when we met the inn-keepers, they offered to open their restaurant for us—an incredibly hospitable thing to do since they were normally closed on Tuesday nights. When the food arrived, it was absolutely magnificent. Hot miso soup, an amazing garden salad, fresh-grilled vegetables, and mouthwatering cuts of lean meat. It filled the stomach and warmed the soul. Remarkably, when I woke up the following morning, my cold was all but gone. What had I said in an earlier chapter about discounting old wives' tales . . . ? Along with my veggies, allow me to officially eat my words.

With a clear head and a fresh outlook, we started on our way. I'd been told that the New Hampshire course was beautiful, and I was glad to be feeling better so that I could enjoy it. The unusually small size of our running group made it even easier to focus on the natural splendor surrounding us. The local officials had capped our field at five participants because of the narrow, winding roads and dangerous blind corners—not that there was any traffic on these roads today. I think a sum total of five cars passed us the entire time.

The course and surrounding scenery were classic rural New England. We ran past rustic old barns, through charming little townships, and along numerous rivers, all the while circumnavigating Newfound Lake, one of the cleanest in the country, whose pristine surface was like mirror glass. We had picked the perfect time of year to run in New Hampshire, as the autumn foliage presented a kaleidoscope of bright red, rich orange, and deep yellow colors.

At several points along the course, we were greeted by the fourth-grade class of Towle School. The students had been following the Endurance 50 as a lesson plan, and had planned this field trip to experience the event firsthand. They'd made a number of signs and banners, with messages that included the following:

ENDURANCE IS FAITH AND SPIRIT!
ENDURANCE IS PUSHING YOUR LIMITS!
ENDURANCE IS TRYING YOUR BEST AND NEVER GIVING UP!
TRUST YOUR FAMILY
EXPRESS YOUR FEELINGS
ROSES ARE RED, VIOLETS ARE BLUE, DEAN IS RUNNING,
    AND SO CAN YOU!

And my favorite Karno's Kids' saying: NO CHILD LEFT INSIDE.

One of the girls had baked some homemade brownies for me. More home-cooked food! I felt like I'd found nirvana.

"Those look great!" I said, and thanked her before stuffing one into my mouth. It tasted as great as it looked.

"And guess what, Mr. Dean," she said. "They're one hundred percent natural!"

Day 33
October 19, 2006
Stowe Marathon
Stowe, Vermont
Elevation: 722'
Weather: 59 degrees; partly cloudy
Time: 4:19:93
Net calories burned: 107,171
Number of runners: 30

There are people who believe that anyone who runs even a single marathon is some sort of maniac. The Marathon Maniacs would certainly take issue with this definition. Yes, there is actually a national running club that calls itself the Marathon Maniacs. To meet the minimum qualifications for membership (Bronze Level), you must complete one of the following:

1. Back-to-back marathons (two marathons on consecutive weekends)
2. Two marathons in three weeks (two marathons within a sixteen-day time frame)
3. Three marathons in three months (three marathons within a ninety-day time frame)

And that's just the *minimum* qualifying standard. The levels get progressively more difficult from there. Okay, maybe they are maniacs after all.

I was fortunate to be joined by many Marathon Maniacs during the Endurance 50. Amy Yanni, the only runner to keep me company in the Deadwood Mickelson Trail Marathon in South Dakota (marathon number ten), was one of them. Much later, in my six-day tour of New England, I was joined by a pair of Marathon Maniacs who happened to be married to each other. Joe Poliquin, fifty-four, and Bekkie Wright, forty-four, make their home in Manchester, Connecticut, and each had completed more than sixty marathons and ultras when they decided to take a week's vacation from work and attempt what they called the "New England Six-Pack."

They not only completed all six marathons, but Bekkie managed to cartwheel—literally cartwheel—across all six finish lines.

Joe and Bekkie were lucky even to start the New Hampshire Marathon, due to the small number of permits we had been granted. Aware of what they were attempting, the folks handling Endurance 50 event registrations at the Squires Sports Group made sure that Joe and Bekkie were included among the handful. The Stowe Marathon in Vermont had a much larger field, which included a seventeen-year-old first-time marathoner named Rick who had only recently taken up running. A potential future maniac? I wouldn't bet against it.

It was interesting to watch Rick, the teenage beginner, running alongside Joe and Bekkie, the mega-veterans. They all seemed so vibrant and full of life. My earnest wish for Rick was that his journey as a runner would be a long one. *May he still be fit, healthy, and enjoying running for decades to come*, I thought. Who knows? Perhaps the Endurance 50 experience increased the chances that Rick will still be running strong in the latter part of his life. Seeing how full of vitality those two Marathon Maniacs were, and how much joy they still derived from running after so many years, might have strengthened Rick's desire to make running a lifelong pursuit.

They say you revert to your childhood as you get older. That has certainly been the case with me. Some of my fondest childhood memories are of running the mile home from school. Kindergarten, to be specific. I was the oldest of three children in our family, and my dad worked two jobs to make ends meet. We were a working-class family in LA, and I could sense my

How Young Is Too Young?

There is no generally recognized minimum appropriate age to run a marathon. I ran one when I was fourteen years old, so I'd be a hypocrite to state that doing so in your teens is too young. However, there are many examples of gifted runners who pushed themselves too hard in their youth and found themselves past their running prime by the time they graduated from college. Therefore, as a rule of thumb, I recommend that highly motivated young runners concentrate on challenging themselves in school races and 5k and 10k road races at least until they graduate from high school, and only then attempt their first marathon, if they can't wait any longer. As the Marathon Maniacs and countless others illustrate, running is an activity that can last a lifetime. It would seem prudent not to risk your future running prospects by going too far too young.

mother having a difficult time getting me home from school with the added responsibility of a third child and a constantly working husband.

"Mom," I finally said to her, "there's no need to get me home from school."

"How are you going to get home, darling?"

"I'll just run," I told her.

At first, I took the most direct route back to the house. Eventually, I started to take diversionary routes through the park and by my favorite construction site on Century Boulevard to check out the heavy machinery in action. I came to look forward to my after-school runs with great anticipation and enthusiasm. Sure, it was about the running, but it was more about the adventure and the exploration.

As I grew older, my love of running continued to flourish. I joined the junior high and high school track and cross-country teams and placed fairly well in most races, periodically winning a few of them. Even as I raced, however, I continued to enjoy running down a trail for hours on end as the ultimate running experience.

It has long been my contention that there is a fundamental difference between a racer and a runner. I like to race, to run marathons and ultras to see how fast I can go, to compete against others, to watch the clock in the hope of beating my previous best time. But in racing, there is a finish line. I don't like finish lines. It is the journey I cherish, not crossing the finish line. In racing, there are boundaries, preset courses, rules that must be abided by. Racing, in short, is a construct of man.

Running, to me, is the purest expression of absolute freedom. There are no boundaries; there are no finish lines; nothing is contrived. There is only never-ending liberty to go as you please, to savor and explore, to immerse yourself wholeheartedly in the experience of being completely alive for this fleeting moment in which we inhabit the universe.

As I've matured over the years, my preference has gravitated toward running for the adventure of it versus the racing element. Yes, I've certainly crossed my share of finish lines, though most of the medals and trophies I've received over the years are stuffed in boxes in my garage. Somewhere. I much prefer walking out my front door, setting a course north, and running for a few days with nothing more than a backpack and some provisions. To me, that is the ultimate running experience.

I always encourage runners, young and old, to do what they love. Running is as much an art form as it is a competition. Some people love to compete, to count the number of races they've finished, to win, to set PRs. Other people prefer to run, just to run, because it liberates their soul and makes them feel most alive. I say, do what's in your heart. Be true to yourself.

People ask: When are you going to stop running? I like to tell them my finish line is a pine box (that is, a grave ten feet under the earth). Truth is, as long as the fire still burns within my heart, as long as the passion for running and exploration remains strong, I'll continue running. Running is one of life's simplest joys; why complicate matters? If I wake up one morning and no longer feel like running, then I'll stop. It's as simple as that.

But enough about me. I bet you're wondering how the lads of the Endurance 50 crew were getting on. Bristol, New Hampshire, population 1,674, for instance, didn't exactly have a raging nightclub scene, to put it mildly. So how *were* the young men faring? They were happy to report that after thirty-three days, their record was untarnished as well: thirty-three states, thirty-three phone numbers! As they say, where there's a will, there's a way.

CHAPTER 24

Mind Over Miles

Day 34
October 20, 2006
Cleveland Marathon
Cleveland, Ohio
Elevation: 1,168'
Weather: 50 degrees; rain
Time: 4:12:34
Net calories burned: 108,358
Number of runners: 50

You can control many things as a runner: your training, your nutrition, your shoe selection, and much more. But you can't control the weather. Mother Nature calls her own shots. Knowing this as well as anyone, I did not expect the weather to cooperate on every single day of the Endurance 50, and I wasn't disappointed.

We enjoyed a streak of pleasant autumn weather throughout our six-day tour of New England; that ended when we moved west to Ohio. Cold rain fell in sheets from a leaden sky and fierce winds blew those sheets sideways, straight into our faces and bodies, as our group of fifty runners shuffled along the streets of Cleveland in a tight, self-protective huddle. The damp chill of the air seeped through my skin and muscles to the marrow of my bones. My legs felt cold, heavy, and stiff. Worse, my joints started to ache, and each foot strike sent a bolt of pain radiating through my system.

My mind sought refuge from my body's misery with visions of relaxing at home with Julie and the kids—maybe fixing a hot meal together and then settling down on the sofa to watch a movie, down comforter snugly draped across us. It wasn't just the unpleasant weather that inspired these thoughts. My mind and body were feeling the cumulative toll of running more than eight hundred miles and traveling more than fifteen thousand miles over the past thirty-four days. With only two weeks plus a day left before we rolled into New York for the grand finale of our adventure, I could now see a faint glimmer of light at the end of the tunnel, and I was starting to crave that light.

Looking around, I saw that everyone else in the group was suffering as much as I was, and this observation brought me a small measure of relief. Misery truly does love company. All fifty of us shared the same goal: to reach the finish line. This common sense of purpose created a transcendental strength that each of us could draw upon to keep moving forward. The tougher the going got, the harder we struggled together, and the stronger our bond became.

After ceremoniously crossing the finish line and sharing hugs and high fives, we sought refuge in a nearby office building, where an improvised Finish Festival took place. Later, as I walked back to the bus with Robin, Garrett, and the rest of the crew, I passed a corner Chinese take-out restaurant and suddenly experienced a powerful memory from many years ago, when I cracked open a fortune cookie and read the following message: *He who suffers remembers.*

This proverb had an immediate impact on my spirit, and has remained a favorite saying ever since, because it captures one of the reasons I love running. When I push my body through running, as I did in the Ohio stop of the Endurance 50, I suffer intensely. While I can't say I like the suffering, per se, I do like its intensity, because it fills me with an extraordinary sense of being alive that is truly unforgettable. These intense experiences never lose their immediacy; they become timeless memories, and I can remember intimate details of such events even years afterward.

More than once, I have been accused of masochism on the basis of my attitude toward the suffering of running. I am no masochist. A masochist views pain as its own reward. I do not view pain as its own reward. I merely enjoy the challenge of overcoming the pain and suffering of extreme bodily fatigue in my quest to explore how far the human body can go. The thrill I get from testing my mental toughness on the run isn't really much different from the kick others get from testing other strengths, from the ability to shoot a perfect round of golf to the ability to express impassioned emotions through music. The harder I push myself in a run, the more satisfied I am afterward. And it's the same for most runners. Giving a 95 percent effort in an event leaves you feeling a little hollow. But when you're hanging out with friends or family, drinking water and stretching after finishing an event in which you know you left it all out there, the feeling of pride and accomplishment can't be beat. You did your best; you gave it everything you had.

I believe all of us have enough mental toughness to achieve the impossible in running—in other words, to run farther and faster than we ever thought we could. Throughout the Endurance 50, I saw mental toughness in men and women, in young adults, senior citizens, and kids, in persons of every ethnicity, and in folks from all fifty states and every corner of the globe. Every runner has the potential for mental toughness somewhere inside. Whenever runners allow suffering to defeat them and consequently fail to do their best, it is not because they lack mental toughness but because, for some reason, they just didn't have the courage that day to access it.

When you're running, 90 percent of your conscious attention is absorbed in one thing: resisting the feelings of fatigue, suffering, and weakness that are telling you to slow down and quit. Through the act of running, we can all learn to push farther than we ever thought we could.

As Ken Chlouber, race director of the Leadville Trail 100, is fond of saying: "You're better than you think you are."

On the drive to Michigan, my thoughts turned to Julie. I missed her deeply. So I picked up the phone and called her at

Just One More

Personal trainers, coaches, and drill sergeants sometimes practice an effective technique to help their clients access their mental toughness that I call "just one more." (In the movie *Animal House,* they called it "Thank you, sir! May I have another?") It works like this. Suppose a trainer is counting a client's push-ups. When the client begins to tire, the trainer says, "Do five more." The client struggles increasingly through the next five, barely completing the last one, only to be told, "Just one more." More often than not, the client is able to do it. I mean, it's just one more!

You can do the same thing in some of your workouts. If you set out to do six hard hill repetitions, put everything you have into those six. Then challenge yourself to do "just one more." Or try running as far as you can *out* in one direction, with no way back other than by foot, and when you're thinking about turning around and heading *back,* force yourself to run "just one more mile" farther (which actually adds two more miles to the total run). This type of mental training builds both toughness and character. The next time Mr. Drill Sergeant pulls a "just one more" on you, hail its completion with a "Thank you, sir! May I have another?"

work, something I rarely do. She's built an incredibly busy and thriving dental practice, and I don't like to interrupt her when she's seeing patients.

They got her on the line.

"Hey, Doctor K," I said, using the colloquial name her staff and patients sometimes refer to her by.

"Hi, sweetie," she answered. "What a pleasant surprise!"

I proceeded to thank her for all her sacrifices and hard work in making the Endurance 50 a reality. She really had poured her heart into it, not to mention her endless hours of planning and preparing. I was very worried about the health of her practice, given that she had been so distracted with helping me, and I expressed this concern to her.

"Are you kidding?" she said. "All of the staff and most of my patients are following your progress. Everything's great!"

I've sometimes described Julie as part saint, part angel. Now you can see where I get that description.

Day 35
October 21, 2006
Grand Rapids Marathon
Grand Rapids, Michigan
Elevation: 748'
Weather: 51 degrees; cloudy
Time: 4:06:03
Net calories burned: 111,545
Number of runners: 50

Among the fifty runners who ran with me in the Grand Rapids Marathon was the first challenged athlete to participate in an Endurance 50 event. Her left leg had been amputated at the knee, and she ran with a prosthetic lower leg. Not only did this young woman cover the same distance as the rest of us, but she did so with fewer muscles available to propel her forward. I could see determination written all over her face and was awestruck by the relentless consistency and indefatigable strength of her pace throughout the entire 26.2 miles.

I am fascinated by how many challenged athletes get back into sports or become athletes for the first time only *after* suffering an accident. You wouldn't necessarily expect so many people to respond to setbacks that reduce their physical capabilities by demanding more from their bodies than they ever did before, yet they do, and they are rewarded for it in the same way every athlete is rewarded for exercising mental toughness against physical challenges: with feelings of accomplishment, pride, and great triumph.

Challenged athletes set a great example that reveals the true secret of accessing mental toughness, which is this: You have to want it. The determination we see in these athletes comes from

Tough Guys (and Gals)

Some runners are especially known for being mentally tough. Three-time New York City Marathon winner Alberto Salazar was legendary for being able to push himself harder than any of his rivals. Current women's marathon world-record holder Paula Radcliffe of Great Britain has a similar reputation. What makes such runners mentally tougher than the rest? Sports psychologists believe there are many ingredients, including genes and impactful childhood experiences.

I believe that mental toughness also comes from your conscious willingness to push aside pain. You can't change your genes or your childhood experiences, but you can control your ability to tolerate increasing discomfort and pain when running hard. Building mental toughness really comes down to saying yes with your heart when your body says no, and getting the job done despite the pain.

the importance they place on squeezing every last drop of potential out of their bodies. If they are more mentally tough than the average able-bodied runner, it's because they've had to work harder to get there, and they want it more. For them, pushing through fear, discomfort, and limitations in running is really about choosing to live wholly instead of halfway.

And there is a lesson here for every runner. After all, running is a microcosm of life. The lessons you learn and the breakthroughs you make as a runner have a way of affecting your whole person. By challenging yourself to overcome your limitations as a runner, you will cultivate inner qualities of determination, focus, and perseverance that will help you overcome limitations in every part of your life. Live as though every step, every breath, is a precious gift. Push yourself relentlessly and learn to tolerate untold amounts of pain. Die trying. It is worth the price.

As one first-time marathoner succulently put it: "I wasn't sure if I could make it. But then I realized the only way I could fail was if I didn't try."

CHAPTER 25

Running Green

Day 36
October 22, 2006
Chicago Marathon
Chicago, Illinois
Elevation: 620'
Weather: 44 degrees; cloudy and windy
Time: 3:28:19
Net calories burned: 114,732
Number of runners: 42,000

One of the most hazardous places to run is near heavy automobile traffic, not just because of the risk of being struck by a vehicle, but also because of the air pollution emitted by gas-burning vehicles. The main ingredient in smog is ground-level ozone, which is produced when natural ozone reacts with sunlight and human-made chemicals (especially hydrocarbons, a major component of vehicle exhaust). Even more dangerous than ozone is the slew of fine particulates that are also released into the atmosphere in automobile exhaust and are toxic to the human body. Ozone damages lung tissue, causing it to age at an accelerated rate. Pollution particulates find their way into the blood vessels, causing oxidation (free radical damage) and inflammation. Over time, frequent exposure to polluted air during exercise can cause the arteries to harden, predisposing the individual to heart attacks and strokes, just as smoking cigarettes does.

When you breathe air with unsafe pollution levels, you may experience tightness in your chest, shortness of breath, wheezing, and coughing. Runners and other outdoor exercisers are especially susceptible to these effects not only because we spend more time outdoors, but also because during exercise we may breathe ten or twenty times as much air—and ten to twenty times as much air pollution—as we do at rest.

In addition to irritating your respiratory tract, working out in smoggy air may also affect your performance. Air pollution causes the airways to constrict during intense exercise, reducing oxygen delivery to the muscles.

In American cities that have the worst air quality, doctors are seeing an alarming trend of more and more outdoor athletes and exercisers coming to them with complaints of asthma, allergies, and breathing difficulties. It's a frighteningly ironic phenomenon. These people are getting outside and sweating every day in part to improve their health, and due to factors beyond their control, they wind up harming their health in certain ways.

There are some simple precautionary measures you can take to help protect yourself from traffic pollution. First of all, time your outdoor workouts for periods of the day when pollution levels are lowest, typically the morning or evening, rather than at noontime. Photochemical smog levels increase after the morning rush hour as the exhaust travels through the bright sunlight.

Also, do your workouts far away from high-traffic areas. Pollution levels tend to be highest within fifty feet of major roadways. Finally, check the air quality in your area before you work out. You can do this by logging on to www.epa.gov/airnow. On days when the air is rated "unhealthy for sensitive groups" (orange) or worse, do your workout indoors.

Thankfully, ozone levels are lower now than they were thirty years ago, though they remain problematic in some areas. One such place is Chicago, where I ran the live Chicago Marathon on Day 36 of the Endurance 50. Unfortunately, Chicago ranks among the fifteen worst cities for air quality in the United States. Don't get me wrong: I love Chicago for its vibrant people, rich culture, colorful history, great food, and musical heritage,

Large Versus Small Marathons

With forty-two thousand runners, the Chicago Marathon was one of the largest marathons in the Endurance 50. This massive scale has its advantages and disadvantages. Small marathons typically have a different set of advantages and disadvantages. Here's a comparison.

	LARGE MARATHONS (10,000+ RUNNERS)	**SMALL MARATHONS (1–5,000 RUNNERS)**
Advantages	Usually very well organized	Fewer hassles (parking, bathroom lines, and so on)
	Lots of spectator support	More personal atmosphere
	Exciting atmosphere	Often held in beautiful non-urban locations
	Mostly in major cities (cool tourist destinations)	Easy to start near the front
Disadvantages	Crowd-related hassles (picking up race number, parking, and so on)	Sometimes not as well organized
	Difficult to start near the front	Not as much spectator support
	Slow early miles due to tightly packed crowd	Fewer perks (free product samples, race photography, and the like)

and I had an absolutely stellar time completing the Chicago Marathon alongside forty-two thousand other runners. It's truly one of the most exciting and upbeat marathons I've ever run. Yet as I ran, even though it was a smog-free and breezy day, I couldn't help thinking about the world that we've created and how we runners are subjected to all kinds of environmental insults that our bodies were not designed to tolerate.

I did not brood on such unhappy thoughts very long, though. The Chicago Marathon offered too many happy distractions for that. The aid stations were well stocked with the usual stuff from start to finish, and the outside support was even better. During the course of the race, I had a container of chocolate-covered espresso beans handed to me, a slice of Chicago-style deep-dish pizza delivered up piping hot, and a platter of freshly made baklava offered at the twenty-mile mark. The air was good in Chicago today, and the food was even better.

And it didn't stop with the race. At the Finish Festival, a large contingency of Greeks had gathered to greet me and my family. Most were relatives, including Uncle Leo, Aunt Sophia, and cousin George. I watched Alexandria and Nicholas socialize with the group. They looked totally at home among cousins, aunts, and uncles.

"Here, you look skinny. I brought you this." Aunt Sophia held out a bag to me.

"Thanks, Sophia," I said, "but I just had lunch."

"It's okay, it's just something light," she said. "Eat."

I took the bag, and it nearly pulled my arm off.

"That's light?"

Inside was a gyro sandwich the size of a cantaloupe.

"I used lamb instead of meat. It's very light. Now eat."

Uncle Leo and cousin George approached.

"We saw you at mile twenty," Uncle Leo said. "You looked like you were in pain. Have some of this. It will help."

They handed me a cup with some clear liquid inside. I thought it was water and downed it.

Immediately I started choking and coughing on the contents. "What is this?" I gasped.

"Ouzo. You won't be feeling much more pain."

I instructed the Endurance 50 team to get me out of there as quickly as possible. If we hung around too much longer, the Greeks were sure to end this tour right here in Chicago.

> *Day 37*
> *October 23, 2006*
> *City of Lakes Marathon*
> *Minneapolis, Minnesota*
> *Elevation: 834'*
> *Weather: 38 degrees; overcast and chilly*
> *Time: 4:22:06*
> *Net calories burned: 117,919*
> *Number of runners: 55*

The City of Lakes Marathon was different from any other marathon in the Endurance 50 in one key respect: It doesn't exist anymore. Held for the first time in 1963, the City of Lakes Marathon (initially called the Land of Lakes Marathon) continued through 1982, when it merged with the St. Paul Marathon, moved to a different course, and became the Twin Cities Marathon. When the folks from The North Face contacted the Twin Cities Marathon organizers about our running a re-created version of their event as part of the Endurance 50, they responded by proposing that we instead use the old City of Lakes Marathon course, which takes place entirely on footpaths, so we wouldn't have to deal with traffic. This not only allowed us to accommodate more runners but also ensured that we breathed cleaner air throughout our four-hour run.

At the finish of the marathon, there was a young girl holding up a sign. She had been following the Endurance 50 in her class and had convinced her mother to take her out to the finish so she could be part of the event. Her sign read:

ENDURANCE IS . . .
E *FOR* EFFORT
N *FOR* NEVER GIVING UP
D *FOR* DARING
U *FOR* UNBELIEVABLE
R *FOR* REACHING FOR YOUR GOAL

A *FOR* ATTITUDE
N *FOR* NOTHING STANDS IN YOUR WAY
C *FOR* COMMITMENT
E *FOR* ENERGY

If this is the future generation we're leaving the world to, I'm encouraged.

During the Finish Festival ceremony, our crew presented a tree to a Twin Cities government official. We did the same thing at numerous stops throughout the Endurance 50. Our intent wasn't only to give beautiful thank-you gifts to our host communities. We also wanted to offset the carbon emissions produced by our tour bus and other official vehicles as we crisscrossed the nation. Since trees consume the carbon dioxide that vehicles emit, planting them is an effective way to fight global warming.

The Conservation Fund operates a program called Go Zero that enables individuals, families, businesses, and other organizations to calculate their carbon footprint, or the amount of carbon dioxide they release into the atmosphere, and also pro-

A Breath of Fresh Air

According to the Environmental Protection Agency, the ten United States cities with the cleanest air are as follow:

1. Cheyenne, Wyoming
2. Santa Fe, New Mexico
3. Honolulu, Hawaii
4. Great Falls, Montana
5. Farmington, New Mexico
6. Flagstaff, Arizona
7. Tucson, Arizona
8. Anchorage, Alaska
9. Bismarck, North Dakota
10. Albuquerque, New Mexico

vides guidelines for offsetting these emissions through tree planting and other means. We worked with them on our tree-planting mission. Our carbon offsetting was achieved primarily through the planting of more than five hundred trees—which was the number Go Zero calculated was needed to cover the emissions from the Endurance 50—across the nation.

There are some environmentalists who dismiss the practice of carbon offsetting as a gimmick that allows people to essentially buy the right to continue polluting guilt-free. The real solution, they argue, lies in reducing pollution, not offsetting it. I agree that the endgame is to reduce pollution, yet I celebrate the carbon-neutral movement because it's just that: a movement. Within the past few years, we've seen the beginning of a major shift in the public attitude toward protecting the environment. While I know we must progress beyond carbon offsetting if we are to adequately safeguard our planet, it's a start—and more than that, the very acceptance of carbon offsetting is a positive sign for the future. Baby steps add up.

Runners should be leaders in the fight to save the planet. Along with cyclists, surfers, skiers, hikers, and other outdoorsy types, we make a regular habit of immersing ourselves in nature and enjoying all that it has to offer. We appreciate the fragile health of the environment more than a lot of people do, in part because we experience the negative effects of pollution more than a lot of people do. Those of us who live in places like Riverside, California, may suffer from headaches and chest tightness for the rest of the day after running outside on a morning of especially poor air quality. People in places like Penticton, British Columbia, might miss snowshoeing in the winter—as they did in childhood but can do no longer, because of global warming. These are very real effects of the damage we have already done to our global home, and there will only be worse effects if more runners and other outdoor enthusiasts don't do their part to defend it.

What actions have I taken, personally, to do my part? First, at the beginning of the Endurance 50, I sold my car. That was more than a year ago now, and I haven't owned one since. How do I get around? You got it: on foot. I have different-size backpacks for use in different types of excursions. For trips to the bank, for instance, I've got a small mesh backpack that is really light (not much heavy lifting going on in my bank account, unfortunately). For trips to the post office, I've got something slightly larger. And for trips to the hardware or office supplies store, I've got an even larger, sturdier backpack.

For more major outings, like to the grocery store, I use a jog stroller. Sure, you get some strange looks when people see a bag of produce inside rather than a baby, but I'm just trying to do my part to save the environment. In fact, we've now adopted a policy in our household. For all trips of less than a mile—if we have sufficient time—we walk. At first, Alexandria and Nicholas moaned and groaned. So we amended the dictum to include any human-powered mode of locomotion. Skateboards, Razors, in-line skates, and bicycles are acceptable. Anything goes, so long as it doesn't involve the burning of fossil fuels.

The kids seem to truly enjoy it now. And, interestingly, most of the time they end up walking with us. We see their friends along the way (most waving out SUV windows), talk to neighbors, enjoy the fresh air, and feel rejuvenated when returning through the front door.

Granted, it might not sound like a Herculean effort we're putting forth to save the planet. But if everyone were to adopt this policy and start walking, we could collectively have a massive impact on the environment. Yep, I'm on my soapbox. Let's collectively give new meaning to the phrase *running an errand.*

CHAPTER 26

The Art of the Stride

Day 38
October 24, 2006
Green Bay Marathon
Green Bay, Wisconsin
Elevation: 591'
Weather: 43 degrees; partly cloudy
Time: 4:07:26
Net calories burned: 121,106
Number of runners: 46

The Green Bay Marathon in Wisconsin fell on Nicholas's ninth birthday. In the spirit of the Endurance 50, he decided to celebrate by running the last nine miles of the marathon—his longest run ever. Alexandria, bless her heart, stepped up to the challenge and ran with him, even though her birthday falls in January.

They timed the start of their endeavor so that, if things went well, our group of forty-six runners would catch them about half a mile away from the finish line and we could all cross together. Indeed we did. The Green Bay Marathon finishes with a lap around historic Lambeau Field, where the Green Bay Packers football team plays. Running in that hallowed venue with my two children and the other runners was a magical experience. My heart swelled with pride as I watched the birthday boy and his big sister dash through the finishing tape, beaming with a sense of accomplishment and looking as though they could run another nine miles.

Something else I noticed during that lap around the football field was how gracefully Alexandria ran. She exhibited the fluid, efficient gait of a naturally gifted distance runner. Younger children look more or less the same when they run, but by the time they reach ten or eleven years—Alexandria's age at the time— you can easily spot the boys and girls who have the potential to excel as distance runners, if they so choose.

There is no single correct way to run. There are, however, certain characteristics that are almost universal in the strides of faster runners and are less often seen in the strides of average runners. These characteristics include a high stride rate (relative to speed), a tendency to strike the ground on the midfoot rather than heel-first, less ground-contact time and more time floating in the air, more bend in the knee during ground contact, less twisting of the hips and spine, and a more relaxed upper body. In a word, the best runners run more efficiently than the rest of us.

Although these stride characteristics come naturally to some runners and not to others, any runner can consciously cultivate them to some degree. There is a persistent myth in running that better stride form cannot be learned. This belief is demonstrably false. Just look at me. Starting off as a ground-pounding Cro-Magnon who lumbered through the miles with my knuckles dragging, I somehow adapted to run with a midfoot landing.

Now, perhaps you're thinking, *Why should I bother trying to run like those sinewy Olympic marathoners? There are lots of reasons I'm not as fast as those folks. Running form is only one of them.* That's a good point. I don't mean to suggest that trying to emulate the form of elite runners will make you an elite runner. What I am suggesting, though, is that making this effort will probably make you a stronger runner than you are today. If you have any interest whatsoever in running faster, improving your form is probably worth trying as a means toward this end. Also, and more important, improving your running form may significantly reduce your risk of developing many of the overuse injuries that are common among runners.

Drill It

Some runners find that performing technique drills helps them improve their running form. Here's a selection of technique drills to try.

Butt Kicks

Run in place for thirty seconds with your thighs locked in a neutral position and try to kick your butt with your heel on each stride.

High Knees

Run in place for thirty seconds, lifting your knee as high as possible on each stride.

One-Legged Run

Run (hop) on one leg for twenty strides, then switch to the other leg for twenty more.

Eighty percent of runners overstride, and this is the most common technique error that causes running injuries, which causes runners' feet to land incorrectly, heel-first, instead of on the midfoot. Why is this error so common? The short answer could be running shoes. Nobody overstrides when running barefoot, because landing heel-first without any cushioning between your foot and the ground would hurt your heel. But as soon as we lace up our shoes, four out of five runners unconsciously switch to a heel-striking stride pattern.

Correcting this problem is simply a matter of shortening your stride. Instead of extending your leg ahead of your body and landing heel-first with your foot well in front of your hips, consciously drop your foot to the ground directly underneath your hips. Leaning slightly forward, not at the waist but from the ankles, might help you make this adjustment more easily. At first, it will probably feel strange. Keep at it and soon enough your new stride will be second nature.

No matter how good your stride is, fatigue will change it for the worse. As fatigue sets in during a run, your stride begins to deteriorate. Initially, the changes are subtle, but as you draw near to the point of complete exhaustion, your loss of running form becomes quite obvious. The unraveling of the stride due to fatigue causes a loss of efficiency that hinders performance, and it also increases injury risk since it involves a loss of stability in the joints. So it's important that you try to hold your form together as well as possible when fatigued.

Highly trained runners are better able to maintain their form despite fatigue than their less well-trained counterparts. Simply being in better physical condition is helpful, though you can also make a conscious effort to resist stride deterioration. When I run, I consciously involve as much muscle tissue as possible in the stride action. I actively push off my toes to increase the involvement of my calf muscles, and I swing my arms a little harder than necessary to get my upper body in on the act. By relying on more muscle groups, I distribute the effort more broadly, and as a result it takes longer for individual muscles to fatigue. Experiment with doing the same thing when you run and see how it works for you.

Another method I use to prevent fatigue is to periodically alter my stride during long runs. I might begin with a neutral, upright torso posture; later switch to a slight forward lean; and still later, switch to a slight backward lean. These small changes in running style serve to distribute the stress of the effort more evenly throughout the body, which enables the hardest-working muscles to last a little longer before they reach exhaustion.

Fiddle with your stride during training runs to find efficiencies and learn ways to shift the load off certain areas by recruiting other muscles to do some of the work. Determine your ideal form by really tuning in to your body and paying attention to the ways you compensate for fatigue, both good and bad. Instead of treating your body like a temple, treat each component of your running system—quads, calves, forearms, abs, et cetera—like a valued team member, with its own unique strengths and weak-

The Power of Visualization

Athletes in many sports use a technique called visualization, or mental rehearsal, to improve their technique. As a runner, you can do it too. All you have to do is sit or lie still with your eyes closed and spend ten minutes imagining yourself running smoothly, efficiently, and powerfully. The more vivid and realistic you can make these images, the more effective they will be. When you visualize yourself running, you activate the same parts of the brain's motor centers that become active when you actually run. But the advantage of mental rehearsal is that you can change these brain patterns for the better by seeing yourself running more efficiently and powerfully than you really do. Then your goal becomes turning visualization into reality.

nesses. Focus on making the total package greater than the sum of its parts. May you live long, and run longer!

After crossing the finish line, we were greeted by the mayor of Green Bay, Jim Schmitt, who presented Nicholas with an enormous Green Bay Packers birthday cake. Then he proceeded to give Nicholas the most remarkable birthday gift ever: a football signed by the Green Bay Packers team. Nicholas was speechless. Watching him on stage with Mayor Schmitt was like witnessing a fairy tale unfold. In the heart of a nine-year-old boy, it was the best birthday he could have ever asked for.

Nicholas is a generous soul, and after blowing out the candles, he offered cake to all the runners.

"You must be very proud of him," said a voice behind me.

I turned to find my good friend and fellow ultramarathoner Roy Pirrung, who had just completed the marathon with me. I smiled at him in agreement.

"When I was his age," Roy went on, "other kids used to make fun of me because I was so fat."

I looked at Roy in shock. He was the absolute picture of fitness and health. A multiple Ironman finisher and ultrarunning masters world champion, the man was capable of running 150 miles in twenty-four hours. Apparently he hadn't always been this way. An obese child, Roy reached a point where he could hardly run around the block, let alone run nine miles without stopping. When his five-foot-six frame hit two hundred pounds, he said enough was enough.

Roy taught himself to eat better and to exercise. Gradually, his endurance improved and the pounds began to disappear. His stride is extremely efficient. I should know: I've spent many miles behind him. Apparently, however, even this needed improvement. Over the years, Roy taught himself how to run with greater economy.

"My stride is not natural," he told me. "I was a heavy heel–toe striker and adapted to become a midfoot striker." It took him five years to learn to become a more efficient strider.

Nicholas came bounding over. "Check this out!" he said, showing us the autographed football.

Roy grabbed it. "Go long!"

Nicholas bolted across the empty lot.

"Pirrung," I shouted, "that's a commemorative ball!"

It was too late. The ball went sailing over Nicholas's head as he dashed to try to catch it. I watched in horror as the meticulously autographed football skidded along the pavement. Nicholas just wasn't quite quick enough to reach it in time.

"Oh well," Roy ribbed. "At least he's got quick foot turnover and a good stride."

CHAPTER 27

Getting Back Up

Day 39
October 25, 2006
Tecumseh Trail Marathon
Bloomington, Indiana
Elevation: 591'
Weather: 44 degrees; partly cloudy
Time: 4:45:21
Net calories burned: 124,293
Number of runners: 55

Running is not a contact sport—at least, not usually. But every once in a while, a rare, freakish moment of bruising or bloodshed occurs, usually quite suddenly, like when you slip and fall on a patch of ice. Runners have a high tolerance for pain, but we prefer the slow-burning pain of creeping fatigue to the hard-hitting pain of sudden impact. If we had any taste for the latter, we would have taken up rugby or karate.

The Endurance 50 was largely free of such freakish moments of brutality—until I ran the Tecumseh Trail Marathon outside Bloomington, Indiana, when it suddenly became a full-contact affair.

The run started in a thickly wooded wilderness, off a desolate roadway. When my crew and I arrived there, we encountered fifty-five exuberant runners raring to go, fourteen of whom had never run a marathon before. Other than a couple of participants who had run here before, I'm not sure many of us had any idea what we were in for.

Watch Where You're Going

It's tempting to look off in the distance and enjoy the scenery when running on wilderness trails, though it's not always safe. When the path is narrow and the footing uncertain, keep your eyes on the trail. Look ahead about ten feet and find a line—the route where you're going to step for the next four to six strides. With practice, you will become more confident and more comfortable in choosing the right place to put your foot down. Rock surfaces can be slippery, as can tree logs. Scan for flat patches of earth to plant your foot on, and slow down when you can't actually see the surface of the trail—such as when it's covered with leaves. You never know what might be lurking underneath.

The course almost immediately hit a technical singletrack trail, with numerous stream crossings, hordes of logs and branches to climb over and navigate around, deep pockets of mud, slippery rocks, and gnarled tree roots hiding silently under thick canopies of fallen leaves. Within a mile, I had an inkling that this was going to be an interesting and different sort of day. My expectations were fulfilled.

The switchbacks were difficult to follow, but to look up for a trail marker was to risk tripping over an unseen obstacle and performing an inglorious face plant. I did precisely that on a harrowing descent less than two miles into the marathon, catching my toe on a hidden root and somersaulting forward. I stood up with nicks and scratches on my arms and thighs. My pride remained intact, however, as most of the other runners were falling all around me as well.

The primary effect of my fall was to increase my fear of falling again, which caused me to run with extra tension in my muscles in a continuous state of bracing for another tumble. My level of concentration also increased. I focused my vision intensely on the trail ahead, trying to pick the safest line and spot camouflaged obstacles. Not only were these efforts physically and mentally exhausting, but they were also ineffective. I fell at least a dozen times. So I forced myself to slow down. I had hoped to run each of the fifty marathons in fewer than five hours, but I began to think I would have to make an exception today given the difficult terrain and the thirty-five hundred feet of vertical ascent and thirty-eight hundred feet of vertical descent along the Tecumseh Trail Marathon course. (By comparison, the infamous Heartbreak Hill along the Boston Marathon course rises eighty vertical feet.)

To make matters worse, the group I was running with got a little lost on a number of occasions. To make up time, we pushed hard on the flat sections and along areas in the trail that were clear of debris. When we crossed the finish line at last, in a time of 4:45:21, my GPS watch indicated that we'd run 27.5 miles.

Throughout the Endurance 50, there was a running joke among the crew about the number of reporters and media personalities who asked us how far our marathon was today. Each time it happened, we hid our exasperation and patiently explained that every marathon was the same distance: 26.2 miles. After asking me this very question and receiving my rote explanation, one radio DJ (who obviously wasn't listening very well) asked whether today's marathon would be my longest.

"Yes," I told him, "today will be the longest 26.2-mile marathon I've ever run. I tried to get the organizers of the Endurance 50 to choose the short marathons," I goaded, "but they all seem to be the same distance."

On Day 39, it was this disc jockey who got the last laugh. That was the longest 26.2-mile marathon I'd ever run.

Day 40
October 26, 2006
Otter Creek Marathon
Otter Creek, Kentucky
Elevation: 568'
Weather: 52 degrees; light drizzle
Time: 4:16:48
Net calories burned: 127,480
Number of runners: 45

Despite some lingering trauma, I felt increasingly upbeat during the drive from Indiana to Kentucky as I began to appreciate the fact that I had survived the brutal Tecumseh Trail Marathon and the worst was certainly behind me. It was nothing more than wishful thinking.

The Otter Creek Marathon is grueling under the best of circumstances. Another trail marathon, it combined a highly technical route with more than twenty-seven hundred feet of hill climbing. The path was tricky, mostly singletrack, with plenty of roots and trail debris—loose rocks, stumps, broken branches—strewn across it. The flat sections were few, the descents were treacherous, and the climbs were arduous. Worst of all, it had rained the previous night, and a steady drizzle continued to fall throughout our struggle to survive the course. As a result, the large slab rocks that dotted the trail were as slippery as sheets of ice.

Runners began falling before we had even lost sight of the starting line. In the third mile, despite every precaution, I put my foot down in the wrong spot and felt it slide out from underneath my center of gravity. I fell backward, landing hard on my rear end. More than anything, it upset me.

Why were we running these technically challenging and difficult marathons as part of the Endurance 50, let alone back-to-back, not to mention as marathon numbers thirty-nine and forty? Rage bubbled inside me as I resumed running. It seemed like

Stay Positive, Heal Faster

It has always been my nature to deal with setbacks internally and resist urges to complain about my suffering to others. A recent study suggests this habit is healthier than I'd realized. Researchers from the University of Missouri found that injured male soldiers who scored higher on a test designed to assess "traditionally masculine" psychological traits (including unwillingness to complain about internal pain and suffering) tended to heal faster. The authors of the study speculated that men who are more reticent to communicate their suffering to others may also have a stronger belief in their ability to overcome suffering on their own, and that this belief is to some degree self-fulfilling.

The takeaway? Try not to wallow in your misery. Instead, channel the discouragement you may feel into a renewed commitment to overcome your setback. Fight harder and you will heal faster.

cruel and unusual punishment. Cruel, because running fifty marathons in fifty days on smooth roads was punishing enough; unusual, because there were plenty of marathons on smooth roads that I could have run instead of these. *What if I fall and tear a ligament or break a bone?* I kept asking myself. It seemed like a very real possibility, and my mind was reeling at the implications. The Endurance 50 could come to a screeching halt with one misstep.

My anger got the better of me and I began to run recklessly, flying down steep, muddy descents and hurdling obstacles like a steeplechaser. I was disappointed in myself for not having scrutinized each of the marathon courses more thoroughly to make sure they weren't this difficult, especially at this late stage in the game. I was upset that we had chosen trail marathons at all. Mostly, though, I was furious that the unexpected difficulty of these last two marathons was causing me to doubt my ability to complete the challenge of running fifty consecutive marathons in fifty different settings. Now I had something to prove!

I ran like there was no tomorrow. A group of exceptionally strong runners separated itself from the primary pack with me, and we pushed one another to the brink. It was crazy to be running at a 4:16 marathon pace in these conditions, yet we proceeded with wild abandon, bounding down steep declines and powering up abrupt hills. Luck was on my side and I made it to the finish line with a few fresh cuts and bruises, though otherwise sound. The Finish Festival looked like a MASH unit. Almost every runner in our forty-five-person field had fallen at least once, and many had fallen multiple times. Blood was visible on the arms and legs of soggy, exhausted men and women all around me.

QUICK TAKE: *QuikClot is a consumer version of a rapid blood-clotting sponge already used by the military and EMTs to help stop bleeding and instantly cauterize your wounds. You can purchase it at many pharmacies.*

At the first opportunity, I pulled aside Robin and told her confidentially how unacceptably treacherous the past two marathons had been.

"You're right," she said, immediately detecting both my physical condition and my level of mental anguish. "We messed up. I'm going to check out the rest of the marathons left on the schedule to make sure there are no more surprises."

I breathed a sigh of relief.

"You look strong, Dean," Robin added. "You're going to make it, and we're going to do everything in our power to help."

Suddenly my angst was replaced with a deep feeling of gratitude. The weather was still wet and chilly, but thanks to these welcome words of encouragement, my mood was now warm and bright. I would not have been so easily cheered if I had known what was awaiting us the next day.

Day 41
October 27, 2006
Georgia Marathon
Atlanta, Georgia
Elevation: 1,050'
Weather: 59 degrees; rain
Time: 4:08:00
Net calories burned: 130,667
Number of runners: 50

Robin meant what she said when she gave me that pep talk. There was just no way she could have anticipated the disaster that lay in wait for me in Atlanta. The Georgia Marathon racecourse travels through some of the busiest streets in the large city of Atlanta, which is not a problem when those streets are closed to automobile traffic and turned over to the thousands of runners who participate in the live event in late March. Our fifty-person, late-October re-creation was another matter.

There was a logistical debacle right at the start, and our police escort never materialized. A critical miscommunication had occurred, and as a result the roads we traversed would remain open to vehicle traffic; we were forced to fend for ourselves without the protective shield that normally surrounded us. Cars and trucks whizzed by us one after another, their sideview mirrors coming within inches of whacking our elbows as we strained to take up as little space as possible on the narrow shoulders. For the third consecutive day, it was raining, reducing visibility for motorists, many of whom obviously did not see us until their bumpers were almost on top of our heels. Dirty puddles of rainwater obstructed the roadway and shoulders, leaving us no choice but to clomp through them, soaking our shoes, and leaving drivers no option but to blast through them, splashing and soaking our clothes and bodies.

At mile six, we passed a construction site on the right side of the road, materials from which spilled onto the shoulder, squeezing us even further. I caught my toe on a rusty piece of rebar that was extending into the pathway and went flying forward headlong onto the asphalt, landing with a gruesome-sounding thud. It happened so quickly, I had no time to get my hands out in front of me. My right forearm hit first and suffered a nasty gash. My face must have hit next, because my mouth took in a gulp of puddle water that tasted of grit and gasoline. I came to rest on my stomach with my right arm tucked under my body in an unnatural position. Almost immediately I became aware of a disturbing numbness in my right hand. Had I broken my forearm?

Shocked and concerned faces loomed above me.

"Are you okay?" asked one of them.

"Somebody call an ambulance!" shouted another.

Before I knew it, and without any conscious intent, I was back on my feet and struggling to remember how to run: left leg–right arm, right leg–left arm . . .

It was one of those moments when instinct took over and made decisions for me. Actually, it wasn't instinct, but rather a second nature developed through many years of trying to faithfully practice the advice of my father: "It's not how many times you fall down that matters; it's how many times you get back up." Since he first spoke those words to me, I have tried to accept the inevitability of failure and setbacks in every part of life and to focus on overcoming them when they occur. Yes, you will fall in life; it is inevitable. The strong fall just like everyone else. But the strong always get back up. This particular case of falling down and getting back up was just a little more literal than most.

My first coherent thought was a simple question: How was I going to complete the remainder of this marathon with a bone sticking out of my arm? As I clumsily continued running along under the amazed looks of the other runners, my mind was already going through possible strategies I could use to somehow get to the finish. Stopping was not one of them.

I have taken a lot of tumbles as a runner, though none was nearly as severe as this one. I didn't want to look down because I knew it was bad, and I was afraid to see just how bad. Somewhere in the recesses of my subconscious mind, the thought that I risked jeopardizing a dream five years in the making must have been percolating, and more than anything else this thought compelled me to keep numbly placing one foot in front of the other. And that's what I did.

Blocking out the pain and doubt, narrowing my focus to the next step, I dragged myself through the remaining distance to complete the Georgia Marathon. A team of paramedics met me at the finish line and essentially glued my forearm back together after I refused to be taken to the hospital for stitches. I wasn't trying to be cavalier. It was a purely tactical decision. If I went to the hospital, how long might it take to be treated and released? We might not make it to Florida in time for marathon number forty-two. And if I missed marathon number forty-two, the Endurance 50 was over. I had fought too hard to get back up to now lie down and surrender voluntarily. No bones had been broken during the fall, nor had my fighting spirit been fractured. *Bring it on*, I thought, as we began the long drive south: *Bring . . . It . . . On!*

CHAPTER 28

Second Wind

Day 42
October 28, 2006
Florida Gulf Beaches Holiday Marathon
Madeira Beach, Florida
Elevation: 10'
Weather: 76 degrees; breezy
Time: 4:09:41
Net calories burned: 133, 854
Number of runners: 50

Every runner has experienced or at least heard about the phenomenon of the second wind. You're running along, when you begin to feel the first signs of fatigue: heaviness in your legs, an increase in your breathing, and usually a general loss of energy throughout your body. You keep running and the feelings intensify, which is a problem, because you still have a long way to go. Hoping for the best, you push onward.

Then, just when it begins to seem that you'll never be able to reach the finish line, you experience a sudden infusion of energy that propels you forward with renewed vigor. It's as though you've been given a new set of legs, and you bound onward with confidence that you will finish strong. Chest heaving, muscles aching, drenched in sweat, you do.

Sometimes a second wind has an obvious cause, such as a muscle cramp that dissipates slightly, a few big swallows of a sports drink, or passing by a group of spectators who shout the right words of encouragement. Other times its source is mysterious. One minute, you're sure you are about to fall on your face—the next you're running as well as you were in the first mile. Yet nothing in particular seemed to happen to cause this change.

Until recently, exercise scientists had no explanation for the second-wind phenomenon. In fact, many exercise scientists denied that the phenomenon even existed. Obviously, these researchers were not runners, because sooner or later every runner experiences an undeniably real recovery from fatigue in the middle of a run. Studies involving repeated maximum-intensity sprints, usually done on a stationary bike, have confirmed the phenomenon of a second wind. In one such study, performed by researchers at Charles Sturt University in Australia, subjects performed best in the initial sprints and a little worse in each subsequent one, but then summoned a little something held in reserve and performed better in the last sprint—a classic second wind.

It's now generally believed that you don't slow down because your muscles have hit a hard limit, such as running out of fuel. Instead, you slow down because your subconscious brain decides that you really *should* slow down—perhaps because it's worried that your muscles will *soon* run out of fuel. But if your brain receives new information that allays these fears, it can instantly reverse its decision and allow you to run harder again—in other words, it can choose to give you a second wind. What sort of information might have this effect? Seeing the finish line ahead of you is one good example. Discovering that, despite everything, you're still on pace to meet your time goal is another.

Most often, a second wind is what happens when, in the middle of a run, your brain changes its assessment of how fast you can safely run between where you are now and the finish line. Many different factors can cause this type of reassessment, but perhaps the most common one is simply hanging in there until you're a little closer to the end. The more experience you

Running to the Beat

Many runners like to listen to music through an iPod or other such device while they run. They feel that the right kind of music gives them a sort of continuous "second wind," an extra boost that enables them to run harder or longer. There may be some truth to this perception. For example, research by psychologist Peter Terry at the University of Queensland, Australia, has shown that exercise performance is enhanced by music with a faster beat. In fact, back in 1998, the great Ethiopian runner Haile Gebrselassie set a world indoor record for the 2,000 meters by synchronizing his stride to the beat of a song called "Scatman."

However, other runners—including many who consider themselves competitive—feel that music is an annoying distraction that interrupts their mind's connection to their body and environment when running. Personally, I enjoy listening to music when I run, and do so periodically. I also enjoy listening to audio books on longer runs. However, I never race with headphones on, and encourage others to unplug during competition (primarily as a courtesy to other runners).

The USATF—America's governing body for running and track and field—has banned the use of iPods and MP3 players at events it sanctions. This is not due to any perceived performance advantage but to safety concerns (it's hard to hear the traffic officer shouting "Turn left!" when the *Chariots of Fire* theme song is blasting in your ears). My thought is that if you want to race with music, sign up for events such as the Rock 'n' Roll Marathon San Diego that provide live musical entertainment along the course. Then boogie to your heart's content.

gain as a runner, the more accurately your subconscious brain will be able to calculate your body's actual limit, and the more reliable your feelings will become as guides for your effort. For example, the first time you run a marathon, the level of suffering you reach at mile twenty might cause you to panic and think, *I'll never make it!* And yet, you somehow do make it, perhaps even to your own astonishment when you reflect back on the exhaustion and self-doubt you felt at mile twenty. The next time you run a marathon and reach that same level of fatigue, you don't panic, because you know you can get through it, as you have before.

The more challenges you face as a runner, the more reliable your feel for fatigue will become. Yet this mechanism isn't perfect in any runner, and it may be especially unreliable when you push unusually hard. So it's only to be expected that your subconscious brain will sometimes become a little overcautious and cause you to feel miserable for a while in the middle of a long run, in order to hold you back, and then reassess the situation when you're closer to the finish line and give you a second wind that allows you to increase your pace and finish strong. Therefore, it's unlikely that you will ever "outgrow" the second wind. In fact, on some of the longer runs I've done—in the two-hundred-miles-plus range—I've experienced a dozen or more "second winds."

More typically, a second wind occurs once within a single run. But the Florida Gulf Beaches Holiday Marathon was a different sort of second wind for me—different even from the multiple second winds I've experienced during a long ultramarathon. Specifically, this marathon was a second wind in relation to the entire Endurance 50. I had suffered immensely in the preceding three marathons, hitting the lowest of lows and staying low long enough to wonder whether I would ever recover. The Florida Gulf Beaches Holiday Marathon gave me just the reprieve I needed, and not a moment too soon.

The course winds through scenic parks and along gorgeous beaches on the Gulf side of Florida. It's flat and paved. On the day we ran it, the temperature hovered in the mid seventies, and there was a refreshing breeze. Of course, it was still a 26.2-mile run, though compared with the preceding three it felt like a cruise with the top down.

There was levity along the course, which always helps revive the spirits. I saw the strangest roadkill ever: a fish. This thing must have jumped out of the water—we ran within spitting distance of the ocean—and been struck by a passing motorist. Even the seagulls circling overhead seem astonished by this one.

Coming around the final corner on the course, we heard some chanting. "Forty-two, we love you. Forty-two, we love you . . ." It was coming from a group of uniformed kids up ahead. The members of Team Trilogy, a youth triathlon club, had finished a "Mini Tri" earlier this morning and were now getting ready for a long cool-down. We ran the final stretch together, chanting their mantra along the way. Second winds don't get any better than marathon forty-two ("We love you!") was for me.

Day 43
October 29, 2006
Marine Corps Marathon
Arlington, Virginia
Elevation: 365'
Weather: 60 degrees; very windy
Time: 3:37:27
Net calories burned: 137,041
Number of runners: 34,000

My second wind continued through the Marine Corps Marathon, which I ran as a live event with thirty-four thousand other runners the following day. I felt very comfortable running at a pace that brought me to the finish line in 3:37:27, despite the blustery headwind. *I just might make it through this thing after all*, I thought as I ran the final stretch toward the patriotic Marine Corps War Memorial, which depicts the planting of the American flag on the island of Iwo Jima after one of the bloodiest battles of World War Two.

I have had more second winds than I can remember. One of the more unforgettable cases was my experience at the An-

Preventing Muscle Cramps

It is widely believed that exercise-related muscle cramps are caused by dehydration or depletion of electrolyte minerals through sweating. But research does not support this. Rather, exercise-related muscle cramps appear to be caused in most cases by a sort of tendon fatigue that occurs when exercise is unusually prolonged. Some runners are more susceptible to muscle cramps than others, but all can reduce their suscepti-bility by gradually increasing the duration of their longest runs in training. There are few shortcuts when it comes to pre-venting muscle cramps. Those who pay their dues reap the re-wards, or in this case avoid suffering the consequences that come with every shortcut.

gela's Crest 100-Mile Endurance Run a few years back. I devel-oped severe cramping in my left calf muscles twenty-five miles into the race. My first thought was that my day was coming to an abrupt and disappointing end before I'd even reached the marathon mark. But then I thought, *Well, let's just see what hap-pens if I walk for a while*, since I was able to walk relatively pain-free.

I walked for five miles and was passed by roughly forty other runners. At the thirty-mile mark, I started running again, slowly, cautiously, experimentally. My muscle cramps were gone. Over the next seventy miles, I overtook all of the runners who had passed me while I walked, plus a few others, and fin-ished the race in fourth place. I learned an important lesson that day: It ain't over till it's over.

When the early onset of fatigue causes you to have serious doubts about whether you can finish a run, try not to give in to those doubts. Instead, buy some time for a second wind. How do you do that? First, slow down, or even walk. Second, reflect back on any previous experiences when you felt just as bad as you do now, but still managed to get through it, and remind yourself, *If I could do it then, there's hope.* Finally, don't allow yourself to quit until you've gone at least one step farther than you thought you could go when your doubts emerged.

Sometimes quitting is necessary. My filter for determining when to stop is when I believe that continuing onward could cause serious acute or long-term harm. In these cases, *DNF* stands for "Did Nothing Fatal." However, you don't want to quit with that nagging feeling in the back of your mind that perhaps you could have finished after all, if only you hadn't given up too soon. One way to avoid this scenario is to make the commitment that you won't stop until the course is officially closed. This tactic is especially useful in ultramarathons. In a fifty-miler, for example, the course might be open for fourteen or fifteen hours. If you commit to keep going until the course is closed, rather than quitting before time runs out, you will go home with a confident certainty that you truly gave it your all.

Some people have the wrong idea about second winds, just as they do about the mythical runner's high. A second wind will not necessarily make running easy; it just helps you continue running hard. It will still hurt. If you pace yourself appropriately and apportion your effort well, your second wind can carry you a measurable distance, perhaps even to your stopping point, be it a finish line or your front door. You can't always count on a second wind. Some days you just have to put your head down and grind it out. Those runs can be the most satisfying ones of all.

I was reminded of this during the Marine Corps Marathon. There is a sculpture along the course called *The Awakening*. On this marathon route filled with prominent memorials and historic monuments, *The Awakening* remains oddly obscure, seemingly beneath the fanfare surrounding other popular sites along the way. Perhaps for reason. Most statues, you look at. *The Awakening* forces you to look in.

Situated at the terminus of a desolate and windswept promenade on the Potomac River, the haunting, massive, hundred-foot-tall figure embedded in the earth, struggling to free himself, is an unforgettable image. As runners round the tip of Hains Point at mile eighteen, *The Awakening* emerges into view. It's a time when you are deeply questioning your own resolve to keep scratching onward—possibly wishing for a second wind to come save the day. Shocking and unexpected, this massive apparition crawling out of the earth is a lugubrious, eerie sight to behold.

The statue consists of five separate pieces buried in the ground, giving the impression of a horrified giant trying to pull himself to the surface. The left hand and right foot barely protrude; the bent left leg and knee jut into the air. A colossal right arm and hand reach skyward, while the bearded face, mouth wide open and howling in apparent agony, thrashes violently to exhume the creature from the entombing soil.

Awakenings are always terrifying, as they force you to realize that your past has been lived in confinement. The most disturbing part is when you recognize that the shackles holding you down are largely ones you have placed upon yourself. The prison is self-constructed. "We are all living in cages with the door wide open," George Lucas once said.

It is so easy to live a life that has been scripted for you by others, to fall into the mire of conformity by following a path that society has laid before you, rather than heeding your own unique calling. Comfort, complacency, routine, the path of least resistance, the easy road—these things are the bane of humankind. It is a disquieting moment when you awaken to realize the trappings of conventionality have created a life for you that is entirely different from the one you wish to live.

This giant figure seems at war with his greatest adversary, himself. He appears to be struggling with the decision to follow what is in his heart, to buck convention and pursue an alternative course, a road less traveled. The grimace on his face comes from knowing that his past may have been a numb existence, and that he will require great courage and conviction in the future if he is to avoid sinking back into the tomb of conformity.

There will be untold battles waged within himself, wars that will test his every thread of persistence and commitment. Yet there is a slight hint of pride in his contorted face, perhaps because he also knows that if he follows his passion with heartfelt intensity, if he dedicates himself unreservedly to his calling, he will persevere and ultimately find fulfillment, no matter where his life may lead him.

We all have dreams and ambitions, though few of us ever become all that we could be. We fight a silent war over purpose, over reaching our farthest destination. Onlookers watching us marathoners pass by today may have only seen the act of running, but as anyone on the course could tell you, there was a powerful, complex conflict under way. William James said, "War is, in short, a permanent human obligation." The runner fights this war against the most savage of enemies: himself.

And, as with any war, this one comes with misery and suffering. War is hell, it has been said, and this marathon is nothing short of war, a raging battle to keep moving forward, to stay the course in the face of unimaginable pain. The marathoner asks more of himself than is reasonable. He commands his body and mind to do the unthinkable, to endure inconceivable hardship, all in the name of accomplishing something he deems noble and worthwhile.

By mile twenty-three, many of us racers were staggering haplessly, fighting with all our might to remain steadfast. People watching may have only seen the horror of it. Though in the horror, there is honor. To march proudly against a formidable adversary, to stand resolute for what you believe in while every shred of your material being is ripped to pieces: As marathoners—as warriors—this is our obligation. For with this struggle comes renewal. The marathon is not about running; it is about salvation.

The Marine Corps War Memorial—the finish—finally beckoned within eyesight. A gust of wind blew sideways across the racecourse, howling shrilly and sending great plumes of leaves and dust skyward. Through the swirling particulates, I saw a runner ahead stagger, then fall to the ground. It was a dream-like, surreal sight, his weary body simply collapsing under the immense physical strain it had been forced to endure over the past several hours.

Immediately, people rushed to his aid. It was a disturbing spectacle to behold. A brother had fallen short of his destiny; a soldier had lost the war in front of thousands of curious on-lookers. The crowd was dismayed. Still, there was no cynicism or scorn—only sadness.

Crossing the finish line, I was not filled with joy or relief. The scene that had just unfolded before me left me feeling grief-stricken and empty. *So close to the finish line*, I thought. *So close*. What a tragedy.

Then I heard the roar of the crowd swelling. There were screams of encouragement, commotion, hands waving, though I did not know why. I found myself being shuffled forward with the other finishers, wrapped tightly in our Mylar space blankets, unable to see what was causing the uproar. I asked a marine in uniform what has just happened.

"A man crawled to the finish line," he said.

My heart raced, my blood pulsed. He had awoken, dug deep into his soul and done the heroic. It was a poignant moment, one that no one present will ever forget. A man had arisen from the ashes, refused to give up, and fought the war crawling bravely on hands and knees through the finish line. His victory was shared by all of us and would inspire each one of us who was there to keep trying, even in the face of seemingly insur-mountable odds and incomprehensible pain.

Life is a struggle. Life will always be a struggle, though we must never give up the fight. A man reminded us today that as human beings, this is our obligation.

CHAPTER 29

It's the Shoes

Day 44
October 30, 2006
Kiawah Island Marathon
Kiawah Island, South Carolina
Elevation: 100
Weather: 75 degrees; sunny
Time: 4:23:37 (27.8 miles, made wrong turn)
Net calories burned: 140,228
Number of runners: 31

---

alfway through the Kiawah Island Marathon, my
feet began to feel constricted inside my North Face Arnuva 50 Boa running shoes. My feet always swell a bit
during long runs (as do the feet of most runners), especially on warm days, and today was warm, in the mid
seventies. So I did what I had done throughout the Endurance
50 when this situation arose: I stopped, bent over, and dialed
the knob on the heel of my shoes a couple of clicks counter-
clockwise to loosen the thin metal wires that substitute for shoelaces. Three seconds later I was running again. And, as always,
a couple of runners who had witnessed this quick adjustment
wanted to know what had just happened.

The Arnuva 50 Boa running shoes were developed in con-
junction with the Endurance 50. Ironically, The North Face did
not make "road shoes" prior to our running expedition. That's
one of the reasons the company sat on my proposal for so long
before finally getting behind it. It didn't make sense to pour a

227

lot of resources into a major marketing outreach to road runners if the company didn't make a road running shoe. The Endurance 50 might never have happened if the top executives at The North Face hadn't decided to create a line of footwear for road runners. Once this decision had been made, my proposed challenge of running fifty marathons in fifty states in fifty days suddenly seemed like a good "fit," so to speak.

The development process began with the hiring of a team of new in-house footwear employees and an outside company that specialized in running shoe development. All of the North Face–sponsored runners, including me, were asked to share information about needs that were unmet by existing shoes. This process led the developers to focus on creating a new lacing system that would allow quick and easy micro-adjustments of fit, as traditional laces do not.

The technology required to fulfill this need already existed in snowboard boots, but it was too bulky and heavy to be transferred directly to running shoes. So the engineers assigned to the project were challenged to shrink it down, and they did a remarkable job. The "reel" that you use to adjust the fit is smaller than a poker chip and not much heavier. The Arnuva 50 Boa allows you to micro-adjust the shoe's fit on the fly, rather than having to stop and fuss with traditional shoelaces. It's revolutionized endurance running.

Fit is the most important factor to consider when choosing a running shoe. Every major running shoe manufacturer makes high-quality shoes that provide cushioning, stability, and a host of other features. None of those features matters, however, if the shoe does not fit properly. Feet come in such a tremendous variety of shapes and sizes that there's just no telling how any given shoe will work on your foot until you try it on.

The best way to determine how well a shoe fits you is to simply put it on and assess its level of comfort. Your feet are smart. If the shoe is too loose or too constricting in a certain area, if it is too stiff or too flexible, too firm or too mushy, your feet will know it right away. The shoe should *feel* perfect right out of the box.

That said, you can't thoroughly assess fit and comfort until you start moving. Most good running shoe stores let you wear-test a shoe before you buy it. Basically, this means taking a spin in the shoe around the block or around the store. Try to avoid talking yourself into buying a pair of shoes that is *mostly* comfortable but has just one or two small points of discomfort. Those small imperfections can become major annoyances once you start logging serious miles in the shoes.

Of course, there's no guarantee that the shoe that felt most comfortable during a brief trial run at the store will feel the same way ten miles into a long marathon training run, due to foot swelling, fatigue-related stride changes, and other factors. Lightweight trainers might feel terrific in the store, but ten miles into a long run, you might find yourself wishing you were wearing a shoe with more cushioning. Take note of such experiences and apply them when choosing your next pair of shoes.

Like so many other aspects of running, finding the type of shoe that works best for you is a learning process. Footwear is the most important component of your running gear, so it's worthwhile to invest some time and effort in the process of

Arch You Glad You Picked the Right Shoe?

Runners with high foot arches tend not to absorb ground impact forces as well as those with normal arches, making them more prone to bone strains and stress fractures in the lower legs. Wearing a running shoe with extra cushioning can attenuate some of this risk. Runners with low arches tend to have less stable hips and knees than their normal-arched counterparts, predisposing them to overuse injuries in these joints. Selecting footwear from the motion-control category of running shoes may help reduce your risk of experiencing knee and hip pain if you have low arches.

learning what works for you and what doesn't. Your feet will be forever grateful.

Day 45
October 31, 2006
Triple Lake Trails Marathon
Greensboro, North Carolina
Elevation: 15'
Weather: 71 degrees; partly cloudy
Time: 4:18:12
Net calories burned: 143,415
Number of runners: 55

A friend of mine, Kevin Paulk, heads up the Advanced Design team at Nike Running. Basically, he and his team create footwear designs for three to five years in the future. Talk about a fun job! Several years ago, Kevin invited me to visit his office at the Nike headquarters and discuss ideas for innovative new running shoes with his team. During the meeting, Kevin showed me all kinds of cool designs and prototypes for shoe technologies that would provide more cushioning, more stability—more, more, more. After seeing all this stuff, however, I started to wonder if perhaps *less* could be *more.*

"Have you ever thought about going in the other direction?" I asked.

"What do you mean?" said Kevin.

"I mean taking stuff away from running shoes instead of adding more stuff to them. Let's face it: Humans are really designed to run barefoot. I realize that's not practical for most runners today, but couldn't you still design a shoe that allows us to run more like we do *without* shoes? My stride never feels more natural than when I run barefoot on the beach sometimes. What about developing a shoe that just lets your foot be, well, *a foot?*"

"Yes, as a matter of fact I have thought about that," Kevin said, "and I agree with you. I think we should look at the possibility of moving in the other direction by taking away things instead of adding more."

A few years after that meeting, Nike launched a shoe called the Free. A minimalist, barefoot-like running shoe, the Nike Free allowed the foot to be the foot better than any other running shoe I'd ever seen. Although I was now affiliated with the North Face running project, I have to admit that I was very impressed with the Nike Free. I called Kevin and asked him how much influence our meeting several years back had had in the development of the shoe. He chuckled.

"I could tell you," he said, "but I'd have to kill you."

My loyalty to The North Face notwithstanding, I believe that the Nike Free is a truly revolutionary piece of footwear and a representation of the future of running shoes. It's not the only minimalist running shoe on the market, though. Others have entered the race. Most of these shoes have deep grooves in their soles that help make them extremely flexible, allowing all the tiny muscles and bones of the foot to work naturally, unlike conventional running shoes. When your feet can function as they were designed to do during running, they absorb impact forces better and make a bigger contribution to forward thrust. Also, the minimal heel cushioning of this type of running shoe encourages a more natural midfoot landing, which can help to reduce injury and enhances the stability and efficiency of the stride.

As much as I like and appreciate minimalist running shoes, I would never go so far as to suggest that they'll definitely work for you. I know of runners who have tried the Free and developed transient plantar fasciitis and other strains, forcing them to go back to their conventional shoes. It's best to operate without any preconceived ideas about what a running shoe should be in your search for the perfect footwear for you. Try lots of models, experiment with different styles, and learn as you run.

If you're an ultrarunner logging big miles, a minimalist running shoe is unlikely to be your best choice. You'll probably fare better with something more durable, like the North Face

> ## Minimalist Running Shoes
>
> Running shoes that are lightweight, flexible, and light on cushioning and stability features allow the foot to function more naturally during running. Here's a selection of minimalist footwear for runners:
>
> - Adidas ZX Racer
> - ASICS GEL-Piranha
> - Nike Free 3.0
> - Nike Waffle Racer
> - Puma H. Street
> - Vibram Five Fingers (not a shoe at all, actually; more like a glove for the foot)

Arnuva 50 Boa shoes I wore throughout the Endurance 50. (I went through five pairs of them, by the way.) Wisely, in developing their running shoe line, The North Face did not seek to compete directly against the major manufacturers for the masses, such as Nike and New Balance. Instead, their goal was to focus on the endurance category, something more consistent with the expedition heritage of the company.

It so happened that Mackey McDonald, chairman and CEO of VF, parent company of The North Face, came to witness marathon number forty-five of the Endurance 50 in North Carolina. He didn't have far to travel, because the company headquarters is right in Greensboro. After the marathon was completed, the runners, our crew, and my family went there for a luncheon with twelve hundred VF employees. Afterward, a ceremony was held, during which I was called on stage to accept a bronze shoe commemorating the Endurance 50 (it was an Arnuva 50 Boa) and a five-thousand-dollar donation to Karno's Kids, reaffirming the company's commitment to getting kids into the great outdoors.

I took Alexandria and Nicholas on stage with me to accept these honors. The whole time we were up there, Nicholas stared

at the bronze shoe with a look of unease that I did not understand at first. Later, as we made our way back to the tour bus to
prepare for the drive to Baltimore, Maryland, Nicholas voiced
his concern.

"Dad, do you really have to wear that?" he asked.

I chuckled. Poor kid had never seen a bronzed shoe before.

"No, Nicholas," I said.

"What is it?" he asked. I thought about his question.

"It's the perfect anti-Free," I answered with a smile.

CHAPTER 30

The Clock Is Running

Day 46
November 1, 2006
Baltimore Marathon
Baltimore, Maryland
Elevation: 95'
Weather: 75 degrees; sunny
Time: 3:49:40
Net calories burned: 146,602
Number of runners: 30 (filled to capacity, permits for only 30 runners)

They say that running saves lives. On Day 46 of the Endurance 50, it did so quite literally. We began the Baltimore Marathon with a police escort eleven strong. As our group was proceeding down a street just past the two-mile mark, one of the runners noticed smoke coming out of a second-story window in a building up ahead. By the time we reached the building, flames were erupting from the window and the heat from the fire reached us all the way down in the street. The police instructed us to dash ahead and wait at the next intersection. Then the officers broke down the door and rushed inside. They pulled three people out of the building, including a baby.

Eventually, the fire department arrived and began dousing the flames. The police turned the situation over to them and pulled back up to us, seemingly unfazed by the heroics they had performed just moments earlier.

I expressed to one of the officers how amazed we were by what they'd just done.

"They're lucky you guys happened to be running down this particular street, on this particular day, at this particular time," he said. "We rarely patrol this area."

The episode seemed surreal, like a dream, yet it's true, and its implications are undeniable: If the Endurance 50 hadn't been proceeding down this path at precisely this moment in time, there's no way the police could have responded as quickly. In a very direct sense today, running did save lives.

We started off again, a bit shaken but still intact. The Baltimore Marathon runs past some incredible places, including Fort McHenry, the birthplace of our national anthem. You actually see the cannons and the place where the harbor was bombed. As we ran by, I could envision Francis Scott Key watching, ". . . the rockets' red glare, the bombs bursting in air . . ."

At mile fifteen, as we passed through a rustic area of downtown, a local tavern was awaiting our arrival and had set up an aid station with water, Gatorade, and—get this—beer. About half the runners partook (several of the latter too). If you've got to get down the carbohydrates, I guess that's one way to do it.

The Baltimore Marathon finishes at historic Camden Yards. As we made our way down the final stretch, the streets were crowded with people watching us run by. Someone yelled, "Why are you running?" One of the runners yelled back, "Because we can." Everyone on the street cheered his response. Even though most of them were clearly not runners, I think they got the gist of his comeback.

At the finish, I spoke with a gentleman who was cramping a bit but absolutely gleaming. He had originally planned on doing the half, but decided at the midpoint to try the full marathon, and made it beautifully! I asked him if he had learned anything from the experience. "Yeah," he said, "I learned that limitations are between my ears." He went on, "I'd been putting off running a marathon for years. You know the excuses: work, family, other obligations, yada yada yada. I didn't have time. Well, today I made the time."

The past is the past, the future's uncertain, and today is a gift. That's why they call it the present.

I now spotted Julie walking across the parking lot and decided to seize the day in a different way.

"Psst," I whispered at her.

She turned and walked over. "Yes? Can I help you?" she responded playfully.

"Why don't the two of us quietly slip into the bus and explore the limits of human endurance?" I said.

"Here, in the parking lot, with all these people around?"

"Listen," I went on, "the boys have been romping around the countryside collecting phone numbers for forty-six days. When's your hubby gonna get a little lovin'?" I smiled my most winning smile.

She looked totally unconvinced.

"Carpe diem!" I shouted, thinking this proclamation would be the decisive battle cry.

"Nice try," she said. "That's Latin, and you're Greek. You just keep running, ultramarathon man. I'm heading out with your mom and Alexandria. Veni, vidi, Visa." She walked off with a wink.

I thought about what she said: I came, I saw, I . . . *shopped*? Yes, that was precisely it! I was left standing empty-handed while she headed off to the mall with my credit card. If that's not tough love, I don't know what is.

Day 47
November 2, 2006
Delaware Marathon
Wilmington, Delaware
Elevation: 73'
Weather: 59 degrees; partly cloudy
Time: 4:02:58
Net calories burned: 149,789
Number of runners: 50

Everyone is busy these days. Feeling constantly rushed and pressed for time is one of the hallmarks of our modern lifestyle. A steady increase in the amount of time we spend at work and in cars has put a major squeeze on the rest of the day. In fact, a recent national survey found that many workers are starting their morning commute earlier than they used to because of the terrible traffic congestion problems affecting almost every major city. Of course, waking up earlier means sleeping less, and the average American adult is sleeping less than ever. It's the only way to make time for all the things we need to accomplish in a day outside of working and sitting in cars: helping the kids with homework, doing laundry, preparing meals, paying bills, cleaning the house—and, oh yeah, running.

I suppose you could say that non-exercisers have an advantage over runners in the sense that workouts are just one more thing runners have to squeeze into their day—one more thing that non-exercisers, by definition, don't have to worry about. Finding time to run each day is a major challenge for many runners—especially those who, like me, have demanding careers and children at home. Meeting this challenge requires a great passion for running, plus discipline, sacrifice, and sometimes a little creativity as well.

Lack of time is the most often cited excuse for not exercising. Yet it is just that: an excuse. In reality, regular exercisers have no more free time than non-exercisers. Non-exercisers are simply more likely to devote their free time to other activities, such as watching television, playing video games, and surfing the Internet, instead of exercising. None of us has time to do everything we would like to do, so we conscientiously choose our priorities. When a person says, "I just don't have time to exercise," what that person essentially means is, *Exercise is not a high priority for me.* Though I think exercisers and non-exercisers both know this.

I used to think I managed time efficiently, until I met Martin Franklin. Martin is CEO of Jarden Corporation, a multibillion-

Better Than Nothing

Many runners operate with a tacit belief that if they don't have at least twenty-five or thirty minutes available to run, it's not even worth bothering to lace up their shoes. That's not true. An aggressive ten-minute run is worth the effort. You can burn more than 150 calories in a hard ten-minute run, which is also long enough to make a noticeable difference in terms of how you feel for the rest of the day. Plus, ten-minute blocks add up quickly. If you do a ten-minute run instead of saying "Aw, forget it" once every week, you will complete thirteen more hours of running over the course of a year—enough to prevent roughly four pounds of weight gain and to produce a measurable in- crease in your cardiovascular health and fitness.

dollar company that owns such familiar brands as Coleman and Mr. Coffee. Needless to say, that's a busy job. Martin is also an attentive husband, devoted father, and committed philanthro- pist. On top of that, he is an accomplished marathoner, ultrama- rathoner, and Ironman triathlete. Martin manages to do it all, and is living proof that a person *can* do it all.

How, exactly, do folks like Martin make it work? First, they prioritize what's important to them, realizing that nobody can have it all. As a former boss once said to me, "You can have any- thing you want, you just can't have *everything* you want." Second, they make sacrifices. I, personally, have absolutely zero social life. None. I don't go to bars or restaurants, or even to the movies anymore. My life consists of family and training, in that order. Until someone figures out how to put twenty-eight hours in the day, something's got to give. Sacrifices must be made. Lastly, high achievers don't make excuses. There is *always* time to exercise, and they take it upon themselves to make the time. No excuses.

Of course, discipline also helps. If you plan ahead, budget your time, and avoid distractions, you will have a much better

Running at Home

Treadmills offer a great solution for busy runners who struggle to squeeze workouts into their day. If the only free time you have is before the sun comes up or after it goes down, a home treadmill allows you to train without having to run in the dark. If you have small children at home, making it difficult or impossible to leave home to run sometimes, you can watch your kids and run at the same time with a home treadmill. A well-built treadmill for home use costs fifteen hundred to three thousand dollars. They're not cheap, but if it keeps you going, it's well worth the price.

chance of accomplishing everything you wish to accomplish in a day—including your run. Our team relied heavily on disciplined time management throughout the Endurance 50. Each day's marathon was scheduled to begin at 8:00 AM. It was important that the events begin on time, not only because the participants expected them to, but also because we promised the local officials at each venue that we would not tie up their roads, police support, and other resources after a certain hour, and because we had to allow time to pack up the Finish Festival in the afternoon and drive to the next marathon location in the evening. So we had our morning routine worked out with military precision.

My alarm went off at six o'clock on mornings when I did not have a blood draw, five o'clock on mornings when I had to get poked. My running clothes, foot lube, and other necessary items had been laid out the night prior for easy access. By seven o'clock I was on the bus, eating my breakfast, and perhaps doing interviews over the phone. If there were any interviews scheduled to take place at the starting area, we made sure to budget time for them.

As the poet Robert Burns said, however, the best-laid plans of mice and men often go awry. Believe me, the best-laid plans

Never Too Busy

Here are some other tips to maintain a consistent running regimen despite a busy schedule:

- *Plan ahead.* Make a habit of knowing when and where you will run tomorrow before you go to bed each night. Set your alarm clock, and stick with the plan.
- *Stay on schedule.* In addition to planning your running opportunities, you might find it useful to create a schedule for your entire day. This will help ensure that your other daily activities don't spill over into the time slot you had reserved for your running.
- *Do what works for you.* Consider all options when trying to determine your best running opportunities. Late-night and predawn runs can be invigorating.
- *Don't be afraid.* Many runners fear that running will sabotage their careers or lead to social ostracization at work or elsewhere. In my experience, however, people actually respect the discipline and commitment required to make these sacrifices.
- *Use teamwork.* Building relationships with other runners is another great way to reduce the frequency with which you find yourself "too busy to run."
- *Multitask.* One great way to save time is to try to accomplish something else while you run. For example, you can literally *run* short errands—to the post office, to the bank, to the market, or wherever.
- *Be flexible and opportunistic.* Creating plans and schedules will certainly reduce the number of running opportunities you miss, though it will not eliminate them. Try to be flexible and adaptable, and seize on gaps in your schedule to get a quick run in. That way, if something unexpected disrupts your normally scheduled run, you don't feel stressed about missing a workout. (And if something unexpected doesn't disrupt your normally scheduled run, you can get in *two* workouts that day!)

of the Endurance 50 went awry more than once. Still, the show always went on. In Minnesota, there had been an electrical fire in the hotel we were staying at, and the building was evacuated in the middle of the night. The fuse box that caught fire happened to be right next to my room. Just this morning, we were delayed leaving for the start by a bomb scare. It was unnerving, to say the least. All we could do was try to remain calm and hope that we were not to be blown to smithereens. We weren't, so we kept going.

Don't get discouraged if you get waylaid by unforeseen events, whether it's a meeting running late, a fire in your hotel room, or a bomb scare. Never write off the run! Deal with the setback and remain steadfast. Despite the obstacles you face daily, apply the universal logic that's gotten me through a midlife crisis and through other, more imminent, stressors (like an explosive device about to detonate within close proximity): *When all else fails, start running.*

CHAPTER 31

Adapt and Thrive

Day 48
November 3, 2006
Philadelphia Marathon
Philadelphia, Pennsylvania
Elevation: 45'
Weather: 57 degrees; partly cloudy
Time: 3:57:17
Net calories burned: 152,976
Number of runners: 50

---

began to entertain some wistfully retrospective thoughts about the Endurance 50 before it even ended. When we rolled into Philadelphia for marathon forty-eight, I suddenly realized that the crew and I would awaken from this crazy dream in fewer than seventy-two hours. While I was looking forward to completing the mission and moving on with my life, I also knew that I would face a post-event comedown in relinquishing our amazing voyage to the past. Anticipating the perspective that my mind would soon have on the whole Endurance 50—that of fond memories and affectionate recollections of adventure—I naturally found myself reminiscing on the many highs and lows of the preceding forty-seven days.

In remembering the first few marathons, I was struck by how differently we had operated then compared with now. We fumbled and bumbled like the Keystone Cops during the first week, whereas lately the Endurance 50 crew had functioned with the efficiency and precision of a highly trained production unit. Our early Finish Festivals had been especially chaotic.

Their physical layout was completely non-intuitive and confusing to everyone, including our own staff. Nobody was in charge—the events seemed to drift along rudderless in no particular direction.

The problem was that the Finish Festivals had been designed before the Endurance 50 began, when we didn't have a clear understanding of what things would *really* be like. When our great expedition got rolling, those of us charged with executing the plan quickly discovered that it needed modification. Knowing we would never survive fifty days unless changes were made, we created a new Finish Festival layout with a more natural flow, which helped everybody in the end. Things improved even further when Hopps stepped forward to create a more formal post-race ceremony that brought a satisfying closure to each event, whereas previously it had just sort of dissolved. This is but one example of the many ways in which the Endurance 50 evolved in response to specific problems and challenges that threatened our mission.

Adaptability is also critical to success in running. Each runner is unique. There is no single formula for running success that works equally well for everyone. Some runners are naturally speedy and struggle to build endurance; others are the opposite. Some runners are injury-resistant, others are injury-prone. Some runners recover quickly from hard workouts while others take longer.

To continually improve as a runner, try to really tune in to how your body responds to training and continuously evolve your training methods accordingly. When you're a beginner, the best you can do is follow one-size-fits-all training guidelines obtained from a coach, a book, or a more experienced runner. As you do so, however, you are sure to discover that they don't always meet all your individual needs. Eventually, these general methods will need to be modified and tweaked to better fit your personal goals and approach. As Charles Darwin has written, "It is not the strongest of the species that survives, nor the most intelligent, but the one most responsive to change."

As your running progresses and evolves, try to never lose sight of running for the sheer enjoyment of running. When I watch the elite African runners, one thing that strikes me—beyond their incredible athletic talent—is that they always seem to be smiling and laughing. Could there be a connection between their smiles and their speed? Perhaps so. Kids sometimes ask me who the best runner is. "The best runner," I tell them, "is the one who's having the most fun."

If you enjoy running, if you embrace it as a priority in your life as important as any other, you are sure to keep it up and will probably even excel in your racing, if that's the path you wish to follow. As the former marathon world-record holder Ian Thompson once said, "When I am running well I am happy, and when I am happy I am running well."

The worst thing that can happen to a runner—besides injury—is burnout. How do you avoid burnout? That's easy: Do what you love. "Every run is a great run!" said Sasha Azevedo, film star and runner.

Finally, don't be afraid to celebrate your quirkiness as a runner. Yeah, we do something that a lot of people view as a minor form of torture, but so what? We also do a lot of zany and wacky things that only us runners can relate to, like peeing in a shrub during a desperate moment, changing in the backseat of a car, or wearing a pair of running shoes to a social function. Sure, you might get some strange looks; probably some envious ones, too. With all the running you've been doing, you're probably not such a bad sight to behold, sneakers and all! Wear your runner's stigma like a badge of honor. Take pride in the fact that you are a little different, perhaps even a little eccentric, and enjoy every step of the way. Yes, you are a runner, and running is life—the rest is just details.

The Philadelphia Marathon was another incredible, and entertaining, event. As we ran along the Schuylkill River on the path to the finish at Philadelphia's famous Museum of Art, one of the runners, a first-time marathoner who up to this point had looked pretty darn strong, started huffin' and puffin' loudly.

Attack Your Weakness

One of the best ways to adapt your training for improved performance is to identify and attack a weak link in your fitness. Most runners have a clear sense of their greatest fitness weakness. Usually it's one of three things: lack of speed, lack of endurance, or lack of race fitness (or the ability to sustain faster speeds for prolonged periods of time). For me, unfortunately, it's sometimes all three. What are your fitness weaknesses?

Addressing a fitness weakness is simple. If your primary weakness is lack of speed, include more high-intensity intervals in your future training. This might come at the expense of duration (going faster for a shorter distance) in the short term, but building speed may boost your cardiovascular fitness to such a degree that your endurance ultimately gets a lift as well. If your primary weakness is lack of endurance, include more long endurance workouts in your future training. Maybe try dual daily workouts to achieve this end. Running twice a day sometimes makes it easier to build your endurance. And if your primary weakness is lack of race fitness, a great way to work on this quality is to include shorter-distance races as training runs. For instance, if you're training for a half-marathon, sign up for some 10k races beforehand to build your race fitness. If your goal is a marathon, enter a couple of half-marathons beforehand as fast training runs.

"You all right?" I asked him.

"All I wanna do is go the distance," he said in a thick Philly accent.

A bunch of the others burst out laughing. At first, the line flew right over my head. Upon further reflection, however, I recognized the voice he had impersonated so well. It had to be a line from *Rocky*.

When we crossed the finish line, in a respectable sub-four-hour time, I caught the context of the jokester's reference. We were at the base of the steps to the Philadelphia Museum of Art, the ones Rocky Balboa ran up when training for his big title bout. The imprint of Rocky's feet is visible in the cement at the top of the stairs; there's even a larger-than-life statue of the "Italian Stallion" in front of the museum.

If there ever was an individual who adapted and improved over time, Rocky was that guy. Now in its sixth new release (*Rocky VI*) over a thirty-year span, the "Greatest Underdog of Our Time" has definitely *gone the distance.*

After wrapping up the Finish Festival, and of course taking some snapshots in front of the Rocky statue, we headed into Manhattan for a *Runner's World* gala, called Heroes of Running, in which I had been asked to present ultrarunning legend Tim Twietmeyer with an award. Tim is a remarkable example of a runner who has gracefully adapted his running to time's changes. Tim has shifted his focus from speed to longevity. Shortly before the Endurance 50 started, he earned a record twenty-fifth Silver Buckle for a sub-twenty-four-hour Western States 100 finish. It was an honor to present this award to Tim, who remains one of my all-time heroes, and the evening was a regal affair. To be honest, I felt really awkward wearing a suit and being thrust into that formal setting after forty-eight straight days of running and road-tripping across the United States. It must have shown, because for the toast the hostess brought me a shot of Gatorade.

Day 49
November 4, 2006
New Jersey Marathon
Long Branch, New Jersey
Elevation: 5'
Weather: 58 degrees; sunny
Time: 4:09:02
Net calories burned: 156,863
Number of runners: 250

The field of participants for the New Jersey Marathon was capped at fifty. Two hundred fifty runners showed up at the starting line. If this had happened on the second day of the Endurance 50 instead of the second to last day, we would have imploded. Now we were so much better at expecting the unexpected and adapting as necessary that we were hardly fazed.

Koop and Garrett immediately foresaw potential problems in fueling and supporting five times the number of expected runners and made a smart on-the-fly decision. Instead of attempting the impossible task of trying to serve all these participants out the window of the SAG wagon, Koop and Garrett shot ahead and dumped off supplies at aid stations farther along the course, then continued shuttling supplies to these aid stations throughout the event. (Yes, we actually had aid stations set up for this event because of the number of people.) Smart move on their part.

This final re-created marathon was both beautiful and melancholy. It was the perfect day for running, crisp and cool, and the course paralleled the seashore for a stretch, the waves crashing brilliantly in the background. The spirit and liveliness of the crowd was remarkable, everybody smiling and joking as we ran, seemingly understanding that this was the first, and perhaps last, "re-created" marathon they might ever run. Some wore costumes. One guy ran in a blue tuxedo; another, Larry the Lighthouse, covered the full 26.2 miles inside a ten-foot-tall lighthouse costume.

There was lots of local pride in the air. A husky guy with a New Jersey accent running alongside me asked, "Hey, Ultramarathon Man, what's been your favorite marathon?"

I turned to see a big, thick Jersey boy who looked more like a linebacker than a runner. "Favorite marathon?" I said, "Why, this one, of course."

"Good," he shot back gruffly. "If you didn't say that, I'd have to break your legs."

A Marathon Fueling Tip

Protein matters. The addition of protein in your fuel during endurance exercise has been shown to delay fatigue, speed muscle recovery, and enhance rehydration. The ideal ratio of carbs to protein seems to be in the 4:1 range. Several sports beverages now include protein along with carbohydrate, which is a good thing, because they're easier to ingest than solid foods, especially while running. Look for those products that have a 4:1 ratio of carbs to protein.

When the finish came, I didn't want to stop. I was having too much fun. We were all having too much fun. We had just clicked off a 4:09 marathon and it didn't even feel like we'd been running. The finish, however, was a mob scene on an order we hadn't yet encountered. There were simply too many people and not enough Endurance 50 team members to go around—sheer chaos. I knew it was going to take a long time to get to everyone in line, and I hoped they would be patient with me.

I started signing things and taking pictures as quickly as possible, without being disrespectful to anyone. But I could sense my crew getting restless very early on. Hopps, in particular, started suggesting that I should wrap things up shortly. This was uncharacteristic of him. Yes, it was going to be tiring to get to everyone, but I was damn well going to. These people had come out to join me and to support the endeavor and what it stood for; it was the least I could do to make an extra effort to spend some one-on-one time with each of them.

Hopps became more forceful, now insisting that we leave. What was he thinking? There were still hundreds of people waiting. We couldn't just up and go. Then Koop came up behind me and spoke.

"Karno, it's time to go." His tone was emphatic.

Something was up; I just wasn't sure what. As Hopps announced to the crowd that I had to leave and ushered me off toward the bus, my heart was broken. I felt as though I'd just deserted family. Seeing the disappointed looks on people's faces as we left crushed me. For the first time, on this second to last day, I felt as though the Endurance 50 might have become a victim of its own success.

CHAPTER 32

The Home Stretch

Day 50
New York City Marathon
New York, New York
Elevation: 95'
Weather: 68 degrees; sunny
Time: 3:00:30
Net calories burned: 160,004
Number of runners: 38,000

was peeved and grumpy as I settled into a seat on the tour bus for a relatively short drive from Long Branch, New Jersey, into Manhattan. My body felt remarkably good: strong and fit. But the cumulative exhaustion of seven hard weeks of travel and nonstop obligations had hollowed out my mind and spirit, leaving only a brittle shell of emotional stability outside, and the unfortunate manner in which today's Finish Festival had ended had now shattered that shell.

As we drove, Hopps informed me that instead of traveling directly to the hotel in Manhattan to meet up with my family and celebrate the last night of the most amazing adventure of my life, I would have to make a detour to the New York City Marathon Expo and sign autographs at a booth operated by The North Face's biggest East Coast customer for two hours.

"No way, Hopps!" I protested, my blood boiling. "Is that why you guys pulled me out of there?"

"I know it's a drag," Hopps said. "But this is the last one. Two hours and you're free."

"Flannery's behind this, isn't he?" I said. Hopps just nodded. I was referring, of course, to Joe Flannery, vice president of marketing for the The North Face, without whom this amazing adventure would not have happened, but toward whom I was not feeling particularly brotherly at the moment.

Two minutes later, I was shouting at Joe on my cell phone. It was my first, and really only, emotional discharge of the entire event. I told Joe I would not—could not—make the appearance, and he couldn't make me. I read him the riot act. I wasn't going to the marathon expo. I was over it, I needed a break. I was going to the hotel to be with my family. My decision was final.

Half an hour later, I was at the marathon expo. The factor that tipped my hand was the thought of all the runners who might make special efforts to go where others had promised I would be, only to discover that I was a no-show. It was unfair that I hadn't been told anything about this scheduled appearance until after completing marathon forty-nine in New Jersey, but it would be even more unfair if I were to bail on anyone who might be waiting. And as it turned out, there were some three hundred people waiting. I signed and took photos as quickly as I could, but when the expo closed, more than half of these folks were still waiting. Some of them charged forward when they heard the announcement that the expo was closing, and I quickly found myself surrounded by an agitated throng of people all requesting something of me at once.

My nerves were frazzled when I finally made my way toward the exit. I felt like I needed to spend twenty-four hours alone on a mountaintop rather than run another marathon. But within twenty minutes, the lowest moment of the Endurance 50 gave way to the highest when I reached the hotel and reunited with my family—including my brother, his wife, and their kids, who had flown in from Southern California—and the complete Endurance 50 crew, including support staff from The North Face's home office and the other sponsors. All my family and best friends were waiting there, cheering and toasting my arrival. Instantly my extreme mental fatigue gave way to streaming tears of joy and laughter. It was an emotional roller coaster on the order of nothing I had ever experienced before.

We had reserved a block of adjoining rooms on the same floor, as at a wedding, and we celebrated as though we were at a Greek Easter party. We had food delivered to the rooms and flung open all the doors between them so everyone could hang out together. Kids ran up and down the hallways, music blared, and laughter rang out continuously. A football materialized and Omar, an Endurance 50 crew member who had done heavy setup and takedown work, taught Nicholas how to perform "bed dives"—diving from one bed to the next to catch a ball thrown in between. Chaos erupted everywhere. Finally, I felt like I was in my element.

When we finally got to bed, it was past one in the morning. My alarm sounded three hours later. By four forty-five, I was sitting aboard a bus that delivered its nervous, carbo-loaded passengers to Staten Island, where the New York City Marathon begins. Although the main field doesn't start until 10:10 AM, the Verrazano-Narrows Bridge closes at 7:30, requiring runners to arrive very early and kill a lot of time in the marathon staging area at Fort Wadsworth.

I had hoped to find a nice quiet nook to nap in, but instead I bumped into Arkansas governor Mike Huckabee and some other familiar faces, and we chatted away over coffee and energy bars. The race organizers had given me the official race number 50, because it was my fiftieth consecutive marathon, and they had given Governor Huckabee the official race number 110, because he had shed 110 pounds since becoming a marathoner. He told me how inspirational it was to be standing next to someone who had completed fifty consecutive marathons, and I told him how inspirational it was to be standing next to someone who had lost 110 pounds.

"I think it's actually a hundred and nine pounds," he said. "I'm hoping to drop one more during this marathon."

Pre-Marathon Don'ts

Here are five things you should try to avoid doing on the morning of a marathon or other long running event:

1. Don't spend too much time on your feet. Standing around will make your legs feel stiff and heavy in the first few miles.
2. Don't overhydrate. There's little to be gained from guzzling excessive volumes of fluid during the last hour before a marathon. Doing so will only cause you to make time-consuming pit stops during your run.
3. Don't sleep in. It takes at least two hours for the body to achieve an internal state that is conducive to optimal running performance after waking up.
4. Don't skip breakfast. It's important that you top off your body's carbohydrate fuel stores following the overnight fast. Even if pre-race nerves make food unappealing, at least have something small and easy to consume, like a banana or a bottle of Ensure.
5. Don't forget to warm up, especially if it's cold. Your body's systems work better when they're warm. Do a little light jogging and stretching to get the blood flowing and help bring your core body temperature up. It was my fastest yet.

"Well, to be honest, I've only run forty-nine marathons, and I'm hoping for one more during this marathon myself," I shot back.

We toasted our respective goals with our coffees and stood there shivering in the morning cool, waiting to be herded up to the starting area.

At last the race officials called our army-size gathering to the start area. In the corral reserved for those expected to run 2:45 or faster, I spotted Lance Armstrong, running his first marathon after winning his seventh Tour de France and retiring from professional cycling the previous year. A throng of celebrity pacers, including three-time New York City Marathon winner Alberto Salazar, surrounded him. *That's the first and last I'll see of Lance today*, I thought.

The gun sounded, the crowd pulsed forward, and marathon fifty was under way. I settled into a groove at roughly seven minutes per mile as the parade of runners marched through the streets of Brooklyn. The New York City Marathon is remarkable not just due of the sheer number of people involved—along with the thirty-eight thousand runners, there are two million spectators—but also because of the rich and diverse culture you experience along the way. One minute we were running through a Puerto Rican neighborhood with rowdy residents standing five-deep on the sidewalks, shouting in Spanish and English, waving flags and banners and blasting music. The next we were running through a Hasidic Jewish enclave, where bearded men in old-fashioned black suits and top hats stared at us in perfect silence.

Wearing the number 50 made me a bit of a target, and a few of the runners in my vicinity recognized me and struck up conversations. I greatly appreciated their interest in the Endurance 50 and their words of encouragement, though engaging in conversation while running seven-minute miles was challenging. By the time I reached the halfway point, just shy of the border between Brooklyn and Queens, I was more drained from yapping than from running.

"I'm going to try to catch my breath," I said to the runner who was next to me at the time. I quit talking and took a series of deep breaths, staying focused in the moment, just putting one foot in front of the other. I wouldn't allow the gravitational pull of the finish line to affect me just yet, even after forty-nine (and a half) consecutive marathons. There were still thirteen miles left to cover; anything could happen in that distance.

I was approaching the twenty-mile mark in the Bronx when I caught and passed my friend Dane, a gifted runner who looked strong despite the mounting heat.

Going the Distance

Before I started the Endurance 50, I wondered what would happen to my body over the course of fifty days of marathoning. Would I progressively break down and end up hobbling (or crawling) as the days wore on? Was I hurting my body?

The opposite turned out to be true. My body seemed to be growing stronger over the weeks. I was able to run faster, with less exertion, as the days progressed. The human body is a remarkably adaptive machine, and this final of fifty consecutive marathons was a telling indication of how the body responds to a physical load placed upon it over time. It was my fasest yet.

"Dude, Lance is only a few minutes ahead of you," he said, "and he's hurting. Go get him!"

My first thought was, *Lance who?* Then I remembered: Lance Armstrong! The thought of catching Lance didn't entice me all that much, though. All I really cared about was staying the course and not doing anything that might jeopardize the completion of the Endurance 50. Besides, making up several minutes with so little distance remaining wasn't likely.

On the other hand, I felt that I did have a nice little store of energy held in reserve after maintaining a calculated pace for the past twenty miles. So, against my better wisdom, I got a little careless and ran miles twenty through twenty-four at roughly 6:20 per mile, passing many more runners along the way, and answering some questions, too, including one in Italian via a running interpreter.

With two miles left to run, I suddenly realized that I hadn't eaten anything or consumed any liquid for the past thirteen miles. I'd been preoccupied in talking with people and hadn't remembered to refuel. To make such a rookie mistake now, after all that I'd been through, was comical. There was nothing I could do but laugh at myself and try to enjoy those last couple of miles, hungry and thirsty, yet smiling ear-to-ear.

Negative Splitting

My split time for the first half of the New York City Marathon was 1:30:31; for the second half it was 1:29:59—a so-called negative split. The term *negative splitting* refers to running the second half of a race faster than the first. Generally, you will run the best possible time in a marathon if you hold enough back in the first half so that you can run the second half faster—if only by a few seconds. It takes a little practice and a measure of discipline. It's tempting to go out fast in the first part of a race, when you're feeling strong, but if instead you concentrate on holding back and conserving energy, often you can turn in your best performances ever.

When I crossed the finish line, a race official came running over to me.

"That was remarkable!" he said. "You were less than a minute behind Lance!"

Finishing near Lance still didn't mean much to me. I was just glad to have finished in one piece, and perhaps beaten Oprah's marathon time.

Lance was standing off to the side catching his breath. He'd been a hero of mine for years and I really wanted to say hello, but he was surrounded by Nike people and VIPs and who-knows-who, so I didn't think it was appropriate.

Koop emerged from the crowd wearing a big smile and congratulated me on completing my dream. We shook hands victoriously. Over the past seven weeks the Endurance 50 had really become *our* dream.

"C'mon, Karno," he said, "let's go find your family."

We exited onto the crowded streets of Manhattan, which were packed tight with throngs of people as far as the eye could see in every direction. How were we possibly going to locate them in this mayhem? Koop pulled out his cell phone and dialed Julie. At precisely the same time, I heard another phone start to ring no more than ten yards away from where we stood. Looking in the direction of the sound, I saw Julie herself flipping open her phone to answer the call. I started screaming and ran over to her. My entire family was there, and we hugged each other in celebration, cherishing a moment that none of us will forget for the rest of our lives. The Endurance 50 had officially ended when I crossed that finish line in Central Park, but now it was eternally complete.

Well, sort of. There was still the final Finish Festival, press interviews, a signing and photo session, and a charity auction to complete.

Chris Carmichael made an appearance at the Finish Festival.

"I wonder how Lance is holding up to all this stuff," I mused.

"Are you kidding?" Chris said. "I just got off the phone with him. He's sitting in his hotel room's Jacuzzi tub drinking champagne."

Man, Lance is faster than me and *he's smarter than me,* I chuckled to myself.

That evening, The North Face threw a large and lavish party celebrating our successful completion of the Endurance 50. I was pretty tired at that point, but it's amazing what a room filled with your favorite people can do to restore your energy.

Also, I had to get to Garrett to hear the outcome of the boys' mission. He explained that there had been some dicey and desperate moments along the way—one number being obtained at the counter of a fast-food joint, and another in front of a corner liquor store on a drive-by—but they had remained steadfast and determined, and had successfully completed their mission: fifty states, fifty days, fifty phone numbers! Just like my running quest, it hadn't always been pretty, but they got the job done.

We toasted their success and danced and shared other stories about the amazing journey we'd all just been through. Laughter and merriment were shared by all. The Endurance 50 experience had been beyond my most faraway expectations. In a world that sometimes seemed so divided and war-torn, here was an event that brought people together in a beautiful and harmonious way. There was something enchanting, almost magical, about it, an incredible power that touched everyone involved. I felt like the luckiest man alive to have been along for the ride.

Yet as the evening wore on, my mind drifted farther and farther from my immediate environment. A tangled knot of confusion was growing inside me. I'd felt tinges of this emotion for some time, but now it was a raging torrent.

Yes, it was over. But for me, as for so many runners, there really are no finish lines. Runs end; running doesn't.

As I stood there surrounded by family and friends, all celebrating the completion of an extraordinary undertaking, a single thought kept repeating in my head: *What now?*

Run Away

Many people asked me what I was going to do after running fifty marathons. I laughingly told them the next Endurance 50 would consist of "Fifty couches, fifty pizzas, fifty beers." But that was just a joke to buy some time. In my mind I was asking myself the very same question.

The first day of my post–Endurance 50 life began with another five o'clock wake-up followed by interview after interview, for ESPN, the *Today* show, *Late Night with Conan O'Brien*, and ABC News, among others. When I was finally deposited back at my hotel that evening, I felt like crap. Not physically. Emotionally. I was all alone for the first time in a long time. My family had flown back home to the West Coast. After all, it was a Monday, and school, work, heck, life went on. The Endurance 50 team—who had become my extended family—had returned to their respective homes as well.

I sat in my empty hotel room pondering life. Something was wrong. Something was missing. So I decided to do what I always do when I feel this way: go for a run. I ran from my hotel to Central Park and traced the original New York City Marathon course, running 28.5 miles in total. There were lots of runners and bikers out, and the weather was very warm and dry for this time of year.

Also, for the first time in more than seven weeks, I ran solo. After nearly two months of running exactly the same distance, at exactly the same time of day, on predetermined routes in the company of other runners, I set my own course once again. It felt good, rejuvenating. It brought me back to the roots of what I love, running for the pure joy of running.

I couldn't sleep that night. I tossed and turned in a cold sweat until dawn slowly crept over a clouded Manhattan sky. Over the past fifty days, I had experienced some of the most glorious moments of my life; now I was experiencing one of the darkest. *What now?* I kept asking myself. *What now?*

Rain was falling as I checked out of my hotel. It was Tuesday, two days after the New York City Marathon. The bellman waved good-bye with a quizzical look at the baby carriage I was pushing. This carriage—which held a few spare clothes, snacks, and some other bare necessities—was my new support crew, my new tour bus, and my new SAG wagon. I started running. For the people who had asked what I was going to do after running fifty marathons, I now had an answer: I was going running.

Three days later, I was making my way into Philadelphia. I'd been sleeping in parks, eating from street vendors as I ran, asking directions from people standing on random corners along the way. There had been one minor oversight in all the planning: No one had booked me a return flight from New York to San Francisco. So I decided to run instead. Yeah, sounds crazy I know, but on a whim I was running across the country, and it felt pretty good; liberating, actually. After fifty days of knowing precisely where I needed to be at every second, now I had no idea where I needed to be at all. All I knew was that I needed to head west, plain and simple. Just head toward the setting sun and enjoy the run. New York City was on one side of the country, San Francisco on the other; eventually I'd hit it.

I ran all day, and sometimes all night. One day I covered more than sixty miles. Another day—during a severe snow-storm—I covered fewer than thirty. Mostly, I averaged about forty-five or fifty. For a month straight I ran, over mountains, through cornfields, across plains, between cities both large and small. I began running as soon as I awoke in the morning, and stopped when I got tired at night.

Sometimes other runners would come out and find me along the roadside and we would run together; other times I would run alone. Many kind folks out in the countryside stopped to offer a ride, and some even returned with a home-cooked meal. It was all good, except that I missed my family dearly. Not a day, and eventually not a minute, passed without my thinking about them.

One day I crossed the Mississippi River. After thirteen hundred miles of running since departing New York City, I had reached Missouri. A fairly large group of other runners came out and found me there, and a healthy pack of us made our way through quiet back roads. In the early afternoon, we entered a footpath. The path meandered along serenely through the outskirts of town. I vaguely recognized this place; the surroundings seemed familiar. Rounding a curve in the path, it hit me. The memories came flooding in.

Ninety days and a lifetime of experiences ago, I had stood at this very spot. We had stumbled upon the starting line of the Lewis & Clark Marathon, the first stop on my fifty-marathon odyssey. Back then, the trees were full with green leaves and there were thousands of runners lining up; now the trees were brown and barren, having lost their leaves, and just a handful of us jogged along reflectively.

It struck me in the span of several strides that I had run from the finish line of the last of the fifty marathons in New York City to the start of the first marathon in St. Charles, Missouri. Since leaving New York on my journey home, I'd covered roughly the equivalent of another fifty marathons to reach this point. In a strange yet serendipitous way, the circle now seemed complete. San Francisco was still many miles away, but as I passed over this spot in Missouri, I felt an overwhelming sense of contentment.

In a weird, almost Forrest Gump–esque moment, I stopped, turned to the group of runners who surrounded me, and said, "I miss my family. I think I'll go home now."

At first, there were only confused stares. Then someone spoke. "That sounds like a good idea to me."

Others chimed in, and soon there was a chorus of approval. Yes, they were right: Going home to my family was indeed a good idea. I thanked them for running with me, and also for their support and wisdom. We exchanged a few quick hugs and high fives, and just like that it was all over. And this time it felt *really* over.

They say all good things must come to an end. I guess the same holds true for all good runs. For a guy who's never quite sure when to stop, this time I was. I tipped my head to the group with a wink, turned for the airport, and called it a run.

Editor's Note

As this book was going to press, Dean was busy working on his next big adventure. Yes, all good runs must come to an end—at least until the beginning of the next one.

How Do You Train to Run Fifty Consecutive Marathons?

Along with traditional mileage training, one way is to use races as training runs. Below is a lineup of the races I completed in the six-month period leading up to the Endurance 50:

Date: March 18, 2006
Event: LA Marathon plus five miles to start and five miles back
Miles for That Day: 36.2

Date: April 1, 2006
Event: American River 50, Sacramento
Miles for That Day: 50

Date: April 2, 2006
Event: Whidbey Island Marathon, Washington
Miles for That Day: 26.2

Date: April 8, 2006
Event: The Relay, Calistoga, California
Miles for That Day: 120

Date: April 16, 2006
Event: Boston Marathon out-and-back
Miles for That Day: 52.4

Date: April 30, 2006
Event: Big Sur International Marathon out-and-back
Miles for That Day: 52.4

Date: May 6, 2006
Event: Miwok 100k, Marin Headlands, California
Miles for That Day: 62

Date: June 4, 2006
Event: Rock 'n' Roll Marathon San Diego, plus 65-mile run to start
Miles for That Day: 91.2

Date: June 10, 2006
Event: Diablo 50k, Clayton, California
Miles for That Day: 31

Date: June 24, 2006
Event: Western States 100, Squaw Valley, California
Miles for That Day: 100

Date: July 15, 2006
Event: Vermont 100 Mile, South Woodstock
Miles for That Day: 100

Date: July 24, 2006
Event: Badwater Ultramarathon, Death Valley
Miles for That Day: 135

Date: July 30, 2006
Event: San Francisco Marathon
Miles for That Day: 26.2

Date: August 6, 2006
Event: Skyline 50K, Castro Valley, California
Miles for That Day: 31

Date: August 19, 2006
Event: Leadville Trail 100, Colorado
Miles for That Day: 100

Endurance 50
Stats and Musings

Event / Endurance 50	
Duration / 50 Days	
Location / 50 States	
Total mileage run by Dean / 1,310	
Total mileage run by all participants / 3,791,035	
Total calories burned while running / 160,355	
Fastest marathon time (New York City Marathon) / 3:00:30	
Slowest marathon time (Tecumseh Trail Marathon) / 4:45:21	
Average marathon time / 3:53:14	
Hottest temperature (Arizona) / 104°F	
Coldest temperature (Alaska) / 38°F	
Greatest elevation gain (Tecumseh Trail Marathon) / 3,877'	
Smallest elevation gain (Mississippi Gulf Coast Marathon) / 40'	
Total heartbeats while running / 1,374,721	
Starting weight / 154	
Finish weight / 153	
Number of shoes / 5 Pairs	
Number of socks / 18 Pairs	
Number of lost toenails / 3	
Number of blisters / 2	
Longest drive / 12 Hours	
Shortest drive / 55 Minutes	
Average hours of sleep per night / 4½	

Beginner's Marathon-Training Plan

The following is a twenty-six-week training plan for first-time marathoners. It's appropriate for healthy individuals who are currently not running at all. If you're already running, you can still use the plan, but you may want to begin at some point after week one. I recommend that you begin with the first week in the schedule whose Sunday run is equal in distance to the longest run you've done within the past couple of weeks.

	MON.	TUE.	WED.	THURS.	FRI.	SAT.	SUN.
Week 1	Rest	Walk 20 min.	Rest	Walk 20 min.	Rest	Walk 20 min.	Walk 20 min.
Week 2	Rest	10x: walk 1 min., run 1 min.	Optional: Walk 20 min.	10x: walk 1 min., run 1 min.	Rest	10x: walk 1 min., run 1 min.	10x: walk 1 min., run 1 min.
Week 3	Rest	7x: walk 1 min., run 2 min.	Optional: Walk 20 min.	7x: walk 1 min., run 2 min.	Optional: Walk 20 min.	7x: walk 1 min., run 2 min.	7x: walk 1 min., run 2 min.
Week 4	Rest	5x: walk 1 min., run 3 min.	Optional: 10x, walk 1 min., run 1 min.	5x: walk 1 min., run 3 min.	Optional: 10x, walk 1 min., run 1 min.	5x: walk 1 min., run 3 min.	5x: walk 1 min., run 3 min.
Week 5	Rest	4x: walk 1 min., run 4 min.	Optional: 10x, walk 1 min., run 1 min.	4x: walk 1 min., run 4 min.	Optional: 10x, walk 1 min., run 1 min.	4x: walk 1 min., run 4 min.	4x: walk 1 min., run 5 min.
Week 6	Rest	Run 2 miles	Optional: 7x, walk 1 min., run 2 min.	Run 2 miles	Run 2 miles	Rest	Run 3 miles

	MON.	TUE.	WED.	THURS.	FRI.	SAT.	SUN.
Week 7	Rest	Run 3 miles	Optional: Run 2 miles	Run 2 miles	Run 3 miles	Optional: Run 2 miles	Run 4 miles
Week 8	Rest	Run 3 miles	Optional: Run 3 miles	Run 3 miles	Run 3 miles	Optional: Run 3 miles	Run 5 miles
Week 9	Rest	Run 4 miles	Optional: Run 3 miles	Run 4 miles	Run 3 miles	Optional: Run 3 miles	Run 6 miles
Week 10	Rest	Run 3 miles	Optional: Run 3 miles	Run 3 miles	Run 3 miles	Rest	Run 8 miles
Week 11	Rest	Run 4 miles	Optional: Run 4 miles	Run 4 miles	Run 4 miles	Optional: Run 4 miles	Run 9 miles
Week 12	Rest	Run 5 miles	Optional: Run 4 miles	Run 4 miles	Run 5 miles	Optional: Run 4 miles	Run 8 miles
Week 13	Rest	Run 5 miles	Optional: Run 4 miles	Run 4 miles	Run 5 miles	Optional: Run 4 miles	Run 10 miles
Week 14	Rest	Run 4 miles	Optional: Run 4 miles	Run 5 miles	Run 4 miles	Optional: Run 4 miles	Run 11 miles
Week 15	Rest	Run 4 miles	Optional: Run 4 miles	Run 4 miles	Run 4 miles	Optional: Run 4 miles	Run 9 miles
Week 16	Rest	Run 4 miles	Optional: Run 4 miles	Run 6 miles	Run 4 miles	Optional: Run 4 miles	Run 12 miles
Week 17	Rest	Run 5 miles	Optional: Run 4 miles	Run 4 miles	Run 5 miles	Optional: Run 4 miles	Run 13 miles
Week 18	Rest	Run 5 miles	Optional: Run 4 miles	Run 6 miles	Run 5 miles	Optional: Run 4 miles	Run 14 miles
Week 19	Rest	Run 4 miles	Optional: Run 4 miles	Run 5 miles	Run 5 miles	Optional: Run 4 miles	Run 9 miles
Week 20	Rest	Run 5 miles	Optional: Run 4 miles	Run 6 miles	Run 5 miles	Optional: Run 4 miles	Run 15 miles

	MON.	TUE.	WED.	THURS.	FRI.	SAT.	SUN.
Week 21	Rest	Run 5 miles	Optional: Run 4 miles	Run 6 miles	Run 6 miles	Optional: Run 4 miles	Run 16 miles
Week 22	Rest	Run 4 miles	Optional: Run 4 miles	Run 5 miles	Run 5 miles	Optional: Run 4 miles	Run 10 miles
Week 23	Rest	Run 6 miles	Optional: Run 4 miles	Run 6 miles	Run 6 miles	Optional: Run 4 miles	Run 18 miles
Week 24	Rest	Run 6 miles	Optional: Run 4 miles	Run 8 miles	Run 6 miles	Optional: Run 4 miles	Run 20 miles
Week 25	Rest	Run 5 miles	Optional: Run 4 miles	Run 6 miles	Run 6 miles	Optional: Run 4 miles	Run 12 miles
Week 26	Rest	Run 7 miles	Optional: Run 4 miles	Run 5 miles	Run 4 miles	Rest	Marathon!

APPENDIX D

Personal-Best Marathon-Training Plan

Following is an eighteen-week personal-best marathon training plan. This plan is not appropriate for many beginners, because it builds up to more than fifty miles of running in one week, including a fair amount of faster running. But if you've already run one or more marathons, or you're experienced at shorter distances, then this is a plan you could follow.

	MON.	TUE.	WED.	THURS.	FRI.	SAT.	SUN.
Week 1	Rest	Easy run: 4 miles	Easy run: 5 miles	Easy run: 4 miles	Easy run: 5 miles	Easy run: 3 miles	Long run: 7 miles
Week 2	Rest	Easy run: 4 miles	Easy run: 6 miles	Easy run: 4 miles	Easy run: 6 miles	Easy run: 4 miles	Long run: 9 miles
Week 3	Rest	Easy run: 6 miles	Easy run: 6 miles	Easy run: 4 miles	Easy run: 6 miles	Easy run: 5 miles	Long run: 11 miles
Week 4	Rest	Easy run: 4 miles	Easy run: 5 miles	Easy run: 4 miles	Easy run: 5 miles	Easy run: 3 miles	Long run: 8 miles
Week 5	Rest	Tempo run: 10 min. easy, 10 min. tempo, 10 min. easy	Easy run: 6 miles	Easy run: 4 miles	Easy run: 6 miles	Easy run: 5 miles	Long run: 13 miles
Week 6	Rest	Tempo run: 10 min. easy, 12 min. tempo, 10 min. easy	Easy run: 6 miles	Interval run: 1 mile easy, 4x 800m @ 5k pace w/ 2-min. jog recoveries, 1 mile easy	Easy run: 6 miles	Easy run: 5 miles	Long run: 15 miles

273

	MON.	TUE.	WED.	THURS.	FRI.	SAT.	SUN.
Week 7	Rest	Tempo run: 10 min. easy, 15 min. tempo, 10 min. easy	Easy run: 5 miles	Interval run: 1 mile easy, 5x 800m @ 5k pace w/ 2-min. jog recoveries, 1 mile easy	Easy run: 6 miles	Easy run: 5 miles	Long run: 17 miles
Week 8	Rest	Moderate run: 5 miles	Easy run: 6 miles	Easy run: 6 miles + 4x 100m uphill sprints	Easy run: 5 miles	Easy run: 4 miles	Long run: 12 miles
Week 9	Rest	Tempo run: 10 min. easy, 16 min. tempo, 10 min. easy	Easy run: 5 miles	Interval run: 1 mile easy, 6x 800m @ 5k pace w/ 2-min. jog recoveries, 1 mile easy	Easy run: 6 miles	Easy run: 5 miles	Long run: 18 miles
Week 10	Rest	Tempo run: 10 min. easy, 18 min. tempo, 10 min. easy	Easy run: 5 miles	Interval run: 1 mile easy, 3x 1 mile @ 10k pace w/ 2-min. jog recoveries, 1 mile easy	Easy run: 6 miles	Easy run: 5 miles	Long run: 20 miles
Week 11	Rest	Tempo run: 10 min. easy, 20 min. tempo, 10 min. easy	Easy run: 5 miles	Interval run: 1 mile easy, 4x 1 mile @ 10k pace w/ 2-min. jog recoveries, 1 mile easy	Easy run: 5 miles	Easy run: 4 miles	Goal-pace run: 4 miles easy, 8 miles @ goal pace
Week 12	Rest	Moderate run: 5 miles	Easy run: 6 miles	Easy run: 6 miles + 5x 100m uphill sprints	Easy run: 6 miles	Easy run: 5 miles	Long run: 22 miles

	MON.	TUE.	WED.	THURS.	FRI.	SAT.	SUN.
Week 13	Rest	Tempo run: 10 min. easy, 24 min. tempo, 10 min. easy	Easy run: 5 miles	Interval run: 1 mile easy, 4x 1 mile @ 10k pace w/ 2-min. jog recoveries, 1 mile easy	Easy run: 6 miles	Easy run: 7 miles	Goal-pace run: 4 miles easy, 10 miles @ goal pace
Week 14	Rest	Tempo run: 10 min. easy, 26 min. tempo, 10 min. easy	Easy run: 6 miles	Interval run: 1 mile easy, 5x 1 mile @ 10k pace w/ 2-min. jog recoveries. 1 mile easy	Easy run: 6 miles	Easy run: 5 miles	Long run: 15 miles
Week 15	Rest	Moderate run: 5 miles	Easy run: 6 miles	Easy run: 6 miles + 6x 100m up-hill sprints	Easy run: 5 miles	Easy run: 4 miles	Goal-pace run: 4 miles easy, 12 miles @ goal pace
Week 16	Rest	Tempo run: 10 min. easy, 30 min. tempo, 10 min. easy	Easy run: 4 miles	Interval run: 1 mile easy, 6x 1 mile @ 10k pace w/ 2-min. jog recoveries, 1 mile easy	Easy run: 6 miles	Easy run: 5 miles	Long run: 22 miles
Week 17	Rest	Tempo run: 10 min. easy, 20 min. tempo, 10 min. easy	Easy run: 6 miles	Interval run: 1 mile easy, 5x 1 mile @ 10k pace w/ 2-min. jog recoveries, 1 mile easy	Easy run: 6 miles	Easy run: 7 miles	Long run: 14 miles

	MON.	TUE.	WED.	THURS.	FRI.	SAT.	SUN.
Week 18	Rest	Tempo run: 10 min. easy, 10 min. tempo, 10 min. easy	Easy run: 5 miles	Interval run: 1 mile easy, 2x 1 mile @ 10k pace w/ 2-min. jog recoveries, 1 mile easy	Easy run: 4 miles	Rest	Marathon

The Results Are In:
How Dean Held Up

By Bryan Bergman, PhD,
University of Colorado Assistant Professor of Medicine
Carmichael Training Systems Pro Coach

Between the beginning and the end of the Endurance 50, Dean was subjected to ten blood draws and urinalysis. These blood samples were preserved and sent to a laboratory for analysis. The results were then sent to Carmichael Training Systems, where I analyzed them to determine the effect of running fifty marathons in fifty states in fifty days on various parameters of Dean's health, including muscle damage, hydration status, inflammation, and immune function. Below are summaries of our findings with respect to each of these factors.

Muscle Damage

We expected to see fairly dramatic increases in Dean's blood markers of muscle damage. The principal marker was creatine phosphokinase (CPK), an enzyme found principally inside muscle cells that leaks into the bloodstream when cells are damaged. A typical marathon runner has dramatically elevated CPK after one marathon, and it stays elevated for up to a week. Dean, however, is no typical marathoner. He had some muscle damage associated with the event. However, at his muscle damage high point, near the end of the Endurance 50, his CPK concentration was still one-fourth of what it would be for a typical runner completing only one marathon! This was a sur-

277

prise, but shows how well Dean's body has adapted to the demands of ultrarunning.

Hydration Status

Dean's hydration status was monitored rigorously throughout the Endurance 50. We followed several parameters, including the percentage of red blood cells to total blood volume (hematocrit), red blood cell counts per liter (red cell density), and concentration of hemoglobin (the oxygen-carrying protein in our blood). Despite having a crew supporting him and reminding him to stay hydrated during these events, Dean still showed signs of dehydration several times during the Endurance 50. However, this potential problem was quickly remedied with increased intake of sports drinks. His markers of dehydration status never stayed elevated for two or more consecutive blood draws in a row. These data point to the constant challenge of staying hydrated, even with a support team looking after you.

Inflammation

We also measured blood levels of an inflammatory marker called interleukin-6 (IL-6). IL-6 is a cytokine (a special type of white blood cell) that is receiving a lot of attention in the scientific world right now because of the link between inflammation and heart disease. We were interested in IL-6 for two reasons: (1) It is one marker of inflammation during an event in which we expect to see considerable amounts of inflammation, immune system activity, and stress; and (2) IL-6 appears to be involved in glucose production by the liver, as well as glucose uptake by muscles. Thus, tracking changes in IL-6 along with changes in resting metabolic rate and muscle fuel utilization would provide insight into the role of IL-6 in ultra-endurance events.

Much to our surprise, IL-6 concentrations did not change very much during this event. Dean is an elite ultra-endurance runner, and once again he appeared to be in much less physiological stress than would be expected from such an arduous event.

Immune Function

Many publications have pointed to an increased risk of upper respiratory tract infections and decreased immune system function after one marathon. Therefore, we expected Dean's immune system to be compromised during the Endurance 50. However, other than a probable viral infection during the first part of the event, we observed no changes in blood markers that would suggest a compromised immune system. We were also on the lookout for possible suppression of bone marrow red blood cell production that also can occur during periods of high stress. Dean's bone marrow continued to produce red blood cells throughout the event and showed no signs of slowing. Clearly, his body did not perceive this event to be as stressful as we expected!

Summary

Overall, Dean sailed through the Endurance 50, with none of the common ailments that plague the more typical athlete during one marathon, much less fifty. We were very surprised that fifty consecutive marathons were perceived to be so "easy" by his body. This is a testament to Dean's preparation and training, and shows us all what is possible when a very motivated and talented athlete sets his sights on a lofty goal.

References

Chapter 1. The Right Foot

Neilan TG, Januzzi JL, Lee-Lewandrowski E, Ton-Nu TT, Yoerger DM, Jassal DS, Lewandrowski KB, Siegel AJ, Marshall JE, Douglas PS, Lawlor D, Picard MH, Wood MJ. "Myocardial injury and ventricular dysfunction related to training levels among nonelite participants in the Boston Marathon." *Circulation.* 2006 Nov 28;114(22):2325–33. Epub 2006 Nov 13.

Chapter 6. United We Run

Linde K, Barrett B, Wölkart K, Bauer R, Melchart D. "Echinacea for preventing and treating the common cold." *Cochrane Database of Systematic Reviews.* 2006 Jan 25;(1):CD000530.

Chapter 8. Running Wild

Faoro V, Lamotte M, Deboeck G, Pavelescu A, Huez S, Guenard H, Martinot JB, Naeije R. "Effects of sildenafil on exercise capacity in hypoxic normal subjects." *High Altitude Medicine and Biology.* 2007 summer;8(2):155–63.

Chapter 15. The Heat Is On

Tucker R, Rauch L, Harley YX, Noakes TD. "Impaired exercise performance in the heat is associated with an anticipatory reduction in skeletal muscle recruitment." *European Journal of Physiology.* 2004 Jul;448(4):422–30. Epub 2004 May 8.

Byrne C, Lee JK, Chew SA, Lim CL, Tan EY. "Continuous thermoregulatory responses to mass-participation distance running in heat." *Medicine and Science in Sports and Exercise.* 2006 May;38(5):803–10.

Chapter 20. A Full Recovery
Roy BD, Luttmer K, Bosman MJ, Tarnopolsky MA. "The influence of post-exercise macronutrient intake on energy balance and protein metabolism in active females participating in endurance training." *International Journal of Nutrition and Exercise Metabolism.* 2002 Jun;12(2):172–88.

Hartman JW, Tang JE, Wilkinson SB, Tarnopolsky MA, Lawrence RL, Fullerton AV, Phillips SM. "Consumption of fat-free fluid milk after resistance exercise promotes greater lean mass accretion than does consumption of soy or carbohydrate in young, novice, male weightlifters." *American Journal of Clinical Nutrition.* 2007 Aug;86(2):373–81.

Chapter 23. The Long Run
Levy BR, Slade MD, Kasl SV. "Longitudinal benefit of positive self-perceptions of aging on functional health." *Journal of Gerontology.* 2002 Sep;57(5):P409–17.

Chapter 25. Running Green
Miller KA, Siscovick DS, Sheppard L, Shepherd K, Sullivan JH, Anderson GL, Kaufmann JD. "Long-term exposure to air pollution and incidence of cardiovascular events in women." *New England Journal of Medicine.* 2007 Feb 1;356(5):447–58.

Chapter 26. The Art of the Stride
Milner CE, Hamill J, Davis I. "Are knee mechanics during early stance related to tibial stress fracture in runners?" *Clinical Biomechanics.* 2007 Jul;22(6):697–703. Epub 2007 Apr 30.

Hasegawa H, Yamauchi T, Kraemer WJ. "Foot strike pattern of runners at the 15-km point during an elite level half mara-

thon." *Journal of Strength and Conditioning Research.* 2007
Aug;21(3):888–93.

Chapter 28. Second Wind

Kay D, Marino F, Cannon J, St. Clair Gibson A, Lambert MI, Noakes TD. "Evidence for neuromuscular fatigue during high-
intensity cycling in warm, humid conditions." *European
Journal of Applied Physiology.* 2001;84:115–21.

Chapter 31. Adapt and Thrive

Luden ND, Saunders MJ, Pratt CA, Bickford AS, Todd MK, Flohr
JA. "Effects of a six-day carbohydrate/protein intervention
on muscle damage, soreness and performance in runners."
Presented at the 2006 Annual Meeting of the American College of Sports Medicine.

Saunders MJ, Kane MD, Todd MK. "Effects of a carbohydrate-
protein beverage on cycling endurance and muscle damage."
Medicine and Science in Sports and Exercise. 2004
Jul;36(7):1233–8.

Seifert J, Harmon J, DeClercq P. "Protein added to a sports drink
improves fluid retention." *International Journal of Sport Nutrition and Exercise Metabolism.* 2006;16:420–9.

About the Authors

Dean Karnazes might just be the fittest man on the planet, writes *Men's Fitness*. His long list of accomplishments is astounding, though perhaps his even greater gift is his ability to help others achieve their fitness goals and become the best that they can be. A past columnist for *Men's Health*, the world's largest men's publication, Dean was recently voted by *Time* magazine as one of the "Top 100 Most Influential People in the World." He is a frequent public speaker and has traveled the world, meeting and running with people of all ages to extol the virtues of physical exercise, good diet, and healthy, active living.

Dean is a member of the California State Senate Task Force on Youth Wellness, and also serves on the board of Girls on the Run, a nationwide non-profit probram that encourages girls to develop self-respect and healthy lifestyles through running. His foundation, KARNO KIDS, whose motto is "No Child Left Inside," has raised hundreds of thousands of dollars for children's charities and for organizations that focus on environmental preservation and restoration and conservation of urban open-spaces.

When he's not running or chasing his own kids around their backyard—which he insists is he favorite workout routine—you can usually find him surfing, mountain biking, snowboarding, or hiking somewhere in the greater San Francisco Bay area.

Matt Fitzgerald is a runner, coach, and widely published journalist and author. A frequent contributor to *Runner's World,* he has written several previous books, including *Brain Training for Runners*. Matt is also a certified sports nutritionist and maintains a popular Web site featuring training and nutrition information for endurance athletes (www.mattfitzgerald.org). He lives in San Diego with his wife, Nataki.